Relocating Global Cities

Relocating Global Cities

From the Center to the Margins

Edited by
M. Mark Amen, Kevin Archer, and
M. Martin Bosman

ROWMAN & LITTLEFIELD PUBLISHERS, INC.
Lanham • *Boulder* • *New York* • *Toronto* • *Oxford*

ROWMAN & LITTLEFIELD PUBLISHERS, INC.

Published in the United States of America
by Rowman & Littlefield Publishers, Inc.
A wholly owned subsidiary of The Rowman & Littlefield Publishing Group, Inc.
4501 Forbes Boulevard, Suite 200, Lanham, Maryland 20706
www.rowmanlittlefield.com

P.O. Box 317, Oxford OX2 9RU, UK

Cover photos: Cityscapes of Frankfurt, Johannesburg, Bangkok, Manila, Tampa, Sydney, Brussels, and Caracas.

British Library Cataloguing in Publication Information Available

Library of Congress Cataloging-in-Publication Data

Relocating global cities : from the center to the margins / edited by M. Mark Amen,
Kevin Archer, and M. Martin Bosman.
    p. cm.
  Includes bibliographical references and index.
  ISBN-13: 978-0-7425-4121-4 (cloth : alk. paper)
  ISBN-10: 0-7425-4121-5 (cloth : alk. paper)
  ISBN-13: 978-0-7425-4122-1 (pbk. : alk. paper)
  ISBN-10: 0-7425-4122-3 (pbk. : alk. paper)
  1. Metropolitan areas—Case studies. 2. Urbanization—Case studies. 3. Globalization—Case studies. I. Amen, Michael Mark, 1944– II. Archer, Kevin, 1957– III.
Bosman, M. Martin, 1963–
  HT330.R45 2006
  307.76—dc22

                                                                    2005030129

Printed in the United States of America

♾™ The paper used in this publication meets the minimum requirements of
American National Standard for Information Sciences—Permanence of Paper
for Printed Library Materials, ANSI/NISO Z39.48-1992.

Contents

List of Illustrations

FIGURES

TABLES

APPENDIX

BOX

Foreword

Saskia Sassen

SEARCHING FOR THE GLOBAL IN THE URBAN

While confusions reign in the world and global cities scholarship, we have nonetheless made some headway into the work of building an analytics about globalization that incorporates the thick and highly variable world of cities. One of the main aims of the foundational texts of the 1980s and early 1990s in the world and global cities scholarship was to build an analytics about globalization that would incorporate the thick and highly variable character of place. At a time when the advanced sectors of the economy were conceived of as globally mobile and not needing place, bringing in cities with their people, politics, and inequalities was not only messy, it was charged. The global economy was shown to be partly dependent on a rapidly growing network of cities. At the same time, the global could be shown to be a partial condition, one that accounted for only some of what was happening in those cities.

And the emergent city analysis itself was partial. Some emphasized cities as sites for global coordination and the resulting city hierarchies. Others emphasized the need to produce global control capabilities, which led to an analysis of the variety of types of workers, firms, and work cultures—from high-level professionals to low-wage service work—that it took to do global finance or advanced corporate servicing. The decision itself to use the term *global* rather than the older historical term *world city* was itself charged with meaning: the intent was to capture the specific articulation of the world economy and cities as it is getting produced today, thereby allowing for the possibility that cities that are not historically world cities could nonetheless be global. This has all spawned a rather large literature across the world, producing, in turn, many advances and quite a few confusions.

But many subjects remain understudied. Perhaps at the top of the list of incompletely researched and theorized subjects is that of cities that are not self-evidently world or global cities. This volume contributes to the effort of filling that gap. One of the distinct contributions is the emphasis on the weight of local political and economic practices in the constructing of a global city component. This shines through in several of the chapters, notably those on Johannesburg, Sydney, Brussels, and Bangkok. Each one of these brings to the fore the work of local and global elites in making objectives happen. This type of focus also allows us to recognize the case of local elites who do not want to or fail to organize themselves sufficiently even to pursue "the goal of becoming a global city," to the possible advantage of the area, as chapter 6 on Tampa illuminates.

These types of account make an important contribution in filling a void. They also reinforce one of the key premises of the foundational texts on the subject: the importance of searching for the global in the urban rather than simply seeing it in terms of numbers of headquarters. This, in turn, calls for detailed knowledge about the city under study. In this regard, I, for one, have argued emphatically, often to no avail, that *global city* is not a descriptive term meant to capture a whole city. It is an analytic construct that allows one to detect the global as it is filtered through the specifics of a place, its institutional orders, and its sociospatial fragmentations. The extent, composition, and institutional or social locations of the global will vary across cities, including in leading global cities. In some cities, it may be minimal or nonexistent. Thus, I found the Tampa case extremely significant precisely because using this analytic construct in the search for the global showed that not much could be found. And chapter 8 by Erik Swyngedouw and Johan Moyersoen shows us that "the 'glocal' city that Brussels already is remains embedded in a provincial and parochial institutional straightjacket." This illuminates the partial and specific structuration of the global inside the urban.

Another major subject that, at least for some of us, remains in need of much attention is that of labor mobility. Michael Samers (2002) reminds us all of the issue and of its generalized neglect in the world and global cities literature. James A. Tyner's chapter 5 in this volume takes Samers' call a step further and makes a major theoretical and empirical contribution: he discusses how the work of organizing the deployment of low-wage workers has promoted the development of resources and networks in Manila that amount to a capability for organizing global labor mobilities. Tyner finds in this one of the sources for Manila's articulation with and insertion into global networks. Over the years, I have emphasized the ongoing conceptualization of a variety of labor mobilities in the language of immigration and ethnicity when it is actually a series of processes having to do with (1) the globalization of economic activity, cultural activity, and identity formation, and (2) the increasingly marked racialization of labor market segmentation. The result is that work belonging to the advanced global information economy but executed in immigrant work environments is not recognized as part of that advanced economy. Tyner's chapter also brings into the world and global city literature the fact that women migrants have become critical actors in several of these new intercity mobilities; we need to link the city scholarship with a growing body of research about the so-called new serving classes and global care-chains (e.g., Ehrenreich and Hochschild 2003).

A third subject that remains underdeveloped is the multisitedness of the global and the fact that it is marked by various incipient divisions of labor, or, to use more familiar language, functions. The overwhelming emphasis in the cities literature has been on competition. "Seeing as a city" tends to produce an image of sharp competition, while seeing as a global firm or market is seeing the need for a growing network of global cities. This network is one mechanism for the expansion of the global economy; it is also an organizing infrastructure for extracting the specific forms of wealth in a country, with its global city functioning as a key gateway. Already in my research in the 1980s, I was detecting that the emerging globalized financial system operating out of New York, London, and Tokyo had a distinct division of labor: Tokyo was the leading global exporter of money as a raw, unprocessed commodity; London was the ultimate entrepot, a legacy of its imperial past; and New York was the Silicon Valley of financial innovations.

Chapter 2 by Jonathan V. Beaverstock, Michael Hoyler, Kathryn Pain, and Peter J. Taylor explicitly seeks to detect the networking infrastructure at work in what is so often presented as rankings or global hierarchies of cities. Without having this as an explicit aim, chapter 9 by Miguel Lacabana and Cecilia Cariola also makes a contribution to the issue of a division of functions among global cities in its emphasis on oil as the key sector that articulates Venezuela to the global economy and makes Caracas the site for the necessary managing and servicing of oil exports and process earnings. To repeat, Tyner's examination of Manila as specializing in the organization of global labor mobilities also contributes to the subject.

A fourth subject is the internal socioeconomic and cultural restructuring of these cities. While this subject has received considerable attention and generated heated debates, there is room for much more research. The particularities of each city, the multiple cities that inhabit each city, and the variety of coping strategies that people invent all generate a need for much detailed investigation of particular cities. Mike Douglass and Pornpan Boonchuen show us in chapter 4 how this diversity gets constituted and reconstituted in the case of Bangkok as it is catapulted into massive capital investment projects and subjected to relentless imaginaries about globalization. Scott Salmon tries in chapter 7 to decipher the multiple interactions among xii Saskia Sassen

processes of gentrification that underlie capital realization in Sydney and the variety of political bodies that get going, or at least get agitated, in this process. Keith S. O. Beavon shows us in chapter 3 how these types of dynamics play out in Johannesburg, one of the most acutely fragmented cities, both historically and today. The case points to the use of territorial reorganization as a powerful weapon in a larger sociopolitical battle. Perhaps the most detailed attention to the subject of the internal fragmentation of cities is in Lacabana and Cariola's chapter 9 on Caracas. They show us the vast growth of poverty, the shifts in the middle class, with some sectors becoming richer and others poorer, and the growing segregation of top income groups in luxury enclaves. These outcomes get constituted though a variety of socioterritorial fragmentations, which, for the authors, engages the larger analytic question of how to grasp urban divisions. All of us who have done research in cities have been at that juncture where we need to decide between a more analytic move or a more descriptive one: do we seek to capture the major dynamics underlying an empirical situation, or do we want to capture the full diversity and fluidity of an empirical landscape? As the authors argue, cities help us explore these questions of method.

In an unusually candid conclusion, the editors reveal their doubts about the whole project and ask many a pertinent question. I agree with them that we need much detailed research on specific aspects of specific cities. I have found in my own research that the deep history of a city becomes more, not less, significant under conditions of globalization. There is indeed a somewhat homogenized landscape that cuts across place and history, but this is merely an infrastructure of state-of-the-art buildings, systems, and talent pools to facilitate the work that takes place in global cities. That homogenized hyperspace of global business should not be confused with the work of articulating the specialized advantages of a country and place with global circuits. The editors also ask a series of questions that get at politics. Urban politics tends to be quite specific as it is conditioned by the thickness of the urban; it is indeed a critical variable. And yet, as social scientists, we need to work at developing an analytics, and much work has indeed been done on the subject. We cannot simply stay at the level of empirical description and confine the project to maximizing the collection of empirical details. In that regard, one of the major contributions of this volume is guided by the editors' notion of searching for the global rather than taking it as a given.

REFERENCES

Ehrenreich, Barbara, and Arlie Hochschild, eds. 2003. *Global Woman: Maids, Nannies, Nurses, and Sex-workers.* New York: Metropolitan Books.

Gugler, Joseph, ed. 2004. *World Cities beyond the West*. Cambridge: Cambridge University Press.

Krause, Linda, and Patrice Petro, eds. 2003. *Global Cities: Cinema, Architecture, and Urbanism in a Digital Age*. New Brunswick, NJ: Rutgers University Press.

Paddison, Ronan, ed. 2001. "Introduction." *Handbook of Urban Studies*. London: Sage.

Samers, Michael. 2002. "Immigration and the global city hypothesis: towards an alternative research agenda." *International Journal of Urban and Regional Research* 26, no. 2 (June): 389–402.

Acknowledgments

This book is the first stage of a project on globalizing cities established by the Globalization Research Center (GRC) at the University of South Florida (USF) in 2002. To launch the project, the editors of this volume invited scholars to write case studies on globalizing cities normally not considered in the global cities literature. These researchers presented their work at the annual meeting of the International Studies Association (ISA) in February 2003. Following the ISA meeting in Portland, Oregon, we invited them to revise their cases for publication in this volume. We are especially grateful to the authors whose work appears in this volume. Their analyses and insights have helped us reconsider our initial interpretation of the current global cities literature.

This project has been generously supported by the GRC (now the Dr. Kiran C. Patel Center for Global Solutions), which was established in 2001 as a member of the Globalization Research Network (GRN), a consortium of four research centers, including the University of California, Los Angeles, the University of Hawaii, Manoa, and George Washington University. The GRN and its member centers would not exist without the funding support provided by the U.S. Department of Education, Fund for the Improvement of Post-Secondary Education (FIPSE).

Special thanks to Barry Gills at the University of Newcastle upon Tyne in the United Kingdom, who chaired and served as discussant for both panels at the ISA meeting. Barry's commentary during the sessions helped us revise the cases after we left Portland. We are also grateful to Saskia Sassen, who came to USF in the fall of 2003 and, during her visit, advised us on both this manuscript and the future direction of the USF project. We also thank her for taking time from her busy schedule to write the forward to this volume. Manfred Steger, now at the Globalism Institute at the Royal Melbourne Institute of Technology in Australia , has given us crucial advice on our project since we first met him in February 2004. We are indebted to Manfred for his counsel.

We could not have been more fortunate to work with our editor at Rowman & Littlefield, Jessica Gribble. Jessica has made an otherwise tedious translation of manuscript to publication far easier than we ever could have expected. Finally, we have had the good fortune of assistance from the excellent staff at the GRC in Tampa. In various ways, Carylanna Bahamondes, Anand Bhat, Rebecca Harris, Robin Leiby, Richard Martin, Jurgen Smit, and Marilyn Leon have nudged us along to complete this volume.

List of Abbreviations

ACHR	Asian Coalition for Housing Rights
ADB	Asia Development Bank
AIDS	Acquired Immune Deficiency Syndrome
APB	Asia Pacific Bulletin
APEC	Asian Pacific Economic Cooperation
BES	Bureau of Employment Services, the Philippines
BMA	Bangkok Metropolitan Administration
CBD	Central Business District, Sydney
CDE	Centre for Development and Enterprise, South Africa
CENDES	Centro de Estudios y Desarrollo, Universidad Central de Venezuela
CIC	Cagayan de Oro-Iligan Corridor, the Philippines
CONAPRI	Venezuelan Council for Investment Promotion
DOLE	Department of Labor and Employment, the Philippines
ECB	European Central Bank
EMU	Economic and Monetary Union
EU	European Union
FDI	Foreign Direct Investment
FOCUS	Focus on the Global South
FPECM	Fundación Plan Estratégico Caracas Metropolitana
GaWC	Globalization and World Cities
GDP	Gross Domestic Product
GRP	Gross Regional Product
HIV	Human Immunodeficiency Virus
IAC	International Advisory Committee
IFSL	International Financial Services London

IMF	International Monetary Fund
JICA	Japan International Cooperation Agency
MSA	Metropolitan Statistical Area
MSS	Municipal Substructures
NATO	North Atlantic Treaty Organization
NCR	National Capital Region, the Philippines
NEDA	National Economic and Development Authority, the Philippines
NESDB	National Economic and Social Development Plan, Thailand
NHA	National Housing Authority, Thailand
NRDP	New Regional Development Paradigms
NSB	National Seaman Board, the Philippines
NSW	New South Wales
OCMW	Openbaar Centrum voor Maatschappelijk Welzijn, Antwerp
OEDB	Overseas Employment Development Board
OPEC	Organization of Petroleum Exporting Countries
PDVSA	Petroleos de Venezuela S.A.
POEA	Philippine Overseas Employment Administration
PWV	Pretoria-Witwatersrand-Vereeniging, South Africa
RAGE	Residents against Glebe's Expulsion, Sydney
SADC	Southern Africa Development Community
SFD	Siam Future Development, Thailand
SMA	Standard Metropolitan Area
SRT	State Railway of Thailand
SSCC	South Sydney City Council
SWIFT	Society for Worldwide Interbank Financial Telecommunication
TBP	Tampa Bay Partnership
TNC	Transnational Corporations
UCF	University of Central Florida
UCLA	University of California at Los Angeles
UK	United Kingdom
UNCTAD	United Nations Conference on Trade and Development
UNDP	United Nations Development Program
USF	University of South Florida

1

Thinking through Global Cities

M. Mark Amen, Kevin Archer, and M. Martin Bosman

Over the past three decades, there has been much discussion in the literature regarding the nature of contemporary globalization in terms of its causes, extent, and ultimate effects on nation-states, cities, and social relations. Much of this discussion has focused on the changing nature and functions of cities as sites of command and control over globalization processes. Such *global cities* are generally considered to include those that have evolved some level of service–sector capacity, most often in finances and producer services, that reflects an appropriate adaptation to the overall restructuring of advanced capitalism from an industrial to a service base. Global cities, then, are considered those which include an above-average number of top-level management service–firms that generate and coordinate the ongoing expansion and now globalization of capitalism in what has been called the post-Fordist era of less regulated, increasingly footloose and flexible capital accumulation.

While there is a vast and rapidly growing literature on the effects of globalization on cities (e.g., INNURA 1998; INNURA 2004; Hamel, Lustiger-Thaler, and Mayer 2000; Falola and Salm 2004; Bishop, Phillips, and Yeo 2003; Gugler 2004), by far the most dominant theme within the more specific global cities literature is that which emerged from the early work of Friedmann (1986, see also Friedmann and Wolff 1982) and Sassen (1991, 2002) and which continues to evolve in the work of, for example, Short and Kim (1999), Taylor (2000), Godfrey and Zhou (1999), Abrahamson (2004), and Yeung (2000). In its most general form, this approach holds that the forces of the global economy produce conditions, through the global expansion of capital accumulation, to which humans located in multiple places must respond. This "global cities," "city-regions," and "world cities" literature derives from the common premise that the status or strategic position of cities in the

1

world today results from the services they provide to the global economy. In most cases, those working within this paradigm conceive global city status as something to be attained, or not, through the active promotion and development of high-level service management functions on the part of cities worldwide. As a result, most empirical work generated by such scholars tends to generate varying and changing hierarchies of global city status on the part of cities of the world. For our purposes, we will call this global cities approach *market driven* as by far the most emphasis is put on the global expansion of capitalist relations, particularly those of finance and producer services.

A second, although clearly much more diverse and loose, paradigm that has arisen as a direct response to this global cities approach focuses on how all cities and city-people are affected by globalizing processes in varying ways, not just economically (Smith 2001; Alsayyad 2001; Flusty 2004; Nederveen Pieterse 2004). This paradigm includes those who consider human agency on both a global and local level to be the most appropriate way to understand changes taking place in the contemporary world. Analytic focus is put on the creation of new "hybrid," "transnational" identities and social relations as a means to deepen the analysis of globalization to include the realm of real, concrete social activities, most often considered to be somehow "below," and yet ultimately constituting, the very structures of global relations described in more market-driven approaches from "above." This *agency-driven* analysis of global cities seeks not only to determine the diversity by which all the world's city-people may, or may not, be globalizing in some significant way, but it also includes consideration of how human agents, as active, knowledgeable, and creative beings, both create and potentially alter the so-called global networks described by more structural, market-driven approaches.

The market-driven approach certainly points to what may actually be considered new in the contemporary period of globalization with its emphasis on the rise and rapid expansion of capital accumulation in finances and producer services worldwide. That, with recent innovations in telecommunications soft- and hardware, has extended the spatial reach of capitalist firms, both industrial and service based. Yet, as the agency-driven approach underscores so well, this spatial expansion of capitalism is neither an inexorable and transparent teleological process nor one that takes place somehow "above" people's heads or behind their backs. In this respect, the world is a messier place than such an economistically determinist approach can possibly capture.

The overall goal of this book is to move farther toward a synthesis of these two paradigmatic approaches in order to make better sense of a complex, unevenly globalized world of cities. Accomplishing this will require no little theoretical work of integration, which we will begin in this chapter by reviewing the contributions and limitations of both approaches in more depth. Taking our cue from the agency-driven approach, we believe that, in order to determine how cities of the world are globalizing, we need to consider those cities that do not typically show up on the radar screen of the global cities literature or, as Robinson (2002) has put it, those "ordinary cities" quite literally "off the map" charted by most of the current literature on the subject, whether market or agency driven. It is to this end, then, that the following chapters are about cities not often considered in the current literature. In the final chapter, we attempt to tease out the more theoretical implications of the various empirical case studies included in chapters 2 through 9.

THE MARKET-DRIVEN APPROACH TO GLOBAL CITIES

While it may seem a stretch to characterize the ever-expanding literature on global cities as fitting within one paradigmatic worldview, it is surely the case that the most dominant argument made by authors like Sassen is that fundamental changes in global capitalist accumulation have created new city forms and functions on a global level. That is, the main emphasis throughout this literature is on how rapidly globalizing *economic* and derived *technological* processes are reshaping urban landscapes and creating a hierarchical structure of global city powers. Indeed, authors as seemingly diverse as Castells (1996, 1997, 1998), Harvey (1989), Scott (2001), and Storper (1997) have all been characterized in this manner, although, for our part, we find that such a characterization is much too simplistic. In any case, we are not the only ones to make such a distinction. Those adopting a more agency-driven approach, such as Smith (2001) and Flusty (2004), have staked their very position largely on a critique of such a seemingly economistically and technologically determinist focus. Yet, as will be made clear in later sections, we do not take our criticism this far. Suffice it to say here that the market-driven global cities literature treats economic and technological processes as first-order causal forces behind globalization and, then, the evolution of global cities, and thereby puts by far the most empirical emphasis on such processes.

To illustrate this point, we will examine here briefly the work of Saskia Sassen, arguably one of the most sophisticated market-driven analysts of the emergence and evolution of global cities. In 1991, for example, Sassen wrote that "the combination of spatial dispersal and global integration has created a new strategic role for major cities. . . . Thus, a new type of city has appeared. It is the global city" (3–4). Since that now well-known declaration, Sassen's growing body of work has carefully charted the direction of the "market-driven city status" literature. Her work constitutes an interlocking body of theses that collectively form a materialist analysis of the relations of production of the global economy, relations that require actual work in particular places, with particular resources and personnel, so that the global economy can function. This claim is of central importance to the global cities literature. As Sassen puts it, "there is no such entity as the global economy 'out there,'" so "understanding how global processes locate in national territories requires new concepts and research strategies. The global city is one such new concept" (2000a, xvi–xvii). This global city concept, in her view, "presumes that global processes, from the formation of global financial markets to the rapid growth of national labor markets, can be studied through the particular forms in which they materialize in places" (Sassen 2000a, xvii).

Sassen's work indicates that a small number of global cities across the world are foremost in the new geography of globalization and function as major centers of coordination, control, and servicing of global capital. The localization of the global happens in only very specific sociospatial formations, in "major cities [that] can be thought of as nodes where a variety of processes intersect in particularly pronounced concentrations . . . [and] assume concrete, localized forms. Their localized forms are, in good part, what globalization is about" (Sassen 2000b, 146–47). She finds that corporate headquarters and specialized command and control functions for the most dynamic and global industries are, to a large extent, concentrated and embedded within and operate through particular strategic locations. Thus, on this basis, strategic locations such as Tokyo "emerged as the main center for the export of capital; London as the main center for the processing of capital . . . ; and New York [as] the main receiver of capital, the center of investment decisions and for the production of innovations that can maximize profitability" (Sassen 1991, 327). In other words, these and a handful of other cities are constitutive elements of globalization and, therefore, have become centers of transnational and global significance, no longer solely representative of their national economies and societies. At the same time, as Sassen (2000b, 146) is quick to point out, "cities emerge as one scalar moment in a trans-urban dynamic." Moreover, this city network and transurban dynamic are made up of cities not as bounded territorial units but as "node[s] in a grid of cross-boundary processes" (Sassen 2000b, 146).

In a recent edited volume, Sassen extends the global cities model to cities in the South, claiming that this "allows us to capture a dynamic in formation, unlike what is the case with global cities already well established" (2002, 3). Sassen says that some of these cases provide examples for what she claims are "three main reasons that explain the trend toward consolidation in a few centers rather than massive dispersal" of economic function along global networks: social connectivity and central functions, cross-border mergers and alliances, and denationalized elites and agendas (2002, 21–25). Contributors to the volume consider how cities located only in the global South become part of existing global circuits by engaging in cross-border economic transactions or transnational business diasporas.

Transforming cities into strategic spaces for global capitalist coordination and accumulation has significant impacts on their local politics and power structures. For instance, Sassen (1998) shows that the superprofits generated by finance and other capital- and skill-intensive industries raise the price of commercial real estate and industrial services. To keep costs down, small-to-medium-size firms often dodge local zoning, health, fire, and labor codes, creating sweatshop conditions in the process. Simultaneously, transnational corporations and their highly paid, often politically connected, workers impose their exclusive demands on the city (see Zukin 1991), be they for more office space, bigger airports, more trendy loft condominiums, or other large office complexes. Due to the money and influence these interests wield in cities, their demands are more likely to be reflected in city and metropolitan budgets than are the needs of poorer residents. The end result, according to Sassen, is an increasing polarization of wealth and power between cities' residents, on the one hand, and the corporations and their new breed of "global" workers located in those cities, on the other. In the end, Sassen claims (1998), this "dual-city effect" occurs because the current globalizing processes are not expanding the middle classes like they did under the earlier era of Fordist accumulation.

Finally, Sassen's work (1996) considers the implications of an emerging global economy for the sovereignty of the modern state. She concludes that both sovereignty and territory "have been reconstituted and partly displaced onto other institutional arenas outside the state and outside the framework of nationalized territory"; that is to say, sovereignty has been "decentered" and "is now located in a multiplicity of institutional arenas" (Sassen 1996, 28, 29). Sassen reaches this conclusion after considering three areas in which the modern state has developed a tradition of authority: regulation of the economy, the economic rights of citizenship, and immigration policy. Yet, in later writings, Sassen acknowledges the ultimate "failure" of the global cities "model to include the state and other political forces" (1998, 479).

THE LIMITS OF THE MARKET-DRIVEN APPROACH

While such a market-driven global cities approach represents a provocative understanding of contemporary changes in the world economy, it poses a number of obstacles to the creation of theoretically grounded accounts of the relationship between globalization and cities. For our purposes, the most critical obstacle is that such an approach offers no explicit theory of the precise causal relationship between globalization and cities. Instead, the approach adopts a number of paradoxical or ambiguous propositions that reduce it to a series of descriptive rather than analytical global cities hypotheses. None of these hypotheses effectively addresses the precise conditions under which cities become global or why they might fall from that status.

Sassen, for example, rejects the outside-inside duality of the model, claiming instead that it is an "analytic strategy . . . to show that economic globalization is not just capital flows but . . . the work of coordinating, managing, and servicing these flows . . . in more than one country" (1998, 478). "The global city network is the operational scaffolding of that other fuzzy notion: the global economy" (1998, 479). But what replaces this duality? We are instructed to use sociological and anthropological approaches to examine globalization processes as they take place in cities. This means conducting descriptive studies that go

> all the way from the top levels to the bottom levels in an effort to capture the variety of work processes, work cultures, infrastructures, and so on, that are part of the global control capacity concentrated in cities and that is one of the features of the global economic system. (Sassen 1998, 479)

Yet, is this fuzzy global economy an independent variable wherein the "agency of finance capital" assigns a central role to cities in the logic of the accumulation process (Smith 2001, 2)? Since its hypothesized relation to cities is never clearly articulated, we are left with many descriptive answers but no questions. Yet, questions abound. Is the global economy a structural backdrop or foreground with which all cities must contend? Do the structures and institutions of capital accumulation stand independently of the particular city parts, yet require centralization of command and control in them so that accumulation can continue? While capital accumulation requires material and space to "conduct its business," does it need cities?

Sassen is clear that, however such questions might be answered, global cities do not converge. Cities like New York, London, and Tokyo have different functions, a division of labor vis-à-vis the financial market. At the same time, she claims the model's point of convergence is "the development and, yes, partial importation of a set of specialized functions and the direct and indirect effects this may have on the larger city" (1998, 480). But Sassen does not tell us from where and why these sets of specialized functions are imported. Does global finance capital force some cities to perform these functions, however they are divided? Sassen answers in her account of capital mobility versus fixity, "The mobility of capital, whether in the form of investments, trade, or overseas affiliates, needs to be managed, serviced, and coordinated. These tasks are often rather place-bound, yet are key components of capital mobility" (2002, 9). Such claims, however, do not explain if, and in what respects, capital mobility and fixity are mutually constituted or the causes of the former's location in some cities rather than others.

This global cities literature is rich with descriptions of the globalizing processes between and within global cities. Therein, however, lies a paradox about the city's status. At times, cities appear to have power over the global economy because they have the institutional and legal "resources necessary for the management and servicing" it requires (Sassen 2000, 2). One is thus left with the impression that if cities refused to perform these functions, the global economy would collapse. But do cities have the power to refuse to provide such services? Most times, it appears that cities are merely responding to global economic imperatives. As Short and Kim (1999) suggest, "'wannabe' world cities," in fact, must adopt strategies and projects to conform to the prevailing characteristics of transterritoriality and functional specialization within the global economy.

Instead of problematizing the power relations between the global economy and cities, the market-driven literature focuses mainly on emerging new relationships among cities. Some authors emphasize that there is a centralized hierarchy with which all cities must contend in acquiring global city status (Friedmann and Wolff 1982; Taylor et al. 2002). Furthermore, this hierarchy continues to be based on the view that global cities (Sassen 1991), world cities (Lo and Yeung 1998), or city-regions (Scott 2001) in the advanced industrialized world occupy a hegemonic position vis-à-vis other cities, especially megacities (i.e., the United Nations University research program) in the developing world. These "other cities" (MacGregor and Lipow 1995; Van Vliet 2001) are generally believed to be passive receptors of globalization's negative externalities, such as urban poverty, rising social and spatial inequalities, lack of formal sector jobs and access to development capital, rising crime, weak administrative infrastructures, and dwindling food supplies (Lo and Yeung 1998).

Others have attempted to move away from the one-dimensional nature of the hierarchy model by adopting other metaphors, for example "nodes," "networks," "city-regions," and "cross-border systems." The contributors to Scott (2001), for example, describe the relationship between globalization and new city-regions as "reflexive in nature" and claim that city-regions are arranged in a worldwide mosaic as a function of globalization processes, processes that are mediated through this mosaic. Borders are being redrawn through the creation of new leading complexes of governmental and business agencies, and these contributors want to show how city-regions "increasingly function as essential spatial nodes of the global economy and as distinctive political actors on the world stage" (2001, 11). These scholars acknowledge the need for more grounded empirical research to resolve the debate about city-regions as nodal points where "globalization processes crystallize" as opposed to cities "as active agents in shaping globalization itself" (2001, 7). But their work does not resolve how these spatial nodes and the global economy constitute an order. Similarly, those who adopt the market approach see cities in both the North and the South as nodes articulating national, regional, and international economies into an increasingly global space economy and performing highly specialized organizing functions (e.g., management and services activities). Yet, like those who follow the agency approach, they do not specify the relationship between the nodes and the global.

THE AGENCY-DRIVEN CITY APPROACH

The literature on "transnational urbanism," "transnational networks," and "urban hybridity" puts the emphasis on human agency in terms of the status of cities in a globalized world. As opposed to what Flusty (2004, 4) calls the "top-down bias" of more structural global city approaches, city status, according to this view, results from the mutual constitution of global and local relations. These relations are expressed in the formation of various spatiotemporal networks. Differences in the forms these networks take underscore that a wide range of cities are actually "players" in the globalization process. Although research results derived using this approach are contextually specific, six common attributes can be identified in the literature. First, human relations are considered to be socially constructed and contingent. Second, social relational patterns are contextually specific. Third, agency power varies based on status and position. Fourth, economic status and position are not sufficient to explain the exercise of agency. Fifth, the exercise of agency is influenced by history, culture, and politics. And sixth, city status is determined by the exercise of agency across a broad range of economic, political, and cultural relations.

For our purposes, Michael Peter Smith's work on transnational urbanism (1998, 2001) best exemplifies this approach. Smith analyzes the contributions that national and local public policy, as well as cultural processes, make to the formation of transnational or global processes (Smith 2001, 48–71). Here, political and cultural relations are not taken as derivatives of economic transformation. Nor is the economy itself considered to have its own internal engine of expansion. Instead, global and other forces are what various agents within cities make of them. Thus, a range of public and private structures and institutions are taken into account in explaining the status of cities relative to globalization.

Smith's work begins with the claim that the global cities model posits a structuralist perspective wherein urban hierarchies are constructed on the basis of positivist taxonomies (1998, 482). Smith rejects the essentialist character that underlies such a hierarchy of nested cities whose positions are based on their success in doing the bidding of global capitalism. The global city is a social construct, he contends, not a place or object consisting of essential properties. There is "no solid object known as the global city appropriate for grounding urban research" (Smith 1998, 485). Smith wants to show that the world is a very messy place with globalist manifestations both from above in the commanding heights of finance and from below in the waves of immigrant labor and remittances and festivals and creations of alternative global networks and nodes.

In *Transnational Urbanism* (2001), Smith elaborates his own approach first by registering his objections to the more market-driven, structuralist work of, for example, Harvey, Sassen, Friedmann, Castells, and others noted above. In general, Smith finds that these and like authors continue to suffer from binary thinking involving the modernist conceptualization of the following dualistic relations: global-local, universal-particular, economic-cultural, political-economic, and international-domestic. In turn, Smith rejects the possibility of grand narratives (e.g., "the accumulation strategies of capitalist logics, structures, and actors") that such theorists propose because such views require a universality that, according to Smith, "renders them ineffectual as explanatory frameworks for social change" in any specific, more complex, real context (2001, 6).

The critique leads to an alternative vision that Smith calls "transnational urbanism." The central conceptual innovation in this vision concerns Smith's view that the sources and dynamics of globalization are found inside the linkage "from below" of transnational spaces, networks, and agencies. Smith claims to resurrect the significance of borders, boundaries, and identities and to infuse them with a social construction that produces the "complex, criss-crossing, contingent character of place-making" in these increasingly transnational times (2001, 8). From this perspective, new networks of all kinds of economic, political, and cultural relations emerge within and among cities on a global scale. Smith's goal, then, is to discover what new oppositional spaces and political possibilities various human actors might well have opened up in response to global economic restructuring (2001, 12).

Once the centrality of agency is posited, Smith offers a series of empirical vignettes to illustrate how networks reconfigure past boundaries and borders and alter power relations in ubiquitous ways. Many events, initiatives, and activities can be explained by reference to these transnational networks, and Smith offers a host of them:

- The appropriation of mass media connections and flows by transnational coalitions of human rights organizations
- The construction of new scales of political practice (e.g., the Zapatista movement) that complicate state-centered projects
- The creation of translocal ties through the immigration and emigration of peoples
- The formation of locally based networks between illegal Central American immigrants and residents in Houston, Texas, to resist the landlord's efforts to displace them

- The networking of international monetary agents that created the neo-liberal ideology of globalization
- The transnational urbanism of contemporary Los Angeles emerging from below and through the historical confluence of state policies and the practices of transnational sociocultural networks concerning racial and ethnic relations

While Robinson's work differs from the transnational urbanism approach, she also begins with a critique of the global cities approach. Her concern is with its Western focus, its predisposition to categories, its use of dualism such as West–Third World, and its espousal of hierarchies based on "pre-given standards of (world) city-ness" (2002, 532). Robinson summarizes comparative studies that have identified differences in the relations cities throughout the world have established with the global economy. These differences suggest an alternative way or "broader framework of advancing an understanding of cities and their possible futures." This alternative requires what she calls a cosmopolitan theoretical perspective, the avoidance of structural hierarchies that mask urban distinctiveness, and an emphasis on the diverse sources of transnational links that shape all cities. In short, Robinson's approach demands an explicit acknowledgment of the multiple social networks within cities (2002, 544). Because of this, Robinson turns to the concept of the "ordinary city" (Amin and Graham 1997; Jacobs 1996) as a site of spheres of overlapping reflexive economic action for all kinds of economic interactions, not just those of concern to global cities scholars. Ordinary cities, in other words, are more than simply economic sites. They include networks of human interaction within the city and a diverse range of links between the city and other places in the world.

THE LIMITS OF THE AGENCY-DRIVEN APPROACH

There is much to recommend in such agency-driven approaches. Certainly, the vast complexity of globalizing processes is brought to light, making them that much more difficult to consider as deterministic or otherwise inexorable. In addition, such a focus puts to rest the idea that globalization is a one-way process ultimately resulting in a more homogeneous global culture. Smith's conceptualization of transnationalism constructs an image of globalization that is so economically, politically, and culturally multileveled as to resist inherently the kind of grand narrative theorization that drives the market-driven global cities literature. It also thereby resists attempts to flatten causal power to one or another of these levels. Indeed, globalization, in this view, is an ever-ongoing process constructed by agents in their activities in all realms now stretched across the planet. Such an agency-driven conceptualization of globalization explicitly and significantly underscores the very real possibilities for alternative globalizations. And this is extremely important. The grand narrative market-driven approach makes it very difficult even to conceive of alternatives; thus, such an approach is largely incapable of providing any effective road maps toward resistance or change.

This is, indeed, a tantalizing social construction of a globalizing world. We are, it turns out, what we make of ourselves, and how we construct meaning within this process, in turn, drives us in various directions of self-construction. Cities and city-people are not the dupes of globalizing "forces," "processes," "networks," and so forth, whether "economic" or "technological"; rather, they are, in their various and varying social relations, what these "processes" actually are, nothing more, nothing less. Because of this, one needs to examine closely each "real" or "ordinary" place over "real" or "ordinary" time to determine the precise nature of globalizing processes in the form of a specific complex of ongoing social relations.

Yet, where does this conception leave us? Certainly, agency-driven approaches like those of Smith and Flusty, as well as those of more culturally specific, postcolonially positioned authors like Alsayyad (2001) and Nederveen Pieterse (2004), show us a tantalizing, complex, hybrid world. But is it really true that such a world is one, as Smith puts it, where such "transnational," "colluding and colliding" "social practices and networks" construct merely a "disjointed" spatial terrain of contingent complexity "ad infinitum" (1998, 485–86)? Does this not leave us with little more to say than that we need to look at each individual, contingently constructed place to say anything at all about what is going on in the world? How else are we to grasp what Smith calls the "complex, criss-crossing, contingent character of place-making" in today's transnationalizing world (1998, 485–86)?

Yes, in fact, it is a messy, real world out there. But can we not make theoretical sense of the ways such a world "hangs together" in similar— although obviously not the same!—ways in different places? Indeed, can we not make better sense of the very "differences" in the world that an agency-driven approach underscores, even celebrates, by investigating the similarities, which may, in fact, be increasing in the contemporary moment, of what is increasingly being called the process of "globalization"?

The problem with the agency-driven approach is that its adherents focus so much on destroying the grand narrative gestures of more structuralist, supposedly more "modernist," approaches to globalization and global cities that they tend to lose sight of any social structuration whatsoever. This is particularly the case, it seems, with Smith's conception of "transnationalism." Certainly, transnational networks are created by human agency in all realms of social relations, not just the economic. That needs to be underscored, as Smith does so well. Yet, surely, some agents have more power over these networks than others. Surely, those at the top rung of what Flusty, for his part, calls the "plutocratic corporate" world have more power to form the contemporary global urban scene in their image than the "Ghanian taxi driver negotiating the streets of Tokyo" or the "Filipino contract construction worker in Bahrain," whose lives Flusty admirably wants to describe in full detail (2004, 5, 32). Indeed, why, in fact, are these people "misplaced," and how did they get there? Is it really true, as Flusty argues, that in this messy world of such global human relations, we must necessarily remain blind, analytically, to what Massey has called globalization's "asymmetrical power-geometries" (Massey 1993; see below)?

Missing in such accounts is a fuller conception of the differential power among human agents who are constructing the very globalized, transnational world exhibited in such empirical detail. Put differently, while the market-driven global cities literature may put the structures and institutions of globalizing flows, particularly economic flows, apparently above and beyond the reach of most human agency, at least this approach recognizes the powerful agency of those who operate at the highest levels of capital accumulation. Surely, these agents who decide where finance and productive capital will roam and eventually light down on a global basis have more power than those completely out of the decision-making process altogether.

An example from Smith's account of transnational relations may bring this point closer to home. Using Rodriguez and Hagan's (1992) and Rodriguez's (1995) ethnographic studies of the experience of migrants from Central America residing in Houston, Smith argues that these migrants successfully have retained close relations with their home regions while creating new economic, political, and cultural relations in Houston. In this way, such migrants have affected and ultimately changed the nature of both places, as well as themselves. They are transnational actors now, constructing transnational networks of social relations and individual identities. Yet, while such an account reveals much possible diversity of human agency, thereby putting a human face on cross-border flows, it nevertheless can be read quite differently. Similar to the Ghanian taxi driver mentioned above, one might ask why, in fact, these people found it necessary or desirable to move from their homelands to reside and work in Houston. Alternatively, one might inquire as to what changes have taken place in transportation and communications infrastructures that have allowed them to move and, indeed, maintain such close ties to their former homes. Put differently, this account of transnationalism could be seen as merely the result of the immigrants' need to adapt to processes quite beyond their control. Their agency is ultimately being structured in particular ways as a result of differential power within globalizing networks of social relations.

This can be seen quite clearly in the particular example Smith uses to illustrate his case for agency-driven transnationalism. The migrants he describes were able to forge relations with Houston natives to "frustrate, circumvent, and at times even to openly resist [their] landlord's efforts to displace them" from their apartment complex (2001, 7–8). According to Smith, this episode represents the migrants' ability to create a new, transnational space of resistance to otherwise oppressive social forces. Thus, although the migrants are formally subordinated to several authorities and actors in Houston, they nevertheless possess some power.

Yet, again, another reading of the same episode is possible and, in our view, arguably more plausible. That the tenants could not keep up financially with the improvements desired by the landlord is a matter of the continuing overexploitation of the migrants and their relative powerlessness in the informal economy of Houston. The further fact that they were, indeed, successful in resisting the landlord's desire to evict them (for how long?) merely makes it that much easier for their employers to continue to overexploit them by paying them the lowest wages for the most menial work. In other words, their apparent culture of resistance has some unintended consequences that actually help to reproduce general features of exploitative global or transnational capitalism. From this perspective, what Smith calls a "space of resistance" we might call a "space of accommodation" with an obfuscating facade of social empowerment. That is, in the long run, the migrants have merely facilitated their continuing exploitation while thinking that they have won something of enduring social value.

THE SOCIAL STRUCTURATION OF GLOBALISM

But one does not have to push the point this far. The alternative meaning made of the empirical evidence is merely one possible example of constructing a more structurationist understanding of transnational place making. The point is that a more complete understanding can be established if market-driven and agency-driven global cities approaches are somehow integrated. Such an integration requires a better understanding of the contingencies of agency in the former and of the biases of structures in the latter. While global cities may indeed be constructed out of global flows and networks, these flows are nothing but human-agent-initiated activities based on myriad specific interests, intentions, and meanings. At the same time, individual human agency, arising from these interests, intentions, and meanings, does not take place in a vacuum or outside of the concrete context of already initiated, routinized, and ultimately reified structures of previous human agency. Again, this emphasis on the structuration of human agency allows for a better sense of how global relations actually hang together in a more coherent fashion than merely the myriad differences portrayed in the empirical evidence found, as Smith suggests, "below" the gaze of those who see "global networks" in the everyday activities of real, increasingly transnational people in particular places.

This is not a new conceptualization, to be sure. Following Giddens (1984) and Bourdieu (1990), we adopt the view that both agency and structure are mutually, if not equally, constitutive elements of globalization and global cities. The human agency required to generate these two phenomena takes place within structuring paths of its own (ever-past) creation, which biases agency in certain directions, most usually those aimed at (ever) reproducing those social relations that already exist (the ever present). But, because social structures are only the result of human agency, and not somehow existing "out there," beyond it or determining it, they are always in the *process* of construction, never completely established, always prone to change. This conception of social structuration makes clear the need not only to recover and restore the power of human agency in the market-driven global cities literature but also to emphasize the structurationist biases that necessarily direct human agency in some directions as opposed to others, something which is often overlooked, we believe, in agency-driven approaches to globalization and global cities.

But there is more. Human agency is certainly biased in certain directions to reproduce "structural properties (rules and resources)" conducive to the reproduction of, say, forms of capitalism or non-Western communalism in different places and different times among different peoples (Giddens 1984, 48). But it is also true that individual agents, and institutions for that matter, have differing amounts of power to control or modify these structuring properties and paths. This is what Massey, as already noted, refers to as the "power geometry" of globalization; namely, some actors and institutions initiate flows and networks more than others. Massey writes,

> Different social groups and individuals are placed in very distinct ways in relation to [global] flows and interconnections. This point concerns not merely the issue of who moves and who doesn't. . . . It is also about power in relation to the flows and movements. . . . Some are more in charge of it than others; some initiate flows and movements, others don't; some are more on the receiving end of it than others; some are effectively imprisoned by it. (1993, 61)

Notably, this view of differential power accepts the reality of asymmetrical power relations between different agents in space and time without a priori privileging one agent over another. It also intimates that structural constraints work through the differential agency of multiple actors. In the end, merely the structural forms of such relations have differed over time and space, not their substantive characteristics in this respect. Unlike those who argue like Flusty (2004), contemporary globalization can and should be conceptualized as a multilayered fusion of structurating processes continually cobbled together by multiple competing human agents with differing amounts of power to understand such processes, let alone actually to control or even to modify them. No, agents are not determined as the mere dupes of structures somehow above or beyond their actions; however, neither are all agents equally powerful in the production of the "longue durée of institutions" and social structures (Giddens 1984, 35).

With his notion of human "habitus-practice," Bourdieu's conceptualization of the structuration of agency-power is even more explicit than that of Giddens. For Bourdieu (1990), social structure is precisely the distributional order of differential power over what he calls economic, political, social, and cultural (symbolic) capital among human agents. Agents continuously seek to acquire more "capital" in each realm and, in the process, continuously reproduce or, in fact, realign structures of power distribution. The key is that the structuration of power relations is never simply reproduced but, rather, is always open to change on the basis of human agency at any time and in any place. Thus, power geometries in particular cities, as well as globally, using Massey's (1993) terminology again, are always open to change on the basis of the specifics of global-local human agency.

But this is merely a theoretical first cut on the social structuration of global relations. We still need to determine the extent to which a Giddens-Bourdieu-like structuration approach actually aids us in our understanding of the myriad concrete empirical details of the chapters that follow. That is, the theory of social structuration appears to offer a way to integrate the market-driven and agency-driven approaches at this level of theoretical abstraction. However, it remains to be determined whether or not this is, indeed, the case on the basis of ongoing investigation, both theoretical and, importantly, empirical. In fact, this actually follows from our adopted structurationist approach itself. Giddens, for example, explicitly maintains that his approach is an *ontological* one, open to illustration on the basis of all kinds of empirical evidence. In turn, Bourdieu maintains that his "ideas" concerning habitus-practice and the structuration of agency-power "are not a general theory but a method." What readers need to know about his approach, he maintains, is that "it's a very general manner of thinking while at the same time it obliges one to study each case" (quoted in Mahar 1990, 36). It was, indeed, on this theoretical basis that we gave our invited authors the widest possible horizon within which to determine, themselves, what to concentrate on in their particular empirical case studies of "ordinary cities" across the globe. We intend to take more comprehensive theoretical stock of their various contributions in our conclusion.

SOCIAL POWER AND SOCIOSPATIAL OUTCOMES: CAPTURING A MESSY, GLOBALIZING WORLD

By way of sifting through the ever-expanding literature on globalization and global cities, we are thus attempting to move beyond both unicausal determinacy and contingent indeterminacy. Surely, in these poststructuralist times, the inadequacies of the former stance toward causality have been well enough rehearsed (Flusty 2004; Dear 2000). Yet, just as surely, as argued briefly in our discussion of the agency-driven approach, we can do better than to characterize the global present as one filled with "multiple processes" that are "simultaneously social, cultural, political, and economic," equally important, and "unevenly developed over space and time" (Hay and Marsh 2000, 3). While this latter assertion may be descriptively true, such an account does not explain either complexity or contingency. And so, we are left with merely an assertion of overwhelming complexity that cannot be "captured" fully by either those who live it or, apparently, those scholars who seek to understand it.

Others, of course, have similarly attempted to capture conceptually the complex structuration of global relations. For example, the multidimensional and truly profound analysis of Appadurai (1996) of the evolution of global cultural "scapes" that overlap and interact in contingently complex relation unevenly over the planet leads to a much fuller understanding of the complexity of contemporary global relations, well beyond, yet including, the economic. Indeed, his notion of global "ethnoscapes" of tourists, refugees, and the global gentry, "technoscapes" of information technology and information, "finanscapes" of now familiar financial flows and their agents, "mediascapes" of globalized images, and "ideoscapes" of political ideology, both hegemonic and counterhegemonic, certainly provides a path via which the sort of complexity identified by Hay and Marsh can be better comprehended. But, while this account certainly portrays a multicausal, highly contingent, globalizing world, could it not be that these scapes are ultimately linked in some theoretically identifiable way? That is, while Appadurai's analysis certainly identifies the complex guts of globalization in all its realms and with much needed detail, such an approach makes it appear that all of these scapes are evolving, more or less, independently and, indeed, at the same pace.

Marcuse and van Kempen (2000), for their part, offer a similarly complex conceptualization of globalization and cities. They argue first, and quite sensibly, that "'the city' is not an actor; it is a place occupied and used by many actors. A city does not prosper or decline, particular groups in it do, and generally in very different fashion." Further, "a city is not global; some of those doing business (and, we think, doing culture and politics as well) in it are, but others like them will do business (and culture and politics) very similar to that in 'non-global' cities" (2000, 265). From this beginning, Marcuse and van Kempen conjure the notion of the "layered city": layers of residence, work, transportation, school, recreation, and commerce, each of which "reflects a divided city" and none of which "shows the complete city" (2000, 266). This cartographic expression of complexity, much like that in Appadurai's work, is useful in that it suggests that the contingency of time and place can nevertheless be conceived in a more comprehensive, explanatory manner. The scapes and layers of the contemporary globalizing world constitute what Hay and Marsh call the "multiple processes of globalization," which "interact in specific" ways.

What is "contingent," however, is not this interaction itself, as these authors suggest, but rather the particular conjuncture of such interaction in particular places at particular times. Put differently, Appadurai and Marcuse and van Kempen offer a way to conceptualize what actually constitutes the processes of globalization; at the same time, they underscore that while such processes may be unevenly manifested over space and time, this unevenness can be understood not as simply random contingency but, rather, as specified scapes and layers in different forms of interaction. Here, we adopt a similar conception of layers of globalizing flows and spatial networks that can be understood as not only economic but also political and cultural. These constitute the evolving global social relations that are now both expanding and intensifying, although they remain unevenly manifested and materialized across the planet.

But we want to develop this conception further. These social layers and spatial scapes are inherently interrelated, even though exactly how remains an empirical question. It appears to us, for example, that the new, post-Fordist process of capitalist accumulation—the new fast capitalism identified by the market-driven approach or, in Appadurai's terms, the finanscapes and technoscapes—is pacing the expansion and intensification of global social relations. Their actual pace, however, is conditioned by the political and cultural contexts that either facilitate or fetter such accumulation at both the global and local levels. That is, global capitalist accumulation is neither inexorable nor somehow taking place outside of such cultural and political contexts. The point is that one needs to look at each particular conjuncture, global or local, in order to determine the precise interrelations among economic, political, and cultural layers.

This conception, we believe, allows for a more sophisticated understanding of actual global and local social relations as essentially the same process in different concrete spatial contexts. That is, such a conception provides a way in which to make better, more coherent sense of the apparent blizzard of contingencies and complexities identified by authors like Hay and Marsh, Smith, and Flusty. But there is more. In our take on the layers of globalizing processes, they are not only inherently interconnected, but, as mentioned, the spatial flows and networks of some layers are more powerfully biased toward spanning international boundaries than others. Again, the existing literature does not place enough emphasis on differential global and local power relations in the process of globalization. And, now, on the basis of this initial lead, we can be even more explicit. Not only are some social relations more powerfully driven toward globalism than others, but within social

relations, some individuals are more powerful than others either in promoting or resisting such processes. Furthermore, power is not only unevenly
spread socially, but this very unevenness manifests itself in reality at different spatial scales, from the more global to the more local. The captains of the
financial industry, for example, have the power to make decisions that cause
investments to be made on a worldwide basis, thereby ultimately affecting
the lives of many others with much less power. Similarly, those who work
more in the bowels of financial institutions, whether public or private, have
the capacity to shape such decisions. They therefore have power derived
from the institutions of which they are a part. Again, those outside of such
institutions do not have such power but may ultimately be affected by its exercise by those inside. Finally, such power does not necessarily include
power over the outcomes of such decisions, which are instead the result of
some combination of powerful action and concrete context. An example of
this would be decisions made by those in such global institutions as the International Monetary Fund (IMF) and the World Bank with regard to East
Asian financial markets in the 1980s and the ultimate financial "crisis" that
these unexpectedly caused in the late 1990s.

Importantly, this type of power is necessarily spatial as well as social. The
power of financial decision makers and shapers at Citibank, for example, is
more global in its potential exercise than that of, say, more locally embedded banks and, of course, most individual investors. Similarly, the spatial
range of power of decision makers and shapers in the IMF and the World
Bank is much wider, indeed global, than that of those within national banks.
But, again, the exercise of such potentially global power does not ensure
that the final results of this exercise will be those originally intended. This is,
in fact, the very essence of the real contingency of social relations across the
planet. Very similar commands for structural adjustment parlayed globally by
the IMF and World Bank, for example, are experienced in reality quite differently in different countries as a result of more locally based power to resist or modify such commands. The key remains the necessity to examine
each conjuncture of global-local, or "glocal," social relations individually in
order to determine what is actually happening in the world today.

Thus, unlike most who consider power in the globalization literature, we
do not consider it to be only that exercised in the political realm (pace Held,
McGrew, Goldblatt, and Perraton 1999). Rather, power is clearly exercised in
all realms, economic, political, and cultural, as these are, in turn, always interrelated in some specific way in specific places at specific times. Given our
brief example of the local modification of global structural-adjustment policies, in fact, this is already indicated. It is national and local public policies
that lead to such modifications, not the actions of agents in the private economic sector. That is, locally embedded political power has had greater
influence on the different experiences of the IMF- and World Bank–

commanded structural economic adjustment in, say, Korea, Indonesia, and Mexico. While the sociospatial extent of such power may be far smaller than that of those working at the global level, it still exists and succeeds in making for the very unevenness of what we call the process of globalization.

THINKING THROUGH THE GLOBAL CITY

Borrowing again from Appadurai (1996), one must, then, consider individual and institutional power relations in the formation of global-local ideoscapes, as well as ethnoscapes and, of course, mediascapes. Why is it, for example, that "neoliberalism," "democracy," and individual "human rights" are the hegemonic political messages in the growing global village (Falk 2000; Kalb 2000)? One does not have to go to the extreme of Fukuyama (1992) to notice that, despite the emergence of new forms of social resistance, this particular discourse is almost singularly global in extent. Or, why are islands of quite similar recreational, social, and built environments for the global gentry increasingly coming into existence in poor countries, quite detached from local social relations? Or, why is it that the likes of CNN, FOX news, MTV, and the *Wall Street Journal* seemingly rule global media flows?

The full story is, of course, much more complex than this. In the case studies that follow, we hope to determine the precise ways in which this kind of globalization may, or may not, be taking place in cities located in both the North and the South. How, for example, are these global power relations actually experienced, modified, or otherwise attenuated by more locally embedded power sources within the "ethno-," "techno-," "finan-," "media-," and "ideo-" flows that bring about the very uneven sociospatial scapes within and between cities as diverse as Frankfurt and Johannesburg? More specifically, how are the seemingly hegemonic messages of democracy, neoliberalism, or individual human rights variously understood and acted upon in very different ways by those in different locally embedded cultural, economic, and political contexts, such as Caracas, Venezuela; Tampa Bay, Florida; and Manila, Philippines? Or, looking at the same issue at the global level, how are these seemingly hegemonic messages being resisted, or not, in Sydney, Australia, or Brussels, Belgium, by alternative, potentially equally powerful, counterhegemonic messages from other sociospatial flows that are creating global scapes quite different from those usually considered in the globalization literature.

More specifically, the following chapters focus, from different angles, on specific urban-based conjunctures of global-local structurating social relations. Importantly, the authors focus on cities not often treated in the global cities literature. This, we feel, will not only contribute to a more complete understanding of contemporary globalization as affecting all cities, but it will also help to tease out more completely how specific conjunctures of economic, political, and cultural power relations actually manifest themselves quite differently in the uneven spatial scapes of the contemporary flows of globalization.

REFERENCES

Abrahamson, M. 2004. *Global Cities*. Oxford: Oxford University Press.

Alsayyad, N., ed. 2001. *Hybrid Urbanism: On the Identity Discourse and the Built Environment*. London: Praeger.

Amin, A., and Graham, S. 1997. "The ordinary city." *Transactions of the Institute of British Geographers* 22: 411–29.

Appadurai, A. 1996. *Modernity at Large*. Minneapolis: University of Minnesota Press.

Bishop, R., Phillips, J., and Yeo, W. W., eds. 2003. *Postcolonial Urbanism: Southeast Asian Cities and Global Processes*. New York: Routledge.

Bourdieu, P. 1990. *The Logic of Practice*. Cambridge, UK: Polity Press.

Castells, M. 1996. *The Rise of the Network Society*. Cambridge, MA: Blackwell Publishers.

———. 1997. *The Power of Identity*. Cambridge, MA: Blackwell Publishers.

———. 1998. *End of Millennium*. Cambridge, MA: Blackwell Publishers.

Dahl, R. 1961. *Who Governs? Democracy and Power in an American City*. New Haven, CT: Yale University Press.

Dear, M. 2000. *The Postmodern Urban Condition*. Oxford: Blackwell Publishers.

Falola, T., and Salm, S. J. 2004. *Globalization and Urbanization in Africa*. Asmara, Eritrea: Africa World Press.

Falk, R. 2000. "The quest for humane governance in an era of globalization." In *The Ends of Globalization*, ed. D. Kalb, M. van der Land, R. Staring, D. van Steenbergen, and N. Wilterdink. Lanham, MD: Rowman & Littlefield Publishers.

Flusty, S. 2004. *De-Coca-Colonization: Making the Globe from Inside Out*. New York: Routledge.

Friedmann, J. 1986. "The world city hypothesis." *Development and Change* 17: 69–84.

Friedmann, J., and Wolff, G. 1982. "World city formation: an agenda for research and action." *International Journal of Urban and Regional Research* 6: 309–44.

Fukuyama, F. 1992. *The End of History and the Last Man*. New York: Free Press.

Giddens, A. 1984. *The Constitution of Society: Outline of the Theory of Structuration*. Berkeley: University of California Press.

Godfrey, B. J., and Zhou, Y. 1999. "Ranking world cities: multinational corporations and the global urban hierarchy." *Urban Geography* 20: 268–81.

Gugler, J., ed. 2004. *World Cities beyond the West: Globalization, Development and Inequality*. New York: Cambridge University Press.

Hamel, P., Lustiger-Thaler, H., and Mayer, M., eds. 2000. *Urban Movements in a Globalising World*. London: Routledge.

Harvey, D. 1989. *The Condition of Postmodernity*. Cambridge, MA: Blackwell Publishers.

———. 1995. "Globalization in question." *Rethinking Marxism* 8: 1–17.

Hay, C., and Marsh, D. 2000. *Demystifying Globalization.* New York: Macmillan Press.

Held, D., McGrew, A., Goldblatt, D., and Perraton, J. 1999. *Global Transformations.* Palo Alto, CA: Stanford University Press.

INNURA. 1998. *Possible Urban Worlds: Urban Strategies at the End of the Century.* Basel, Switzerland: Birkhauser.

———. 2004. *The Contested Metropolis: Six Cities at the Beginning of the 21st Century.* Basel, Switzerland: Birkhauser.

Jacobs, J. 1996. *Edge of Empire: Postcolonialism and the City.* New York: Routledge.

Kalb, D. 2000. "Localizing flows: power, paths, institutions, and networks." In *The Ends of Globalization*, ed. D. Kalb, M. van der Land, R. Staring, D. van Steenbergen, and N. Wilterdink, 1–29. Lanham, MD: Rowman & Littlefield Publishers.

Lo, F., and Yeung, Y., eds. 1998. *Globalization and the World of Large Cities.* Tokyo: United Nations Press.

MacGregor, S., and Lipow, L., eds. 1995. *The Other City: People and Politics in New York and London.* Atlantic Highlands, NJ: Humanities Press.

Mahar, C. 1990. "Pierre Bourdieu: the intellectual project." In *An Introduction to the Work of Pierre Bourdieu: The Practice of Theory*, ed. R. Harker, C. Mahar, and C. Wilkes, 26–57. New York: St. Martin's Press.

Mann, M. 1997. "Has globalization ended the rise and rise of the nation-state?" *Review of International Political Economy* 4: 472–96.

Marcuse, P., and van Kempen, R., eds. 2000. *Globalizing Cities: A New Spatial Order?* Oxford: Blackwell.

Massey, D. 1993. "Power-geometry and a progressive sense of place." In *Mapping the Futures: Local Cultures, Global Change*, ed. J. Bird, B. Curtis, T. Putnam, G. Robertson, and L. Tickner, 59–69. London: Routledge.

Nederveen Pieterse, J. 2004. *Globalization and Culture: Global Mélange.* Lanham, MD: Rowman & Littlefield.

Robinson, J. 2002. "Global and world cities: a view from off the map." *International Journal of Urban and Regional Research* 26, no. 3: 531–54.

Rodrigucz, N. 1995. "The real 'new world order': the globalization of racial and ethnic relations in the late twentieth century." In *The Bubbling Cauldron: Race, Ethnicity and the Urban Crisis*, ed. M. Smith and J. Feagin, 211–25. Minneapolis: University of Minnesota Press.

Rodriguez, N., and Hagan, J. 1992. "Apartment restructuring and Latino immigrant tenant struggles: a case study of human agency." In *After Modernism: Global Restructuring and the Changing Boundaries of City Life*, ed. M. Smith, 164–80. New Brunswick, NY: Transaction Publishers.

Sassen, S. 1991. *The Global City: New York, London, Tokyo.* Princeton, NJ: University of Princeton Press.

———. 1996. *Losing Control? Sovereignty in an Age of Globalization.* New York: Columbia University Press.

———. 1998. "Swirling that old wine around in the wrong bottle: a comment on White." *Urban Affairs Review* 33, no. 4: 478–81.

———. 2000a. *Cities in a World Economy.* 2nd ed. Thousand Oaks, CA: Pine Forge Press.

———. 2000b. "New frontiers facing urban sociology at the millennium." *British Journal of Sociology* 51, no. 1: 143–59.

———. 2001 (1991). *The Global City: New York, London, Tokyo.* Rev. ed. Princeton, NJ: University of Princeton Press.

———, ed. 2002. "Introduction: locating cities on global circuits." In *Global Networks, Linked Cities.* New York: Routledge.

Scott, A., ed. 2001. *Global City-Regions: Trends, Theory, Policy.* Oxford: Oxford University Press.

Short, J., and Kim, Y. 1999. *Globalization and the City.* Edinburgh Gate, UK: Addison Wesley Longman Limited.

Smith, M. 1998. "The global city—whose social construct is it anyway? A comment on White." *Urban Affairs Review* 33, no. 4: 482–88.

———. 2001. *Transnational Urbanism: Locating Globalization.* Malden, MA: Blackwell Publishers.

Storper, M. 1997. *The Regional World: Territorial Development in a Global Economy.* New York: Guilford Press.

Taylor, P. 2000. "World cities and territorial states under conditions of contemporary globalization." *Political Geography* 19: 5–32.

Taylor, P., Walker, D., Catalano, G., and Hoyler, M. 2002. "Diversity and power in the world city network." *Cities* 19, no. 4: 231–41.

Van Vliet, W., ed. 2001. *Cities in a Globalizing World: Global Report on Human Settlements.* London: Earthscan Publications.

Yeung, Y.-M. 2000. *Globalization and Networked Societies: Urban-Regional Change in Pacific Asia.* Honolulu: University of Hawaii Press.

Zukin, S. 1991. *Landscapes of Power: From Detroit to Disney World.* Berkeley: University of California Press.

2

In London's Long Shadow: Frankfurt in the European Space of Flows

Jonathan V. Beaverstock, Michael Hoyler, Kathryn Pain, and Peter J. Taylor

THE RISE OF FRANKFURT

It is hard to pinpoint the beginning of Frankfurt's transformation from German city to "world city" status. Some academics have put the time as early as the late 1960s when economic activities that were to become the axes of the global economy began to concentrate in Frankfurt (Keil and Ronneberger 2000). But by the late 1980s, Frankfurt had attributes that appeared to set it apart from other cities within Germany as a world rather than a national city. The landmark skyline of the financial and business district today denotes the city's current role as a prominent international hub, and the economic globalization literature would suggest that, as Germany's leading financial center, Frankfurt should be on a rising trajectory (Bördlein 1999; Felsenstein, Schamp, and Shachar 2002; Harrschar-Ehrnborg 2002).

In spite of Frankfurt's ascendancy to Germany's main financial center (see Holtfrerich 1999; Schamp 1999), Germany's historical development and relatively decentralized national political and economic structure have meant that Frankfurt has lacked the prominence that London has had in the UK. Whereas the UK financial and business services industry is centered in London, Frankfurt is one of several German cities with complementary functional specializations (Blotevogel 2000). An important recent question has been whether changes associated with European Economic and Monetary Union (EMU), with the UK outside, would change Frankfurt's status in a "Europe of Cities," bringing it out from London's long shadow. Can Frankfurt rival London? This question stimulated the research reported here.

This chapter is divided into four parts. The first part briefly discusses Frankfurt's position among world cities, which sets the context for the research. Parts two and three constitute the bulk of the chapter and provide a detailed empirical analysis of Frankfurt's relations with London at the onset of the introduction of the euro and of organizational tensions pertaining to firms in both cities. Finally, several conclusions are reported, the gist of which are that, for the foreseeable future, London will most likely continue to cast a long shadow over all of its European world city neighbors.

FRANKFURT IN THE SHADOW

This section reviews the evidence for the importance of Frankfurt as a contemporary world city. The argument begins with the conventional concern for locating cities within urban hierarchies before developing a network approach to understanding the current role of Frankfurt in the world economy. This discussion is important because it is necessary to understand what sort of shadow London casts over Frankfurt.

FRANKFURT IN THE WORLD CITY HIERARCHY

For nearly two decades, studies of relations between world cities have been dominated by Friedmann's (1986) identification of a "world city hierarchy." He classified cities according to the way they "articulated" production and markets in the world economy. In Friedmann's hierarchy, Frankfurt was designated as a "primary world city" (in the core economies), ranked fourth (behind London, Paris, and Rotterdam) in the European space economy (with Zurich fifth and Brussels, Milan, Vienna, and Madrid listed as "secondary" European cities) (see his table A.1, The World City Hierarchy). Of course, such rankings were based upon an analysis of "attribute data," for example the number of headquarters for transnational corporations (TNCs) or international institutions. No other German cities were identified in Friedmann's (1986) hierarchy.

Almost ten years later, Friedmann (1995, 35), drawing on Keil and Lieser (1992), noted that Frankfurt was the "premier German global city." Frankfurt was newly designated in his hierarchy of "spatial articulations" (1995, 24) as a "multinational articulation" for western Europe, along with Miami (which articulated into the Caribbean/Latin America), Los Angeles (Pacific Rim), Amsterdam or Randstad and Singapore (Southeast Asia). Frankfurt was a city that articulated capital in the western European space of flows, primarily through its position as a financial center, but it was not included as one of Friedmann's "global financial articulations," like London, New York, and Tokyo, which sat atop his hierarchy of thirty world cities (1995, 24). Friedmann's (1995) positioning of European world cities identifies as important "national articulations" Paris, France; Zurich, Switzerland; and Madrid, Spain; in the case of Germany, Munich and Düsseldorf-Cologne-Essen-Dortmund (Rhine-Ruhr) have been designated as "sub-national/regional articulations." Thus, there is no German "national articulation"; its world cities are either multinational or subnational articulators.

Table 2.1. London/Frankfurt Attributive Data: Key Financial Market Statistics

(1) Markets for Foreign Equities, 1999[a]					
	Turnover (£bn)	*% of World Turnover*	*No. of Foreign Companies Listed*	*% of Listings*	*Global Rank*
London	1,211		58.5	499	17 1
Frankfurt		104	5.0	195	6.9 4
Totals		2,072	100	2,833	100

(2) International Bond Market, 1999[b] (by nationality of issuer)		
	Value ($bn)	*% Share* *Global Rank*
Germany	223	18.4 2
UK	116	9.5 3
Total	1,215	100

(3) Market for Fund Management, 1999[c] (by institutional equity holdings, $bn)			
City	*Country*	*Equity Holdings*	*Global Rank*
London	UK	2,461	1
Frankfurt	Germany	310	13

(4) Location of Daily Derivatives Turnover[b] (by institutional equity holdings, $bn)		
	OTC Turnover April 1998 ($bn)	*Annual Number of Contracts (millions in 2000)* *Global Rank*
UK	171	223 1
Germany	34	454 5
Totals	474	3,074

(5) Foreign Exchange Dealing, 1998[b] (daily average)		
	Value ($bn)	*% Share* *Global Rank*
UK	637	32.2 1
Germany	94	7.0 5
Totals	1,571	100

Sources:
[a] London Stock Exchange (quoted in International Financial Services London [IFSL] 2001).
[b] Bank for International Settlements (quoted in IFSL 2001).
[c] Thomson Financial Investor Relations, *Target Cities Report 2000* (quoted in IFSL 2001).

Table 2.2.   The Number of Financial Institutions in London and Frankfurt

	Futures/ Derivatives Companies	FOREX/ Money Market Brokerage	Investment Banks	Investment Management Companies	Merchant Banks	Securities/Foreign Brokerage Banks Companies	
London	150	24	168	88	61	477	481*
Frankfurt	63	2	54	13	9	75	191**

Source: Seifert et al., The Performance of European Financial Centers—Indicators and Trends, at www.pal grave.com/business/professional/fcm (accessed November 1, 2003).
Notes:
* As of March 2000 (Source: IFSL 2001).
** For 2001 (*Source:* Deutsche Bundesbank, Vierteljahreszahlen, 3. Quartal, Hauptverwaltung Frankfurt, 2002).

This German particularity will appear in a modified guise in the empirical work below, but the key point to note first is that Frankfurt never makes the top tier in Friedmann's hierarchy: London is consistently shown as Europe's only world city at the hierarchy's apex. The statistics shown in tables 2.1 and 2.2 support the importance of London in comparison to Frankfurt. Using twelve basic indicators of financial prowess, London is found to be leading Frankfurt on ten of them. But it is important to understand that such figures do not indicate that London is above Frankfurt in a new urban hierarchy. These are attribute measures that show London to be a far larger financial center; they say nothing about how the two cities are linked, hierarchically or not. Attributes provide measures of size that allow cities to be ranked but should not be confused with hierarchical processes (Taylor 1997). To demonstrate the latter, there needs to be direction from above impinging on the actions below. This requires measures of relations between cities, not simple ranking by size. Thus, the two tables show London to be more important as a world city, a finding consistent with Friedmann's world city hierarchy, but it does not confirm the existence of the latter. In fact, it is not at all clear in what sense "London" directs "Frankfurt" as a hierarchical process. But such hierarchical theories originated before the contemporary information and communications technology (ICT) era and cannot explain the role of these cities in globalization (Beaverstock, Smith, and Taylor 1999).

FRANKFURT IN A WORLD CITY NETWORK

Because world cities operate as bases for transnational economic activity, they are inevitably tied together through multiple connectivities within a new space of flows that traverses what Castells (2000) calls the old "space of places." This suggests that unpacking the dominance of London's shadow in a Europe of Cities requires more than adding on an extra scale to traditional models of national urban hierarchies (see Taylor and Hoyler 2000; Taylor 2004). In a global space of flows wherein electronic communications eliminate distance costs, there is no intrinsic reason for cities to be arranged hierarchically. For this reason, conventional ways of viewing intercity relations have to give way to more flexible models. In this research, world cities are interpreted as constituting a network: following Castells (2000), they are the nodes that define a world city network. In order to investigate why Frankfurt remains in London's long shadow, despite the introduction of the euro at the end of the 1990s, it is therefore necessary to study the relations between Frankfurt and London within this world city network.

This is a challenging research goal given the multiplicity of material and virtual flows that connect contemporary global cities across geographical space. The starting point is to derive a careful specification of the world city network (Taylor 2001). The world city network is not like typical networks where the nodes (usually members of a group) are the actors that produce the network. In the generation of a contemporary world city network, advanced producer service firms are the key actors in world city network formation. This network is a triple-level structure in which the nodal and network levels are joined by a "subnodal" level of service firms within the nodes (cities). This defines an interlocking network in which the firms link together the cities through their office networks (Taylor 2001). Thus, financial and business service firms are the creators of the world city network through their global location strategies for servicing their clients. These firms have become the dominant internationally organized activities in the world economy because they must operate as cross-border networks (made possible by developments in ICT) to provide a "seamless" service for their corporate customers anywhere in the world (see Dicken 1998; Lee and Schmidt-Marwede 1993; Porteous 1999). To do this effectively and to compete successfully with market competitors, their city-based offices must function as cooperative cells within the global organization. In this way, these myriad office networks constitute a world city network with information, knowledge, ideas, plans, intelligence, strategy, instruction, and all other communication linking the cities together across the globe.

There is a very important corollary to replacing the hierarchical model with a network one. Hierarchies are premised on a process of competition; this is how the basic structure is created and reproduced. It follows that in a world city hierarchy, the prime relation is competitive as cities strive to climb the rungs of the structure. Networks are premised on processes of cooperation; without this fundamental mutuality any network will cease to function and collapse (Powell 1990). It follows that in a world city network, cities share a synergy of roles that are complementary within the operation of the network overall. Cities, therefore, do not themselves compete: the competition is between the firms operating in various global service markets. This has important theoretical and policy implications. There is a large literature on city competition that feeds into city boosterism policy making (encouraging city administrations to compete for mobile financial and business services). This is a place-based discourse and practice that largely ignores "external" factors in the success of cities. Of course, it is important for cities to attend to their locale to attract firms, but this will always be a minor feature compared to the general process of world city network formation. No amount of national and city government boosting of Kuala Lumpur as a place for business will lead to its replacing Singapore as the key Southeast Asian node in the world economy. The message is that cities need to be far less inward looking (place oriented) and to attend especially to their networks (Beaverstock et al. 2002).

Guided by this interlocking network model, data have been collected for 100 global service firms (see appendix 2.1) across 316 cities (Taylor, Catalano, and Walker 2002). Using basic network-analysis techniques, measures of interlocking connectivities between cities have been computed from this data to provide global network connectivity values (Taylor 2001; Taylor, Catalano, and Walker 2002). The global network connectivity of a city indicates its relational importance as a node within the world city network: the top twenty cities ranked by this measure are shown in the left columns of table 2.3. This relational measure confirms the importance of London compared to Frankfurt discussed above using attribute measures (tables 2.1 and 2.2): London is ranked top and Frankfurt ranked a relatively lowly fourteenth (behind four other European cities). Note that this way of portraying Frankfurt compared to London is much more sophisticated because it is a relational measure (involving 315 cities in all) with a specific meaning within a world city network model. In addition, this relational measurement approach is quite flexible. The global network connectivity measure covers firms in six different service sectors; if the connectivity is measured for banking/finance firms only, then a banking/finance measure of connectivity is produced. The results are shown in the right columns of table 2.3. This illustrates two things. First, while London remains number one, Frankfurt rises appreciably to seventh position (still behind Paris for global-scale connections, even in banking). Second, Frankfurt is more narrowly an international financial center rather than a more rounded global service center in comparison to London.

It is this interlocking model that informs the main research reported upon: the focus is on global service firms and how they use cities, specifically how they use Frankfurt and London.

**Table 2.3. Top Twenty Cities for Global Network Connectivity
and Banking Network Connectivity**

Global Network Connectivity			Banking Network Connectivity		
World City	*Rank*	*Score*	*International Financial Center*	*Rank*	*Score*
London	**1**	**1.000**	**London**	**1**	**1.000**
New York	2	0.976	New York	2	0.984
Hong Kong	3	0.707	Tokyo	3	0.943
Paris	4	0.699	Hong Kong	4	0.854
Tokyo	5	0.691	Singapore	5	0.804
Singapore	6	0.645	Paris	6	0.789
Chicago	7	0.616	**Frankfurt**	**7**	**0.698**
Milan	8	0.604	Madrid	8	0.686
Los Angeles	9	0.600	Jakarta	9	0.662
Toronto	10	0.595	Chicago	10	0.650
Madrid	11	0.594	Milan	11	0.633
Amsterdam	12	0.590	Sydney	12	0.625
Sydney	13	0.578	Los Angeles	13	0.617
Frankfurt	**14**	**0.567**	Mumbai	14	0.616
Brussels	15	0.557	San Francisco	15	0.614
São Paulo	16	0.541	São Paulo	16	0.611
San Francisco	17	0.508	Taipei	17	0.600
Mexico City	18	0.486	Shanghai	18	0.592
Zurich	19	0.485	Brussels	19	0.586
Taipei	20	0.477	Seoul	20	0.579

Source: Taylor and Catalano 2002.

FRANKFURT AND LONDON IN A EUROPE OF CITIES

The research phase ran between 2000 and 2001 and was funded by the Anglo-German Foundation for the Study of Industrial Society (Beaverstock et al. 2001). Recent significant developments—the introduction of the new European currency, the euro, and Frankfurt's new role as home of the European Central Bank (ECB), hence, as the capital city of Euroland—were the starting point for our study. An ongoing inventory of relevant information for the period from 1998 to 2001, including UK and German financial press reports, leading trade journal articles, and official data, was compiled to provide an overview of knowledge concerning changing Frankfurt-London relations in the public realm. The primary research was a major face-to-face interview survey. In-depth interviews were conducted with key players at the ranks of senior partner, chief executive, and so on, in top international producer service firms (as listed in the top ten of their respective business sectors) and institutions in each city. Altogether, forty-eight interviews were conducted with firms in banking, accountancy, law, management consulting, and advertising at two census points, and twenty-six interviews were conducted with the senior executives of regulatory, trade, and professional organizations and government agencies.

A COMPETITION DISCOURSE

As expected, the discourse dominating the specific topic of concern at the start of the research was premised on competition. Frankfurt was widely regarded as being at a critical point with respect to its development as a world city in rivalry to London. The particular significance of the euro for Frankfurt's status as a world city was that the new currency, with the UK outside EMU, would give Frankfurt a natural advantage over London in the European region.

First, the German government's success, and the UK government's failure, in securing the location of the ECB in Frankfurt as opposed to London was seen as promoting Frankfurt's position (symbolically at least, relative to London) since, in the future, monetary policy for eleven (now twelve) countries would be controlled there. Second, the concurrent demise of the London International Financial Futures Exchange (LIFFE) and the success of Deutsche Terminbörse in the international futures market suggested that technological developments were allowing businesses to slip away from London. Third, with the advent of the euro, trade and professional reports predicted that Frankfurt would become the city where international banks and other business services (for example, accountancy, management consulting, law, and advertising) would congregate in the future to access an expanding continental European market.

Together, these changes were expected to raise Frankfurt's profile as a world city significantly in relation to London. As the financial center of the most powerful economy in Europe (Germany) and the European financial center for the Eurozone, could Frankfurt emerge from the shadow of London to be the premier world city in Europe? Financial press coverage in Frankfurt and London for the period between 1998 and 2001 depicted a fierce rivalry between the cities. A supposed London-versus-Frankfurt competition was a top news item, with the majority of reports portraying the relationship between the cities as a serious battle for supremacy.

In 1998, the year leading up to the issuing of the new currency, typical commentaries included "Frankfurt's growth is overshadowed by that of London"; "Frankfurt could reduce the lead of London"; "Will Britain's decision to stay out of the first wave enable Frankfurt to wrest leadership from London?." Frequently, the language used to describe Frankfurt-London relations could have been referring to an international war. For example, in the British *Fi-*

nancial Times, the relationship was described as "a bitter war for supremacy" or "a battle between London and Frankfurt," while the German *Frankfurter Allgemeine Zeitung* talked of London as a "threat" and about Frankfurt's "power play."

Frankfurt's Manhattan-style office skyline was depicted as a symbol of the city's success and rivalry with the city of London. A series of articles in the *Financial Times Deutschland* in November 2000 showed a photograph of Frankfurt's skyscrapers and asked, "Wie lange stehen diese Türme noch in Frankfurt?" [How long will these towers still be standing in Frankfurt?]; "Was wurde richtig gemacht, was falsch?" "Wie steht die Stadt im internationalen Vergleich da?" [What has been done right, what wrong? What is the position of the city in international comparison?].

This was the way the Frankfurt-London relation was widely portrayed; through primary research on the cities' relationships as service business hubs within a world city network, we set out to look beneath the surface of this powerful media representation.

PRACTITIONERS USING FRANKFURT AND LONDON

The interviews set out to shed light on the processes underlying relations between London and Frankfurt, drawing on the experience of key business practitioners in the two cities. Questioning was designed to draw out, first, the firms' adjustment to the euro with respect to Frankfurt-London relations and, second, perceptions of how each service sector was responding to the euro with respect to Frankfurt-London relations in the context of wider global relations. Firms were interviewed on two occasions to evaluate the situation one and two years after the launch of the currency. Where a firm had offices in both cities, we investigated the varying importance and functions of offices in both Frankfurt and London. Where a firm had offices in only one city, we investigated how it dealt with business in the other city and how this was changing.

The results reveal a relationship between the cities that reflects their roles in a global context and is much more complex than simple attribute data comparisons suggest. At an early stage, it became clear that it was not possible to single out relations between just two cities, confirming our network theoretical framework. Global service provision involves specific operational practices relating to information, skills, labor, and cultural flow that transcend but also differentiate the "space of places."

THE EURO AS A TRIGGER OF CHANGE?

As a starting point for the interviews, we addressed the popular press contention that the introduction of the euro and the location of the ECB in

Frankfurt would change relations between the cities. Responses across sectors in both cities were highly consistent. The overwhelming finding was, first, that business environment and market conditions take precedence over currency in determining relations between the cities; second, that Frankfurt's recent development as a financial and business services center has not been detrimental to business in London; and, third, that London remains regarded as the unassailable top global city in Europe (see box 2.1).

Surprisingly, the euro was a nonissue. The ECB has been an image boost for Frankfurt but has not had a detrimental effect on London as a financial center. However, it was seen as essential that London ensure its inclusion in European Union (EU) policymaking.

Box 2.1. Effects of the Euro:
Frankfurt's Future as a Global City Relative to London

- No effects from euro; currency is not an issue.
- Shifting business opportunities are critical; however, the euro may be affecting clients, and this could have indirect effects for some professional services eventually.
- UK exchange rate instability and isolationism outside the EMU could be problems in the longer term.
- Frankfurt-London relationships are shifting a little, although the changes are not as strong as expected. Frankfurt is moving toward greater innovation, deregulation, liberalization, and integration of markets and is capturing some parts of the financial services market.
- The German market is expanding and is very important with clients increasingly demanding cross-border professional services. Firms need to be close to the customer in continental Europe.
- Frankfurt is strengthening its position relative to London but will always be in a "second league" of world cities held back by German decentralization.
- The increasing strength of Frankfurt is feeding into London, not draining strength away from it. The EMU is a symptom and facilitator of underlying change, not the cause.
- Frankfurt is a cheaper place to do business than London and is increasingly liberalized, but it remains overregulated with inflexible employment structures, and an undeveloped skills base, high social costs, and a dull living environment compared to London.
- London and its institutions cannot be complacent. London remains the top global center in Europe—it is more liberal and open to foreign investment than Frankfurt. It provides a "level playing field" with greater critical mass, depth of infrastructure, skills, creativity, and employment flexibility, and the international business language is spoken there. However, it is increasingly congested and expensive and social costs are rising.

Comments showing the lack of importance attached to the euro as a cause of change include "The fact that the euro has not been introduced in England has changed nothing in relation to the leading position of London, including the euro-business"; "It's having no effect on business strategy"; "There hasn't been a rush to Frankfurt since the introduction of the euro." These views were strongly reinforced during the telephone interviews of the second census period. No difference of response on the issue of the importance of the euro on service business relations between London and Frankfurt emerged from a comparison of the two sets of interview results. Recent investigations in both Frankfurt (Spahn et al. 2002) and London (HM Treasury 2003) confirm our findings on the minor role of the new currency as an agent of locational change nearly five years after its introduction.

So, if the new currency and Frankfurt's associated new role were not determinants of change, what were? The interviews went on to explore in what ways business and market conditions considered important by interview respondents affected Frankfurt-London relations. A series of crosscutting tensions and relational networks were found to shape the global and local geography of service business.

THE SPACE OF FRANKFURT-LONDON
RELATIONS IN A EUROPE OF CITIES

Markets and Tensions: A Global-Local Space

Competition in globalizing transnational markets was seen as the key driving force behind service network geography. An increasing need to respond to processes of globalization was frequently named as the prerequisite for doing business successfully in the local contexts of London and Frankfurt. In the world of advanced producer service business, relations between the cities can only be meaningfully understood in the context of a "global-local space" that varies considerably within and between the sectors studied.

Banks vary most in the geographical extent of their market operations. Only the largest investment banks claimed to have a truly global business strategy. Most banks were dominant players in a European (or, in the case of some UK banks, domestic) market, but most indicated that "international" ambitions are mounting. The regionalization of European financial markets was seen as a key driver of cross-border market participation and local representation. However, business relations between Frankfurt and London consistently reflected London's specialist role as an "international" hub and Frankfurt's role as a "local" base for continental European and German business. Continental European banks have no alternative than to run two big operations (a national-based headquarters and a London office), but not all German banks are headquartered in Frankfurt, and non-German banks maintain a much smaller presence in Frankfurt than in London—office size is adjusted flexibly to suit market requirements. E-commerce is an increasingly important mode for the development of cross-border ability, suggesting that some business flows could bypass Frankfurt.

In legal services, increasing global reach was seen as essential to maintaining firms' client bases. All major law firms were said to be required to provide an international service. In this context, cross-border relationships between London and Germany have recently mushroomed to enable UK law firms to service transnational clients and access the German market and to enable German law firms to engage with the growing international legal market. Marked national differences in professional practice and business culture have not stood in the way of a spate of mergers. Cross-border relations were seen as essential to business expansion in both countries, but whereas Frankfurt is one of several centers for legal services in Germany, albeit by far the most important for corporate legal work, in the UK, international business law practice is confined to London.

While accounting and management-consulting firms have a tradition of international operations, markets were generally perceived as remaining predominantly local. Yet, the expanding European market is creating a shift in business relations. The size of the German market and latent demand for professional services is increasing business relations between London and Frankfurt predominantly for financial services and high-tech business. National differences in business and professional practice and regulations were emphasized and relations between the cities were seen in terms of a transfer of Anglo-Saxon skills and practice from London to Frankfurt.

Advertising products were regarded as crossing borders more easily than those of other services, yet maintaining a local presence remains vital to reflect cultural diversity. One advertising executive commented, "If you took our advertising in the UK or Germany, it's still the same car, or it's still the same media, so it's the cultural difference which you have to understand." Although London is the European headquarters for most agencies and widely regarded as a global creative center of excellence, the success of all service hubs (including Frankfurt and London) was thought to be essential to network competitiveness. However, whereas London clearly is the major advertising center for the UK market, Frankfurt is one of five main advertising centers in Germany (including Düsseldorf, Hamburg, Munich, and Berlin).

Relations between London and Frankfurt were found to be fundamentally linked to global and local market conditions. The dynamic nature of customer-servicing relationships, labor markets, business products, and technologies results in a complexity of contradictory drivers and tensions that firms must manage continuously to remain competitive. Specific market characteristics for each sector vary, but the basic tension for all firms is reconciling the need for global reach against the need to engage with local

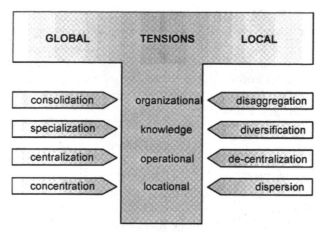

Figure 2.1. Tensions in interfirm competition.

markets. This basic underlying tension shapes the Frankfurt-London network space.

The Global-Local Tension

A global-local tension underpins a series of specific tensions relating to organizational structure, knowledge production, and operational and locational issues, as illustrated by figure 2.1.

Demand for cross-border services gives firms the incentive to expand their geographical market coverage, and many firms insist that failure to do so would seriously damage their ability to win business and remain competitive in their markets, as in the case of London law firms, which perceive an absolute need for a physical presence in the German legal market. At the same time, globalizing market competition means that firms also feel considerable pressure to remain physically close to their customers and to engage actively with local markets. These twin pressures lead to an increase in the size of firms to achieve both local and global market coverage and an integrated, "seamless" service across borders.

Organizational Tension

The perceived need for critical mass to compete effectively on a global scale and the stretching of business organization across geographical space in cross-border markets are associated with contradictory drivers. They lead to organizational consolidation—in legal services, for example, "anything that moves has merged"—and to organizational rationalization to stay economically competitive. At the same time, firms stress the need to focus on core functions (by outsourcing peripheral functions) and to demonstrate flexibility within markets. This produces a counterdriver for disaggregation and the demerging and vertical breakup of traditional organizational structures across business services. The pressures for increased industry representation at the top end of the services sectors and at the bottom "niche" market end are likely to drive continuing restructuring of business relations between London and Frankfurt.

Knowledge Tension

The knowledge products of business services are associated with similar contradictions. Skilled people and their business knowledge are firms' key assets. Competition between firms within labor markets and for market share leads to specialization but also to diversification so that firms can differentiate their services from those offered by their competitors. In accountancy, "Everybody's looking now for more and more specialism"; "We're migrating skills [from London] to other European countries, particularly Frankfurt." In legal services, the need to build specialist teams has led to "whole teams being poached" in Frankfurt and London. In management consulting, intense competition for skills is leading to the formation of new business models, strategic alliances, and market diversification: "Consulting doesn't describe what we do . . . We don't naturally fit anyone's segmentation. . . . Frankfurt will be an important part of that and London will."

Operational Tension

At the same time, operational decentralization and local interpretation is a priority for building customer relationships and engaging with local markets. In law, "If you get to number one or two in the UK, you can't pretend to be a global firm if you're offering a number eight operation in Germany, or France, or Italy. You've got to be in the top three everywhere." A German banker in London commented, "You can't just sit here and expect everyone to come. . . . Increasingly you have to put your resources onto the ground because you want to be close to the customer . . . because there's a lot of competition out there."

Both decentralizing and centralizing tendencies can be seen in operational networks. On the one hand, ICT developments allow functions to be located almost anywhere in the world, yet there are also pressures to control risk and reduce costs by centralizing functions. German and continental European banks are increasingly putting key global functions in London: "Centralization brings control, and it's reinforcing the concept of identity and team";

"You have to have a big critical mass in each location to achieve focus on organizational goals . . . significant, hidden, non-monetary costs . . . turn into monetary costs in decentralizing. . . . Operational risks limit how much division of labor you can have."

Locational Tension

Economic competitiveness also brings a need to disperse functions away from expensive global city locations where possible to reduce space and labor costs. A non-European banker in London told us, "We'll move all our operations out, everything over five years, move them to a cheaper environment. . . . We want to keep the intellectual capital close together at the moment until we can develop the technology that allows [us] to share intellectual learning and capital with each other but do it with technology—that time's probably not very far away."

Yet, proximity in London and Frankfurt is critical to contemporary service business. The presence of skilled labor markets and the agglomeration economies associated with face-to-face contact and knowledge transfer in global cities are also strong drivers for locational concentration. The same banker went on to tell us, "I see more concentration coming in here [London] all the time and less and less in other places. . . . Over time you could see a hell of a lot more trading taking place in this environment." Another banker commented, "The need for human contact is incredible. It's still a very, very strong issue. . . . That's an overriding factor. Despite all the potential the Internet offers, there will still be a very, very strong desire by management to keep everything colocated." A lawyer noted, "Sitting in London, I've got both local and global" and an accountant commented, "the issues about London and therefore whether face-to-face meeting/conferencing are important, in my view that hasn't changed and will not change."

Attempts to resolve these various tensions produce dynamic flows within and between service business networks that play a crucial role in constructing and reconstructing relationships between the cities. But interview discussion highlighted the fact that wider forms of relational networks beyond the discussed office linkages play a key role in shaping London-Frankfurt relations.

INTERWEAVING NETWORKS

Responses revealed the complexity of the space of flows associated with cross-border service business operations. We identified four interweaving, wider relational networks that affect London-Frankfurt relations (figure 2.2).

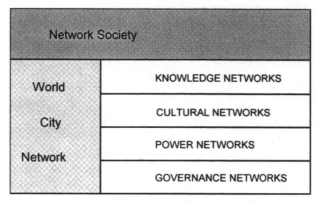

Figure 2.2.   Networks in the global city network.

Knowledge Networks

Knowledge flows from inner-city networks.   "Local" flows of knowledge between London and Frankfurt are highly interconnected with wider,
intercity network flows. Potentially, knowledge can be made available anywhere in the world through a network: "You can do it from almost anywhere, and it's only some of the old regulatory structures and things like that
that are almost keeping the physical" (banking, London). "It is out of the network that ideas are being generated. . . . It doesn't really matter whether this
person is in Hamburg or Frankfurt because they take their network with
them" (advertising, Frankfurt).

Skills are flowing to Frankfurt.   In all sectors, knowledge is being
transferred from London to Frankfurt: "You have to . . . bring the resources
to wherever they're needed," and people from London are being sent to
Frankfurt to develop the skills of people there (accountancy, London).

ICT opens up new spatial relationships.   ICT is allowing the formation of innovative spatial relations between firms and markets and is an important future medium for firms to engage with local markets globally. Local
market knowledge and close client relationships are increasingly important
in a competitive market, causing firms to feel the need for a physical presence in Frankfurt: "One of the advantages of a network [is], if you have to do
something in another country, you can adapt it, [but] you'll have to have the
people there who can smell and feel and know that and who can then realize it" (advertising, Frankfurt). But technology offers economies of scale, "a
bifurcation . . . an execution platform and a research platform that interfaces
with customers with little human touch" (banking, London). These developments open up possibilities of engaging with markets through a smaller local, physical presence (see also Grote, Lo, and Harrschar-Ehrnborg 2002).

Some business flows could bypass Frankfurt. European services headquarters and knowledge concentration remain focused in London. Future business strategies for banking in Frankfurt are likely to be flexible: "There has to be a real business reason. . . . There would have to be a real demand to operate a specific operation out of Frankfurt" (UK bank); "We kept our service functions there [Frankfurt] on the ground and invested in them" (UK bank); "We have a presence in Frankfurt to reflect the current role of Frankfurt in the equity markets. . . . Our options are open with regard to Frankfurt at the moment, but the concentration of investment presently is elsewhere [London]" (continental European Bank). The scale of presence in Frankfurt is likely to be adjusted to suit market needs. European banks use various familiar front-shop brand names to collect business, but the handling of those business transactions is done in London for added value "because that's an efficient place to conduct business" (German bank), and not all German banks will require a substantial physical presence in Frankfurt.

Cultural Networks

Skilled people flow to London. Location of workforce has become more important than location of customers, and where skilled people want to live is a critical labor-market and office-location determinant: "Intelligent people who create something new are concentrated in a few special places" (UK bank, Frankfurt); "We need to be able to recruit good people. As far as our location in London's concerned, we can get good people" (advertising, London); "From the client-service point of view, personally, I don't think it's important that we have an office in London at all . . . but from a point of view of . . . the team of consultants . . . for emotional reasons, social reasons, they might not be so keen [to move]" (management consulting, London).

"City culture" matters. Skilled workforce members are increasingly lifestyle conscious, and even key decision makers have personal (as well as corporate) motivations regarding where they want to work and live. This highlights the importance of the cities as places of consumption: "With modern technology . . . it doesn't matter whether [markets] are in Frankfurt or in London or even Timbuctoo. . . . People have to live somewhere. . . . You could imagine the relative importance of financial centers being dictated by quite different things from where's the most liquid market because the liquidity can flow from anywhere—where's the most pleasant to live, theatres, restaurants, and all sorts of secondary issues" (management consulting, London).

Frankfurt lacks "city buzz." Ambitious people were said to want to work in London, not Frankfurt. The difficulty of recruiting people in Frankfurt was emphasized in both cities. Attitudes to Frankfurt as a place to live were generally negative. Frankfurt is regarded as "boring" and "dead from seven or eight o'clock at night" (law, London); "The quality of people I have recruited has become better, but it is arduous. If we can't find people in Germany, we try it internationally, but it involves higher costs to get people to move to Frankfurt, and there is the language problem" (law, Frankfurt); "It's extremely difficult to attract German top advertising people to Frankfurt. . . . There is no inspiring environment here" (advertising, Frankfurt). "The English, Americans, or French are not very keen to come to Germany; that's almost non-existent" (law, Frankfurt). We were told that even Germans used to living in London, if asked to move to Frankfurt, "think it's like being banished to the Third World" (management consulting, London).

Diversity is a strength of London. Diversity of cultures and languages is essential to engaging with local markets everywhere from a global city hub, and these are available in London. In investment banking, London offices are internationally staffed to incorporate multiple ethnicities in an increasingly "less defined" world: "Part of the supporting infrastructure is . . . the cosmopolitan nature of London as a city. . . . Firms can access any language they need from all the different communities that are actually present in London. . . . It's about the ease of doing business."

Power Networks

Power flows to London. More power is concentrated in London than Frankfurt due to the UK's history of global connections. In general, firms' global leadership positions are located in at most eight to ten cities, and more key staff members are located in London than in Frankfurt, which has implications for decision making and global influence. Power relations are constructed by the scale of existing infrastructure and resource investment. A newly elected European leader based in Frankfurt in one international management-consulting firm would almost certainly have to move to London. "This, rightly or wrongly is where the European leadership sits. . . . If he wanted to change the European location, of course he could do that, but it's a bit of an effort. There's a little bit of infrastructure!" Frankfurt was described in both cities as a service center for the local German/European market held back by a lack of skills and excessive regulation.

London is an international hub and club. The fact that London is favored by Americans, particularly U.S. investment banks, was seen as "absolutely critical" to London's position: "The American banks are at the heart of it. . . . They have a lot less attachment to Frankfurt" (institution, London). The fact that English is the international business language and London's openness and merchant heritage are important and lead to a critical mass of skills and knowledge. London was described as "an ever-shifting club . . . a hub with all of those skills, both local and cross-border, all around me"; "London is so easy as a global hub—it's a great advantage if you're trying to be a global financial city, and you're actually in a global city. . . . There's genuinely global ownership of London" (non-European bank).

The benefits of openness outweigh the risks. London was seen as providing an infrastructure for transnational business—a producer services "Wimbledon"—creating scale and critical mass that would not otherwise be present: "Very few companies in the city of London are owned in this country, or capitalized in this country. . . . They're mainly American or European owned now [but] the decisions are still being made here" (law, London). The volume and strength of business flows was seen as "hard to dislodge" (institution, London).

Frankfurt lacks London's national prominence. Frankfurt's position as one of a number of important German business centers holds back its development relative to London: "Big business is taken away from Frankfurt and is being done elsewhere. . . . The decision center for many things is London and not Frankfurt" (law, Frankfurt); "[For European banks] this is the village where they meet all their competitors and their financiers" (institution, London); "I don't think I could point you to a case where anyone has said, 'Ah, we can do this in Frankfurt, but we can't do it here.' . . . I don't remember anyone who has said . . . 'What we're going to do is beef up our Frankfurt operations and transfer stuff from London to Frankfurt'" (institution, London).

Governance Networks

Regulation matters. Regulatory context is a critical determinant of cross-border business flows, and there are important differences between Frankfurt and London. For London, there is a strong emphasis on maintaining balanced regulation and a level playing field, while, for Frankfurt, there is a greater focus on control and internal growth: "The infrastructure of the market is all privately owned in one way or another. . . . Is that a disadvantage, or does that just reflect the nature of the market place these days? . . . London will do better . . . if you're prepared to be open to new competitors. . . . We don't try to bias things in one direction or another" (institution, London).

Frankfurt is less open, but this could change. In Frankfurt and London, we were told that Germany needs to "open up" and come into line with international business practice to increase its international business activity. European regulatory change and progress toward the single market could force reform within Germany to Frankfurt's advantage as a global city. Enlargement, less regulated labor markets, corporate restructuring, increasing demand for producer services, and the impact of Anglo-Saxon business practice were predicted to increase Germany's power, and this could benefit Frankfurt. Harmonization of accounting standards and growth in European and German equity markets, providing a deep, liquid pool of capital, were said to present an opportunity for Frankfurt's growth.

Cross-border governance is an issue for London. Continuing progress toward a single European market was seen as important for London. A level playing field was said to be needed to remove obstacles to fluid cross-border business flows. Ensuring that the UK has equal access to the single market if it remains outside the EMU and that EU directives be consistently implemented in each member state were key London concerns.

City competition is unhelpful to business flows. Institutional conflicts of interest are damaging to cross-border business, suggesting a need for cooperation across administrative boundaries. In Germany, conflicting interests arise from the decentralized structure of public and private governance and the separation of Frankfurt as a financial center from the political capital. In the UK, more focused governance benefits London, but institutional conflicts of interest are perceived as holding back London's growth.

CONCLUSION

In this chapter, we have gone against the grain of almost all previous world city research (e.g., Friedmann 1986, 1995) and studies of international financial centers (e.g., Lee and Schmidt-Marwede 1993; Porteous 1999) that are premised on hierarchical urban structures, deeply embedded in the city-competition discourse spawned from comparative, attributive data analyses. Instead, we have used a major economic event, the EMU, to investigate Frankfurt and London through a relational discourse as part of a world city network. Three major conclusions are drawn.

London remains the favored European global city service hub. Despite London's being officially outside of "Euroland" and the location of the ECB in Frankfurt, all the evidence shows that international business flows continue to be focused on London, leaving Frankfurt in its shade. We have shown that the reasons for this can be pinpointed as resulting from the global-local tensions and interweaving networks we have identified. Five key factors stand out. First, London's long-term depth of infrastructure and critical mass of knowledge, skills, languages, and power continue to be key business location factors. Second, London is an "open" city for business and a global market location with favorable regulation, taxation, and employment policies. Third, London provides critical agglomeration and scale economies through having the highest international flows of capital, knowledge, and skills in Europe. Fourth, London has a strong, transnational, skilled and specialized labor market with the diversity of languages and cultures required by international business that is unrivalled in Europe. Fifth, London's city culture is important because in "people-driven" business, it is the preferred city to live in; thus, it is chosen as a hub for international business, particularly by U.S. firms.

In short, as with all previous studies of London as an international financial center (see Corporation of London 2003), it is the premier European financial city.

London and Frankfurt complement one another in the contemporary European space of flows. The first finding does not mean that the scale of London's advantage over Frankfurt is necessarily damaging to Frankfurt. London does not win at the expense of Frankfurt because they are both integral parts of the world city network in Europe. Thus, London's concentration and proximity of markets, skills, and experience in a single location within Europe has been shown to be an important benefit to business in Frankfurt. Typical arguments from respondents were, "London has acted as a model for Frankfurt, and Frankfurt has profited from looking to London" (law, Frankfurt); "London is in the space between New York and Europe; it doesn't prevent the euro area developing" (institution, London). Skills are flowing to Frankfurt from London. Frankfurt is close to an expanding market and has strong technology and infrastructure. Frankfurt's importance is growing: "Stock market activity in Frankfurt is going to grow compared with London. . . . The UK is a mature market. German GDP is a good deal higher than ours. When German stock market capitalization to GDP is at a comparable ratio to ours, domestic German market activity is going to far exceed ours"; "[Although] London will remain the center for global, cross-border, international market activity, Frankfurt will grow hugely in terms of financial services on the back of an expanding German domestic market" (institution, London). The key point is that Frankfurt's growing connections with London are seen as essential to the development of international business in Frankfurt, and Frankfurt is increasing its importance as a "gateway city" from London to continental European markets: "London is the European interface, and, so, Frankfurt's strength is good for London" (institution, London); "[The] increasing strength of Frankfurt is feeding into London not draining away from it. . . . Greater volume coming out of Frankfurt actually just builds activity in London" (institution, London). Frankfurt has prospered by being within both similar and different webs of connections to London—the cities have different, complementary roles within a Europe of cities.

The positioning of London and Frankfurt within a European space of flows is necessary for meaningful analyses of their intercity changes in contemporary globalization. All the empirical material reported in this chapter supports our initial theoretical approach to understanding intercity relations. London and Frankfurt are shown to be part of a world city network with an interlocking structure. Financial and business service firms have created this network and continue to attend to it (see Beaverstock et al. 2002). Thus, changing relations between London and Frankfurt are part of this network reproduction that transcends particular events, such as the launch of the euro. After all, it is largely the same banks and service firms that operate in and through both cities. Given that they need to be in both cities, these firms typically have made large investments in each city; therefore, they have vested interests in the success of both cities. In short, increasing city interdependencies are being brought about by global interfirm competition in cross-border markets: it is firms that compete, not cities. For this reason, London's superior strength of global network connectivity does not seem to challenge or to be threatened by relations with Frankfurt. In fact, quite the opposite is the case—the evidence we have presented for 2000–2001 shows the growth of both cities has been boosted.

ACKNOWLEDGMENTS

We would like to acknowledge the Anglo-German Foundation for the Study of Industrial Society for funding this research from the project "Comparing London and Frankfurt as World Cities."

REFERENCES

Beaverstock, J. V., Doel, M. A., Hubbard, P. J., and Taylor, P. J. 2002. "Attending to the world: competition, cooperation and connectivity in the world city network." *Global Networks* 2, no. 2: 111–32.

Beaverstock, J. V., Hoyler, M., Pain, K., and Taylor, P. J. 2001. *Comparing London and Frankfurt as World Cities: A Relational Study of Contemporary Urban Change*. London: Anglo-German Foundation for the Study of Industrial Society, at www.agf.org.uk/pubs/pdfs/1290web.pdf (accessed November 4, 2005).

Beaverstock, J. V., Smith, R. G., and Taylor, P. J. 1999. "A roster of world cities." *Cities* 16, no. 6: 445–58.

Blotevogel, H. H. 2000. "Gibt es in Deutschland Metropolen? Die Entwicklung des deutschen Städtesystems und das Raumordnungskonzept der 'Europäischen Metropolregionen.'" In *Metropolen: Laboratorien der Moderne*, ed. D. Matejovski, 179–208. Frankfurt am Main: Campus.

Bördlein, R. 1999. "Finanzdienstleistungen in Frankfurt am Main. Ein europäisches Finanzzentrum zwischen Kontinuität und Umbruch." *Berichte zur deutschen Landeskunde* 73, no. 1: 67–93.

Castells, M. 2000. *The Rise of the Network Society*. 2nd ed. Oxford: Blackwell.

Corporation of London. 2003. *Financial Services Clustering and Its Significance for London*. London: Corporation of London.

Dicken, P. 1998. *Global Shift*. 3rd ed. London: PCP.

Felsenstein, D., Schamp, E. W., and Shachar, A., eds. 2002. *Emerging Nodes in the Global Economy: Frankfurt and Tel Aviv Compared*. Dordrecht: Kluwer.

Friedmann, J. 1986. "The world city hypothesis." *Development and Change* 17: 69–83.

———. 1995. "Where we stand: a decade of world city research." In *World Cities in a World System,* ed. P. L. Knox and P. J. Taylor, 21–47. Cambridge: Cambridge University Press.

Grote, M. H., Lo, V., and Harrschar-Ehrnborg, S. 2002. "A value chain approach to financial centres—the case of Frankfurt." *Tijdschrift voor Economische en Sociale Geografie* 93, no. 4: 412–23.

Harrschar-Ehrnborg, S. 2002. *Finanzplatzstrukturen in Europa: die Entstehung und Entwicklung von Finanzzentren.* Frankfurt am Main: Lang.

HM Treasury. 2003. *The Location of Financial Activity and the Euro.* London: HMSO.

Holtfrerich, C.-L. 1999. *Finanzplatz Frankfurt. Von der mittelalterlichen Messestadt zum europäischen Bankenzentrum.* München: Beck.

International Financial Services London (IFSL). 2001. *International Financial Markets in the UK* (April 2001). London: IFSL.

Keil, R., and Lieser, P. 1992. "Frankfurt: global city—local politics." In *After Modernism: Global Restructuring and the Changing Boundaries of City Life,* ed. M. P. Smith, 39–69. New Brunswick, NJ: Transaction Publishers.

Keil, R., and Ronneberger, K. 2000. "The globalization of Frankfurt am Main: core, periphery and social conflict." In *Globalizing Cities: A New Spatial Order?* ed. P. Marcuse and R. van Kempen, 228–48. Oxford: Blackwell.

Lee, R., and Schmidt-Marwede, U. 1993. "Interurban competition? Financial centres and the geography of financial production." *International Journal of Urban and Regional Research* 17, no. 3: 492–515.

Porteous, D. 1999. "The development of financial centres: location, information externalities and path dependency." In *Money and the Space Economy,* ed. R. Martin, 96–115. Chichester, UK: Wiley.

Powell, W. W. 1990. "Neither market nor hierarchy: network forms of organization." *Research in Organizational Behavior* 12: 295–336.

Schamp, E. W. 1999. "The system of German financial centres at the crossroads. From national to European scale." In *Cities in Perspective: Economy, Planning and Environment,* ed. E. Wever, 83–98. Assen, Netherlands: Van Gorcum.

Scifert, W. G., Achleitner, A. K., Mattern, F., Streit, C., and Voth, H. J. 2000. *European Capital Markets.* Basingstoke, UK: Macmillan.

Spahn, P. B., van den Busch, U. et al. 2002. *Position und Entwicklungsperspektiven des Finanzplatzes Frankfurt.* Wiesbaden: FEH-Report No. 645.

Taylor, P. J. 1997. "Hierarchical tendencies amongst world cities: a global research proposal." *Cities* 14, no. 6: 323–32.

———. 2001. "Specification of the world city network." *Geographical Analysis* 33: 181–94.

———. 2004. *World City Network: A Global Urban Analysis.* London: Routledge.

Taylor, P. J., and Catalano, G. 2002. "World city network formation in a space of flows." In *Stadt und Region: Dynamik von Lebenswelten,* ed. A. Mayr, M. Meurer, and J. Vogt, 68–76. Leipzig: Deutsche Gesellschaft für Geographie.

Taylor, P. J., Catalano, G., and Walker, D. R. F. 2002. "Measurement of the world city network." *Urban Studies* 39: 2367–76.

Taylor, P. J., and Hoyler, M. 2000. "The spatial order of European cities under conditions of contemporary globalization." *Tijdschrift voor Economische en Sociale Geografie* 91, no. 2: 176–89.

APPENDIX 2.1. GLOBAL SERVICE FIRMS: THE GAWC 100

Accountancy

AGN International
Arthur Andersen
BDO International
Ernst & Young
Fiducial International
Grant Thornton International
HLB International
Horwath International
International Group of Accounting
  Firms (IGAF)

KPMG International
MacIntyre Sträter International
Moore Stephens International
Moores Rowland International
Nexia International
PKF International
PricewaterhouseCoopers
RSM International
Summit International + Baker Tilly

Advertising

Asatsu DK
BBDO Worldwide
Carlson Marketing Group (CMG)
D'Arcy Masius Benton & Bowles
Draft Worldwide
Euro RSCG
Foote Cone & Belding (FCB)
Hakuhodo, Inc.

Impiric
J. Walter Thompson
McCann-Erickson WorldGroup
Ogilvy & Mather Worldwide, Inc.
Saatchi and Saatchi
TMP Worldwide
Young and Rubicam, Inc.

Banking/Finance

ABN-AMRO Holding NV
Bank of Tokyo-Mitsubishi
Barclays
Bayerische
HypoVereinsbank
Bayerische Landesbank
Girozentrale
BNP Paribas
Chase Hambrecht & Quist
CitiGroup (Citibank + SSBCiti
  Asset Management)
Commerzbank
Credit Suisse First Boston

Dai-Ichi Kangyo Bank
Deutsche Bank
Dresdner Bank
Fuji Bank
HSBC
ING Bank
J. P. Morgan
Rabobank International Sanwa
SDI (Sakura + Dellsher Bank)
Sumitomo Bank
UBS AG
Westdeutsche Landesbank
  Girozentrale (WestLB)

Insurance

Allianz Group
CGNU
Chubb Group
Fortis
Liberty Mutual

Lloyd's
Prudential
Reliance Group Holdings
Skandia Group
Winterthur

Law

Allen and Overy
Baker and McKenzie
Cameron McKenna
Clifford Chance
Coudert Brothers
Dorsey and Whitney
Freshfields Bruckhaus
Deringer
Jones Day

Latham and Watkins
Linklaters—Alliance
Lovells Boesebeck Droste
Morgan Lewis
Morrison and Foerster, LLP
Sidley and Austin
Skadden, Arps, Slate, Meagher,
and Flom, LLP
White and Case

Management Consultancy

A.T. Kearney
Bain & Company
Booze, Allen & Hamilton
Boston Consulting Group
Cap Gemini Consulting
Computer Sciences Corporation
(CSC)
Deloitte Touche
Tohmatsu

Hewitt Associates
International Business Machine
(IBM)
Logica Consulting
McKinsey & Company
Mercer Management Consulting
Sema Group
Towers Perrin
Watson Wyatt Worldwide

Note: See also www.lboro.ac.uk/gawc/datasets/da6.html.

3

Johannesburg 1986–2030: A Quest to Regain World Status

Keith S. O. Beavon

Johannesburg at the beginning of the twenty-first century finds itself in what might, in the longer term, be called its midlife crisis. It is no longer the great city firmly based on gold mining or the important manufacturing center it was in the 1960s; instead, it is a focal point for a concentration of sophisticated tertiary and ICT activities that now not only need to be globally competitive to survive and grow but must be provided with a globally competitive urban environment.

It is widely known that the central parts of Johannesburg experienced a sharp decline commencing in the 1980s (Robinson 2000). More recently, both the private sector, through the voice of the Centre for Development and Enterprise (CDE) (a private think tank) in Johannesburg, and the Johannesburg City Council have not only conducted their own research and analysis but indicated what they believe is the way forward for the city in an endeavor to restore its former status. This chapter focuses on the most important of the findings and proposals that have emerged from the two studies just mentioned, some of which have again been aired in the press as part of a local newspaper's evaluation of the current city management (see Bernstein 2003; Bethlehem 2003; Fraser 2003; Moriarty 2003).

Notwithstanding a large volume of literature on "world cities," this chapter references only those aspects of the literature resorted to by those who wish Johannesburg to have world city status once again, albeit only in the second tier, the rank once "conferred" by the influential academic John Friedmann in his seminal study published in 1986.

In the discussion that follows, it must be remembered that by the end of the 1980s, apartheid South Africa and its siege economy, with import substitution, had been isolated from the international community for almost thirty years. Reengagement with the world economy, world sport, and other activities meant that South Africa as a whole, but particularly its major city, had to accept, more or less overnight, the levels of globalization and best practice that other developed and successfully developing nations had been adopting and adapting to over a period of decades. As such, state protection in the form of subsidies and import controls fell away. The effects both in temporal, sectoral, and spatial terms were varied, but Johannesburg business people were quick to react to the changing circumstances by using the strategies of unbundling large conglomerates and substituting capital for labor in order to become globally competitive as quickly as possible; at the same time, for better or worse, they created a new central business district some 10 km north of the original one.

JOHANNESBURG IN ITS REGIONAL CONTEXT

Johannesburg in 2003, with a population of 3.2 million, is situated at the heart of the Witwatersrand, in the core Pretoria-Witwatersrand-Vereeniging (PWV) region of the Gauteng Province of South Africa. The city expanded its boundary in 2000 and now incorporates several formerly independent municipalities, notably Sandton and Randburg (see Carruthers 1980, 1981), which, by the late twentieth century, had constituted the loosely defined Johannesburg Metropolitan Area (Fair and Muller 1981; Beavon 1992), as well as Midrand (figure 3.1). Significantly, almost since its proclamation as a mining camp on the world's richest goldfield in 1886, the areal spread of the city and its near neighbors has been acentric, with most of the richest (formerly whites-only) areas concentrated increasingly to the north of the gold reef (figure 3.2).

THE CITY'S CHANGING INTERNATIONAL STATUS

Whereas Johannesburg was already enjoying something of world city status when it was only forty years old (MacDonald 1926), in its centenary year, it was included on the influential world city list drawn up by Friedmann, albeit as a "secondary [world] city in a semi-peripheral country" (1986). Johannesburg's appearance on Friedmann's 1986 list of world cities was surprising given its segregationist history (see Beavon 1982, 1999) and the fact that it was the premier city of a pariah state increasingly isolated from a shrinking world that was already in the early but accelerating stages of globalization. At the time, Johannesburg was coping with the fact that not only had it lost its gold-mining base through the depletion of the local ore bodies, but it had lost out to other regions of the country with respect to the location of man-

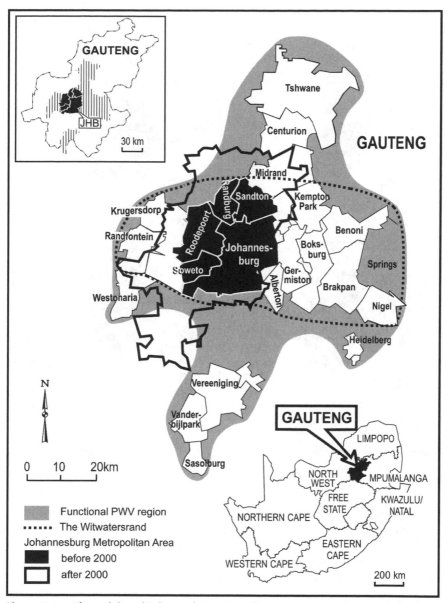

Figure 3.1. The unicity of Johannesburg 2002, its constituent regions, and the functional area of the PWV relative to the province of Gauteng.

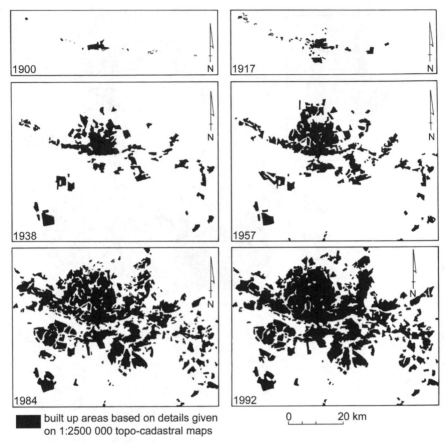

Figure 3.2.   Areal growth of Johannesburg and the central Witwatersrand, 1900–1992.

ufacturing industries in the apartheid economy. Furthermore, by 1986, the country had been ostracized by the whole of Africa, and Johannesburg could not be regarded as the springboard into the continent's economies. In addition, the Johannesburg central business district (CBD), which was long the citadel of South Africa's financial and retail muscle and by then constituted the new economic base of the city, was already in decline as increasing numbers of major businesses sought a new "home" in the then burgeoning and also whites-only town of Sandton.

The first steps toward South Africa's reengaging with the world came with the release from prison of Nelson Mandela in 1990. Although for the following four years, as politicians debated the process of transition to a democracy, the country teetered on the brink of civil war (see O'Meara 1996), both the elections and the transfer of power from the National Party government to the newly elected African National Congress went off peacefully in April 1994. At about the same time, Friedmann (1995) in his review of a decade of world city research, made the point that just as the ability of a city to attract global investment would determine its position in the order of world cities, so it might appear on and disappear from any world list (a similar point is made by Douglas 2000). In light of both those comments and, apparently, the four years of political turmoil in South Africa leading up to the elections, Johannesburg lost its place on Friedmann's list on the basis of what he described as the ongoing political struggle and, presumably, the economic uncertainties that flowed from it.

The fact that Johannesburg still found itself on other lists of variously defined world cities (see, inter alia, Knox and Agnew 1989; Keeling 1995; Finnie 1998; Petrella 1995; Beaverstock, Taylor, and Smith 1999) appears to have cut far less ice among the CDE and city council analysts than did its removal from the Friedmann list. Nevertheless, as a point of reference for people not familiar with Johannesburg, it should be noted that the city appears on the University of Loughborough's Globalization and World Cities (GaWC) inventory of world cities just above Munich and Buenos Aires and just below Mexico City, Montreal, and Seoul (Beaverstock, Taylor, and Smith 1999).

To provide some necessary background, this chapter next sets out a brief outline of some of the most important aspects of the decline of the old CBD and its reconstitution in the north.

THE DECLINE OF THE OLD CBD: 1970s TO 2000

By 1970, one-third of the white people employed in Johannesburg resided outside the municipality (Urban and Regional Research Unit 1973), and a range of decentralized shopping clusters had emerged in the white suburbs of both Johannesburg and its neighboring towns. Then, in the 1970s, two major malls were opened. The first, of 30,000 m², was placed in Sandton, a town where the wealthiest people of the metropolis were increasingly choosing to live. The other, of 90,000 m², was placed at an intercept point on the freeway system used by East Rand people who worked or shopped in central Johannesburg. The two large malls were an immediate success and sparked a massive growth in large malls and shopping centers, particularly in the "northern suburbs" (a term that included not only Johannesburg suburbs but also those of Randburg and Sandton) (Beavon 1997, 1998a, 1998b). The developments impacted negatively on high-order retailers in the CBD of Johannesburg, and they soon departed and headed for the suburbs and the municipalities of Randburg and Sandton, closer to the northward-shifting center of gravity of white purchasing power. Decentralized and speculative office clusters soon followed and increasingly drew office-based businesses from the CBD (Mandy 1984; Beavon 2000, 2003; Goga 2003).

Notwithstanding the major part that economic factors played in the early decline of the CBD, there was also a distinct racial element in the form of "white flight" northward in the years following the 1976 Soweto Revolt (Kane-Berman 1978) and more particularly during the era of rolling mass action against the apartheid regime, with unruly protest marches in the city center from the 1980s. The rush to the north included white residents from the fashionable high-rise apartment blocks of the inner-city residential area known colloquially as "Hillbrow."[1] With the passage of time, Hillbrow not only changed in terms of its racial composition but property values also dropped significantly (see Pickard-Cambridge 1988; Lupton 1992; Morris 1994; Beavon 1999).

By the mid-1980s, despite a significant loss of high-order retailing, the main financial institutions, including in particular the Johannesburg Stock Exchange and the registered offices of a large number of firms listed on its "main board," were still situated in the CBD. In addition, although Johannesburg was administratively and financially separate from the two "newtowns" of Sandton and Randburg, they were perceived by many to be simply part of Johannesburg, or Greater Johannesburg, rather than autonomous places competing with the "City of Gold" for high-value businesses. Thus, when seen from afar, Johannesburg must have looked to be in better shape than it was and was included on Friedmann's (1986) influential list of world cities.

During the political hiatus that extended from the 1980s and included the first period of democratic local government which commenced in 1996, the central area, with its vacated premises, became a zone of rapid change and one increasingly populated by poor black people, many jobless and seeking somewhere to live other than the crowded backyard shacks in the black townships. Indeed, thirty-three thousand people moved into buildings in and close to the CBD in 1991 and 1992 (see Shiceka 1995). Rack-renting took place, followed by rent boycotts; many apartments became overcrowded, health regulations and bylaws were not enforced, and, consequently, the racial transformation, although anticipated, was in fact poorly managed. The situation was aggravated when empty office blocks were occupied by the new wave of inner-city residents and used for purposes for which they were not designed (Beavon 2001). With no one prepared to enforce the bylaws of the city, the demise of the CBD was marked by increasing levels of grime and physical blight as plumbing failed, garbage piled up, and landlords forsook the maintenance of buildings (see, for example, Gifford 1997; Moya 1997; West 1997; Beavon and Larsen 1998). This situation still prevails from time to time in certain buildings (see, for example, Tabane 2000; Cox 2003). Concomitantly with the failure to enforce the municipal bylaws, hundreds and later thousands of street sellers jammed the sidewalks, trying to earn a living by selling low-order items in demand by the new majority of residents. In the process, more of the formal businesses simply closed up shop and left the CBD (Rogerson 1996). In the meantime, numerous shantytowns, or "informal settlements," were springing up on all sides of the urban periphery as people from the impoverished Bantustans of the apartheid period migrated to the city in search of jobs that did not exist. Under such conditions, petty and later serious crime, committed by locals and illegal immigrants and including mafia-type activities like car hijacking, auto theft, drug dealing, prostitution, and heists of cash in transit, began to plague the inner-city areas and the CBD of Johannesburg before spreading to and escalating in other parts of the city as well (Fraser 1995; Beavon 1998c; Leggett 2001, 2003).

An overview of Greater Johannesburg in 1995 and its positioning to come to grips with globalization from its abnormal base has already been published (Beavon 1997, 1998c), and the details are not repeated here. It should be noted, however, that just prior to the first democratic local elections of 1995, in what was a gerrymandering exercise, several of the former independent municipalities were incorporated into four municipal substructures (MSSs) with their own councils, together making up what would formally be called Greater Johannesburg [figure 3.3(a)]. For a variety of reasons, the new administrative model that was also supposed to facilitate the redistribution of local property-tax revenue to the poorer areas of the city failed to function efficiently. Radical action, including municipal reorganization, was deemed necessary to rescue the city from looming bankruptcy and was initiated by the Gauteng provincial government in October 1997. Consequently, in the run-up to the municipal elections in late 2000, the MSSs were scrapped, and a new and enlarged boundary was created to incorporate all of de facto Greater Johannesburg that was to be administered as a unicity headed by an executive mayor (Allan, Gotz, and Joseph 2001).

JOHANNESBURG IN 2002–2003

The new, and current, boundaries of Johannesburg [see figure 3.3(b)] enclose 2,300 km^2 of built-up area and open space (CDE 2002, 14) and now include the booming and formerly independent municipality of Midrand, which is situated approximately halfway between (old) Johannesburg and Pretoria and is the major locus for South Africa's high-tech and information-technology industries (Hodge 1998; Rogerson 2001). Table 3.1 shows the percentage of the population in each of the eleven regions. It should immediately be noted that Soweto is made up of Regions 6 and 10, with 43 percent of the population. As Region 11 is dominated by poor black people, this means that 53 percent of the total population is made up of black people who live in the southwestern quadrant of the metropolis.

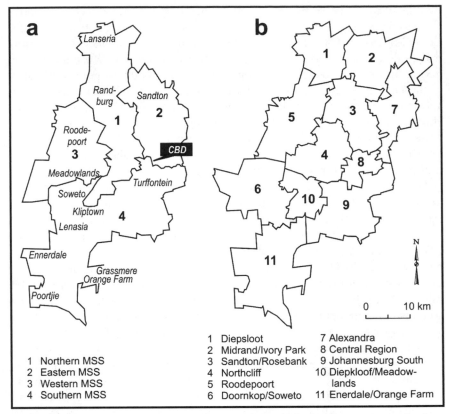

Figure 3.3. (a) The four MSSs adopted in 1995 prior to the local government elections and used until late 2000, and (b) the Johannesburg unicity 2000 and its administrative regions.

Table 3.1. Percentage of the Population per Region as Shown in Figure 3.3(b)

Region	1	2	3	4	5	6	7	8	9	10	11
Percentage of population	1	5	6	6.5	8	22	8	7.5	5	21	10

Source: City of Johannesburg 2003.

TOWARD A MODEL FOR THE FUTURE

With the unicity in place, the new council and its first executive mayor set out to make the city financially sound. Such a goal, they realized, meant making the city not only more attractive but more efficient and safe as a place in which to invest, do business, and live. In order to cut costs and improve efficiency, the city executive began to privatize many of the city's public services (including refuse collection, waste management, power, water, and public transport), and with the assistance of a World Bank team, they put in place a major fact-finding exercise, analyzed the data, and in 2002 produced the council's vision and strategy for improving the city over the next twenty-eight years. This document comes in the form of a 148-page booklet entitled *Joburg 2030* (see City of Johannesburg 2002).

Concomitantly, the CDE was conducting its own research, and in 2002, almost coincident with the publication of the council's *2030*, it produced a 133-page monograph entitled *Johannesburg, Africa's World City: A Challenge to Action*, which contains the CDE's analysis of the city and suggestions for the way forward (CDE 2002). It is important to note that there is clearly common ground between the council and the CDE on what Johannesburg is and what it might be, as is indicated by the citations to both publications in the text below (see also Bethlehem 2002).

Certainly in the case of the CDE publication and apparently in the *2030* document,[2] the writers have been influenced by the allure that has come to be associated with what Friedmann, almost regretfully, has termed "the golden phrase of a world city." The epithet, despite its lack of clarity (Taylor 2000) and "fuzziness" (Short et al. 1996, in Douglass and Boonchuen 2003), has not only become "a badge of status" (Friedmann 1995, 36) but a sought-after talisman, one that will supposedly attract major national and foreign direct investment. In the case of the CDE study, there is also evidence that they have been influenced by the work of E. W. Soja, which is in turn drawn from his 1996 work on the transformation of Los Angeles between 1965 and 1992. In that study, Soja came to the opinion that the urban restructuring in Los Angeles over almost thirty years could be summarized in terms of six "geographies" each "representing an important dimension of accelerated urban change as well as a particular approach to interpreting the 'new' Los Angeles" (1996, 433). In brief (and using some of the terminology from Soja 2000a), they are the

- *Exopolis*, or the restructuring of urban form including the creation of outer or edge cities
- *Flexicity*, or the changing geography of production
- *Cosmopolis*, or the exposure to aspects of globalization and world city formation
- *Fractal city*, or the repolarized metropolis in class and ethnic terms
- *Carceral archipelago*, or the prisonlike city with its multitudes of security and surveillance systems
- *Simcity*, or the restructuring of "workplace" through use of the "information highway"

In a subsequent review of relevant literature, Soja (2000a, 2000b) has argued that the same six themes or geographies identified in Los Angeles are indeed evident in places that are regarded as (or claim to be) world cities (see also CDE 2002, 64). Of course, not all of the six geographies are necessarily "good news." Certainly, the carceral archipelagos would appear to be an undesirable, albeit a currently prevalent, attribute of world cities. Likewise, the fractal component can be seen as a negative aspect if the cleavage lines of class align too closely with those of race or ethnicity. Those who have read Soja's 1996 paper and who are familiar with the current geographies of Johannesburg would probably agree with the claim by the CDE that there "will be few residents in or observers of contemporary Johannesburg who won't recognise at least echoes of Soja's themes in their city" (CDE 2002, 65). For example, it is claimed that Johannesburg is now "host" to several "edge cities," including Sandton and Midrand. In the flexicity idiom, it can be noted that while production-line factories have disappeared, a host of smaller enterprises now offer a variety of high-order and specialized goods and services. Furthermore, Johannesburg is undoubtedly the country's most cosmopolitan city, linked to the world by some sixty airlines currently serving the needs of some eleven million passengers a year. The CDE believes that, increasingly, the cleavage lines of the city are taking on class terms. A word of caution should, however, be added here, namely, that substantially more integration of races within "class-distinct" residential areas is needed before the starker "ethnic" divisions of Johannesburg's past will be erased (Prinsloo and Cloete 2002; Beavon 2003). The carceral archipelagos recognized by Soja are perhaps more in evidence in Johannesburg on a per capita basis than anywhere else in the world. They take the form of "private" security villages and, in many instances, illegally fenced-off suburbs protected by security companies hired by the residents of the enclave (CDE 2002, 66). As such, the Johannesburg carceral archipelagos are more a reflection of a negative attribute than anything else. Finally, Johannesburg is the undisputed simcity of Africa, where not only almost 60 percent of the national information-technology enterprises are located (Rogerson 2001) but the use of new information technologies by the managerial echelons of the city is extremely high (CDE 2002, 66).

Mention was made in this chapter's opening paragraph of the need for Johannesburg to offer a competitive urban environment for world-class businesses it wishes to attract or retain. Simply based on general points made in the body of world city literature, the city must therefore inevitably be or become a place where "top" people would want to live. As such, it should at least be able to offer lifestyles that compare favorably with those offered by world cities in the tier below London, New York, Paris, and Tokyo. The city will have to provide high-quality support services required by major corporations and institutions and at the same time offer excellent physical and cyberspace connections to the rest of the world. Above all, and this is taken much more for granted in many places in the world, the city and its environs must be safe, which means that crime rates for all levels of crime, not just murder, rape, hijacking, and armed robbery, must be at internationally acceptable lows.

AN ASSESSMENT OF JOHANNESBURG'S CURRENT MERITS

Keeping in mind the points just made above, one can now run through a check of some of the major positive and negative features of Johannesburg that are relevant to its current and desired status.

Some of the City's Major Positive Attributes

On the face of it, the "new" (enlarged) Johannesburg [Figure 3.3(b)] with just over 3.2 million people is indeed a rather impressive place. It has 55 percent of the nation's private office space, most of it constructed in the last 10 years (CDE 2002, 38; Beavon 2003). It is the location for 74 percent of national corporate headquarters and 70 percent of national banks, as well as most of the international banks (including Bank of America, Chase Manhattan, Credit Suisse, and Deutsche Bank) (CDE 2002, 14, 38). In addition, it has 20 percent of the country's major malls (i.e., of at least 10,000 m²) in terms of both numbers and gross leasable area (South African Council of Shopping Centres 2002).

Despite its being located inland, Johannesburg is South Africa's largest port by virtue of the Johannesburg International Airport (CDE 2002, 65) and the railways' City Deep container depot. Not only do 20 percent of South Africa's exports still originate in Johannesburg, but 39 percent of all the exports pass through the "port" of Johannesburg (City of Johannesburg 2002, 15).

The gross geographic product (GGP) generated by Johannesburg is nominally R117 billion (approximately US$13 billion in 2002) and equal to 40 percent of the gross domestic product (GDP) of its province, Gauteng, and 16 percent of the national GDP (City of Johannesburg 2002, 24). The city budget of R8.8 billion in 2002 was third in size only to the national budgets for safety and security (R15.73 billion) and defense (R13.8 billion) and R1.16 billion more than the national budget for education (i.e., primary, secondary, and all forms of tertiary education). The current economy of Johannesburg, as one might expect from a postindustrial world city aspirant in the twenty-first century, is dominated by the service sectors, that is, financial and business services (22 percent), retail and wholesale trading (19 percent), community and social services (18 percent), and manufacturing (20 percent). The remaining 21 percent consists of construction (8 percent), transport and communications (6 percent), and public administration (5 percent); mining is now lost in the category of "other," which makes up a mere 2 percent (CDE 2002, 121; City of Johannesburg 2002, 25).

Johannesburg provides 12 percent of the national employment, and although its unemployment level increased by 3 percent between 1996 and 1999, that particular trend reflected in part the substitution of capital for labor (in the realm of services as well as industry) between 1991 and the end of 1999 (City of Johannesburg 2002, 24, 32). Finance and business services account for 35 percent of the city's GGP, with commerce contributing an additional 25 percent. The government sector's share of GGP is only 9 percent, and as such, one must agree with the CDE opinion that Johannesburg is the uncontested, leading professional and private-sector city in South Africa, indeed, in Africa as a whole (CDE 2002, 19). In the above context, the CDE stresses that as Johannesburg is not a leading leisure or tourism center and is no longer the leader in gold mining or manufacturing, it will have to stand or fall by its recognition as a world city, which, it is believed, will reinforce its commercial business strengths and make it an increasingly attractive locus for foreign investment (CDE 2002, 73).

Another plus, one that is linked to the formation of the unicity, is that the negative impact of the stock exchange's move out of the Johannesburg CBD (Robinson 2000) to the neighboring town of Sandton has been countered: with the incorporation of Sandton, the exchange is now back in Johannesburg! So, too, is the world-class convention center announced for Sandton in 1998, which was the venue for the well-managed and massive World Summit on Sustainable Development in 2002. Such sleight of hand aside, however, it should be immediately apparent that what is now being administered as a unicity is an area and functional unit that probably corresponds more closely with what outsiders typically believe the name Johannesburg implies, even if they have no idea of its internal geography. By contrast, for those keenly aware of the city's geography, the massive divide being created between the well-endowed, urban, opportunity-rich north and the decayed areas of the (old) inner city, the impoverished, formal, black townships southwest of the Parktown ridge, and the new, informal townships to the northwest will be obvious (Beavon 2000, 2003).

Based on a survey of 360 businesses in 2000 (as part of the data collection for *Joburg 2030*), the overwhelming majority of firms rated road links, airport facilities, and markets as fair to excellent. Water and electricity utilities were rated as good, but there were increasing concerns about periodic, but prolonged, power failures caused by cable theft, piracy, and system overloads, particularly in the northern areas (City of Johannesburg 2002, chapter 3; Moya 2002). Of the businesses surveyed, 85 percent said that were they to expand their enterprises, they would be happy to do so in Johannesburg (City of Johannesburg 2002, 64).

Consideration can now be given to some of the major negative factors uncovered during the research undertaken for the city by the World Bank team in 2000, which are detrimental to Johannesburg's current and sought-after world status.

Significant Negative Aspects Associated with the City

Before unpacking *only some* of the leading factors contributing to the perceived lowering of the international status of Johannesburg, an important point needs to be made. Once South Africa was readmitted into the community of nations in 1994, a bill of rights was high on the priority list and, once formulated, was a guide in drawing up the country's liberal constitution in which, among other things, the powers and procedures of police and justice officials, as exercised during the apartheid era, were rightly curbed. Unfortunately, the numbers of people available to police the borders and the streets were decreased. Consequently, the numbers of illegal immigrants and international criminals who saw Johannesburg as a launching pad for organized crime in both South Africa and its neighboring countries increased, and the already rising rates of crime were exacerbated (Leggett 2001, 2003).

Business leaders of Johannesburg who participated in the World Bank study cited crime and violence as the single greatest threat to the future development of business and to the success of current businesses (CDE 2002, 64; City of Johannesburg 2002, 20–23, 66). Other negativities were labor relations, interest rates, and exchange rates. Also mentioned were corruption among government officials, shortage of skills and skilled labor, tax rates, laissez-faire urban developments, impediments to smooth trading with the Southern Africa Development Community (SADC), gridlock on the roads, and HIV/AIDS. A brief elaboration follows.

To provide perspective on the crime factor, some contrasting data is presented on rates of crime in Johannesburg vis-à-vis some major cities elsewhere in the world. In Johannesburg during 1999, there were 177 murders, 1,903 residential burglaries, and 272 car hijackings per 100,000 people. Comparatively, for murder, the 1997 rate for Washington, D.C., was 70, for Moscow, 20, for Paris, 4, and for London, 2 (Louw et al. 1998; Schönteich and Louw 2001; CDE 2002, 64). When the rates just mentioned for Johannesburg are converted to absolute numbers, a sharper picture of the situation emerges: there were approximately 5,000 murders, 5,500 burglaries, and 7,800 hijackings in 1999, and in 2001 there were 4,752 rapes.[3] Given the fact that the ratio of hijacking to vehicle theft is approximately 52:48 (Benjamin 2003), the number of motor vehicles lost to crime is approximately 15,000 per year, a demanding statistic for any police force, let alone one that is underresourced in both personnel and matériel. Furthermore, if one takes into account that, in addition to the major crimes listed here, Johannesburg has high rates of assault and petty (but often violent) theft, then it is not surprising to learn that business firms spent, on average, 1.6 percent of sales revenue on crime prevention. In 1999, some 83 percent of firms had experienced some sort of crime, and approximately 61 percent of employees had been victims of street crime while traveling to and from work (CDE 2002, 64). It is little wonder then that the council states in the *Joburg 2030* document,

- "In a survey [by the World Bank team] of 360 Johannesburg firms [in 2000] 70 per cent mentioned crime as a major obstacle to growth" (p. 20).
- "87 per cent of those firms that perceive crime to be a major obstacle have actually been victims of crime" (p. 22).
- "If a firm perceived itself to be located in a high crime area, it would invest 54 per cent less than a firm . . . in a low crime area" (p. 23).
- "Even if all other urbanisation economy issues are dealt with 100 per cent [*sic*], investment in Johannesburg will be 61 per cent lower than in an equivalent location" (p.66),
- "[Hence] crime is the *deal-breaker* for the future of the city" (p. 66) [emphasis added].

In addition to the high crime rates and insufficient policing in Johannesburg, the prosecution service is understaffed. Consequently, the arrest and charge rates are not as high as needed for the levels of crime, and the conviction rates are even lower. A report recently made public by the South African Law Reform Commission shows that between 1998 and 1999, some 76 percent of murders and 92.8 percent of robberies with aggravating circumstances remained unsolved in Johannesburg (Ellis 2003).

Both the council and the CDE also see the shortage of skills and skilled labor as major drawbacks to the development of Johannesburg. Indeed, the council regards them as "the second brick wall [after crime, that is] facing the city" and impeding development (City of Johannesburg 2002, 66). Underlining the seriousness of the matter is the fact that telecommunications, information technology, and financial services are the most rapidly growing sectors in the Johannesburg economy. It is not as if Johannesburg itself and the Gauteng region, with three universities and two large *technikons*, are incapable of training the people needed. The bitter truth is that not only are too few high school graduates qualified to enter the training programs, but the young people once equipped with the skills needed by the sectors just mentioned in Johannesburg are in demand worldwide. So, if the city of Johannesburg is perceived to be dangerous and losing rather than gaining status, then skilled personnel, particularly recent graduates, will leave, as they already do. They will seek out greener and safer pastures in London, New York, and places in Australasia.

The foreign exchange rate of the South African rand is not good and has been subject to some wild fluctuations, from a high of R13 to the U.S. dollar in December 2001 to about R7.30 in August 2003. Prime interest rates were 17 percent in February 2003 but had dropped to 13.5 percent by September 2003. The marginal income tax rate of 40 percent kicks in at R240,000 (approximately $32,000) per annum, and the top marginal rate for corporate taxation is 30 percent. An unfortunate side effect of the current labor laws in South Africa is that the costs of hiring and firing labor, when measured in South African rands, is high. In 2000, the cost of hiring a least-skilled worker was R9,000, and firing a worker at that level ran at between R2,000 to R3,000. On average, it took just under three months to retrench an entry-level worker (CDE 2002, 64), all of which encourages capital substitution, pushes up unemployment, fuels a cycle of poverty, and, thereby, contributes to increased crime.

Both the CDE and the council cite the aging of certain critical components of the infrastructure as detrimental to the current and future standard of the urban environment. For example, the main infrastructure for the distribution and monitoring of electric power is thirty-three years old and was given a life expectancy of only forty years when it was installed and last upgraded. The water reticulation system and the sewers have also been neglected since 1994, when the top financial priority was deemed the provision and improvement of municipal services in the formerly disadvantaged areas (CDE 2002, 31). At the same time, the city has demonstrated an amazing inability to collect payments for services rendered (City of Johannesburg 2002, 49; Cox 2001, 2002a, 2002b; Oliphant 2003) and to prevent the theft of services that are simply pirated off the main reticulation systems, which cause massive budget deficits to accrue.

During the death throes of apartheid, and especially in the years immediately following its demise, informal settlements of shacks and shanties mushroomed on the periphery of the metropolis and often in areas that had previously been zoned for low density, semirural, residential development. Consequently, excessive, unforeseen demands were placed on the existing water reticulation systems, sewers, power lines, and even roads compared to their design standards. The imbalance between demand and capacity has not been restricted to areas where informal housing has sprung up but includes the burgeoning Sandton business node that is located in the heart of what was designed as, and until 1980 still was, a low-density residential area until it developed rapidly into an edge city (the Johannesburg equivalent of Tyson's Corner; see Garreau 1991); it is now effectively the CBD of the new Johannesburg. The converse of what has just been described is also a cause for concern, and the best example is the heavy investment in certain specialized types of infrastructure in the old CBD that are now underutilized.

South Africa, in general, particularly Johannesburg, acts as a sort of entre-pot as well as an origin and destination point for exports and imports within the SADC region, an important attribute for world status. For a whole set of historical reasons, the main links between Johannesburg and SADC countries are predominantly road and rail, and given that transocean links between SADC locations and those overseas will usually have a rail or road interface in the City Deep container terminal, the efficiency of that terminal and the road and rail links to it becomes a key factor in the overall costs of SADC trade through Johannesburg: the hijacking of container trucks is one aspect affect-ing that efficiency (see Oliphant 2002). It appears from comments in *Joburg 2030* that all is not well. Not only does the terminal not operate twenty-four hours a day because of fears associated with crime, but it does not track and trace all containers on a continuous basis, as best practice demands, despite available technology. Overall, the situation is described by the city council it-self as "a major slap in the face for a City that perceives itself, and one of its advantages, as being its operation as a sub-continental hub" (City of Johan-nesburg 2002, 66), a view endorsed by the CDE (2002, 79).

The switch of many CBD businesses from their original setting in the heart of "old" Johannesburg to the Sandton node, the development of a rash of major malls on the northern side of the city, the high-tech industrial devel-opments that are linked to the highway between old Johannesburg and Midrand, and the concentration of cluster-housing complexes, especially in the northwestern quadrant of the city, have all contributed to subsequent changes in the traffic flows. In a sense, the main highways designed to be fast-flowing links around the metropolis and between Johannesburg and Pretoria have become the clogged and slow-moving "main streets" of north-ern Johannesburg. For the record, one should note that many of the minor east-west suburban roads in northern Johannesburg are carrying capacity loads with many major snarl-ups during the day (see City of Johannesburg 2002, 42). Because of excessive congestion, the Sandton node has already lost some of the major corporations that were early arrivals from the old CBD in Johannesburg. Gridlock is now a realistic prospect for the part of the city best placed to enhance the claim for world status. Traffic volumes continue to increase, rising 26 percent between 1999 and 2001 according to research conducted for the CDE (see CDE 2002, 82–83). Despite optimistic claims about the proposed rapid-rail commuter system (the so-called Gautrain) de-signed to run more or less parallel to the existing Johannesburg-Pretoria highway (as opposed to the present circuitous rail route much further east), there is much skepticism as to whether it will prove a panacea for reducing the in- and outbound traffic congestion of the main northern Johannesburg nodes.

Finally, but not least importantly, one needs to be aware of the extent and implications of HIV/AIDS. The council believes that at least 286,000 people in Johannesburg either have AIDS or are HIV positive. That is 10 percent of the 1990s population in general and an even higher percentage of the various strata that one can define within the population using the parameters of race, age, gender, or a combination of the three. The estimate is that for the foreseeable future, the number of people infected will increase by some twenty-six thousand per year, and over the next ten years, the disease will contribute to a decline in life expectancy from sixty-one to forty-eight years. The number of AIDS orphans was estimated to be 76,000 in October 2001 and projected to increase to 139,000 by 2010 (Naidoo 2001; Anonymous 2003).

The implications of the HIV/AIDS statistics just cited, which appear not to have been updated since they were placed on the Joburg website in 2001, are frightening, and not only in terms of how they might contribute to petty crime and unemployment. In addition, there is no unambiguous plan for dealing with and treating people with AIDS/HIV, given the dithering stance of the central government.

JOHANNESBURG 2030: COMMENTS ON THE VISION AND THE WAY FORWARD

In its preface to *Joburg 2030* (p. 5), the council claims that the document attempts to "paint a picture" of what Johannesburg will look like by 2030. Furthermore, it states that the vision is not a utopian shopping list but is rooted in the reality of what is possible given the then (2002) situation. Unfortunately, the vision appears to be nothing but utopian, a view to which the CDE also subscribes. For example, consider the following specific expectations listed by the council:

- "By 2030 . . . the City will be fully exploiting its economies of urbanization . . . and will be viewed as a world-class business location internationally" (p. 108).
- "The labour force of the City will be dominated by white- and blue-collar workers with a culture of numeracy, technology and high service standards" (p. 110).
- "The former CBD, now termed the inner city, will be regenerated to its previous standing as a prime business location, but on a far smaller geographic scale" (p. 112).
- "It will offer the same services, at the same standards and with the same efficiency, as New York, London or Tokyo" (p. 115).

To be fair, however, it must be remembered that quite possibly, any vision of an improved Johannesburg in twenty-eight years time, no matter how soundly based, might well appear utopian to someone in 2003. Furthermore, the vision itself is a desirable one and reflects a city well worth living in were it obtained. Yet, the ultimate test of whether any vision is realistic must depend upon the accompanying strategy for realizing it. Before commenting on the council's strategy, one must note again the two major impediments already identified by both the council and the CDE: the very high levels of serious and organized crime and the shortage of both skilled personnel and young school-leavers sufficiently equipped for training in the high-level skills required in a postindustrial city. Consequently, one must expect the "strategy" for reaching the *2030* vision to describe explicitly how crime will be reduced and how skilling will be brought about. Unfortunately, the strategy statements with respect to both of the drawbacks come across as vague and mealy mouthed in the extreme. This is the case with respect to crime partially because South Africa has a single national police service, unlike America and Great Britain, which have city or regional forces. Consequently, the city has no direct say in the priorities of the force. The Johannesburg Metropolitan Police, despite its grand name, is little more than a unit for enforcing traffic laws and enforcing certain bylaws (Krost and Ndaba 2001). It is neither equipped nor permitted to investigate murders, rapes, cash heists, auto theft, or hijacking, to mention but a few of the criminal ills besetting the city.

Likewise, the council appears to have been unable to produce a convincing strategy for improving the necessary levels of science and mathematics at the school level in order to offer tertiary educational institutions a pool of people equipped for high-level, technical skills training. There appears to be no consideration of how good science and mathematics teachers might be enticed to teach in schools, let alone how students will be recruited and trained to become the good teachers.

Without plausible and workable strategies for how to overcome crime and skill shortages, the vision for 2030, however noble, simply becomes utopian. In part, the lack of conviction in the strategy statements of *Joburg 2030* is related to the caveat contained in its introductory chapter, namely, that the council, its officials, and, indeed, the city itself believe they can only ever operate within the policies set by the central government. As such, by its own admission, the Johannesburg council sees itself only as a policy taker and not a policymaker (City of Johannesburg 2002, 7–8). Yet, the problems of South Africa's leading city are so great, and the implications for Johannesburg are so serious should it fail at least to keep pace with other world cities of similar rank and should it not maintain its role as the postindustrial hub of at least southern Africa, that one must side with the published view of the CDE. The CDE believes that Johannesburg's redevelopment and future development must be viewed as a special case, one that requires a supralocal intervention given that its status in the world has a bearing on international investment links with the country as a whole and, through it, with the SADC and other parts of at least sub-Saharan Africa.

Not all of the CDE suggestions are feasible (see also Bethlehem 2002), not least the first in which the CDE advocates a national partnership to steer Johannesburg toward its goals as set out in the council's *Joburg 2030* and the CDE's *Johannesburg, Africa's World City* documents. The CDE explicitly states that, on the basis of the analyses completed by them and the council, it is convinced that the council on its own cannot turn Johannesburg around. The same is said for business leaders alone or any civic group. The subsequent proposal that the national partnership be composed of, inter alia, three senior cabinet ministers, two newspaper editors, and the governor (or deputy) of the Reserve Bank is really not feasible. Nevertheless, whereas one can argue specifics of how such a national partnership might be constituted, it does appear to be a notion worth further exploration. If such a partnership is given the executive powers it will need, somewhat similar to those of a major urban-development corporation, then the suggestions on what is needed to turn the city around will become more plausible. For example, the policing of the city must embrace a greater degree of zero tolerance for crime, as was adopted by New York City not so long ago. Nationally approved incentives to encourage investment in Johannesburg will be necessary; such incentives could take the form of substantial tax breaks. In order to overcome the skills shortage, an about face is needed. Instead of making it difficult for skilled foreigners, including mathematics and science teachers, to come and work in Johannesburg, the city should encouraged them to do so and aggressively recruit them (CDE 2002, 115–23). But the notion that Johannesburg might be exempt from immigration laws applicable elsewhere in the country must be a nonstarter.

There is no point in unpacking here all the detail set out in the CDE document; the points mentioned briefly above will have to suffice. It is, however, important to mention that the suggestions made by the CDE (and outlined above) are prefaced by what they believe are major fallacies that are detracting attention and resources from the main task of reestablishing Johannesburg's claim to be recognized as an undoubted world city, albeit on the second tier. Before this chapter concludes, four of the major fallacies recognized by the CDE researchers need a brief mention. To wit, they claim the following are fallacies:

- Solving the problems that beset the old CBD of the city is the most important priority for the city.
- The flight of capital to the suburbs is an abnormal process, and it is racially inspired to undermine the city.
- Johannesburg is still primarily a mining and manufacturing center.

- Job creation must be an economic focus. In fact, job opportunities flow out of an enterprise-friendly city that attracts investment.

Certainly, one can endorse the CDE view, especially the folly of trying to reconstitute the old CBD as *the* CBD (City of Johannesburg 2002, 112), given the volumes of capital that the private sector in the main and the council have already invested in creating the Sandton business node, namely, the new CBD. By way of an example, the local authority has indicated that between 1996 and 2000, R2.7 billion of (private) building work took place in the Sandton business node and its environs: nominally, R540 million is spent per year (Eastern Metropolitan Council, cited in Jacobson 2000).

CONCLUSION

To conclude, if Johannesburg is to become a city that enjoys the "fuzzy," but prestigious, tag of a world city, then it must get crime under control. Both the private and public sectors are *ad idem* on that point. Thereafter, the physical problems that beset the city and its businesses must be tackled, and it seems clear that this will be led by the council, which has rejected the CDE suggestion for how a "national partnership" to direct the city should be constituted. Importantly, most of what is regarded as First World in Johannesburg is found and operates in the northern part of the metropolis. Consequently, if the drive for enhancing the city's world status is successful, the benefits will continue to accrue almost exclusively in the still predominantly "white" north. Just how such a divide is explained to those on the other side and, indeed, in the impoverished northeastern black township of Alexandra is a matter for shrewd politicians (see Phahlane 2000).

ACKNOWLEDGMENTS

I wish to acknowledge the help of Ingrid Booysen, senior cartographer in the Department of Geography, Geoinformatics, and Meteorology at the University of Pretoria, for producing the maps in digital format. I also wish to thank Marius Peters, Pauline Larsen, Margot Rubin, and Dirk Prinsloo for helpful advice, some data, and comments.

I also wish to thank the United Nations University Press in Tokyo for permission to reproduce figure 3.2, which originally appeared as Fig. 13.1 in K. S. O. Beavon, "'Johannesburg': Coming to Grips with Globalization from an Abnormal Base," in *Globalization and the World of Large Cities*, Fu-chen Lo and Yeu-man Yeung, eds., 352–88.

NOTES

1. The colloquial term *Hillbrow* refers to Hillbrow, Joubert Park, Berea, and parts of Yeoville.

2. Unfortunately, the *2030* document does not list the bibliographic details of its sources or references.

3. Based on the ratio given in Isserow 2003. The state has placed an embargo on the publication of crime statistics.

REFERENCES

Allan, K., Gotz, G., and Joseph, C. 2001. *Johannesburg: an African City.* Cape Town: Zebra Press.

Anonymous. 2003. "Joburg HIV/AIDS unit," at www.joburg.org.za/health/health_hiv .stm (accessed November 7, 2005).

Beaverstock, J. V., Taylor, P. J., and Smith, R. G. 1999. "A roster of world cities." *Cities* 16: 445–58.

Beavon, K. S. O. 1982. "Black townships in South Africa: terra incognita for urban geographers." *South African Geographical Journal* 64: 3–20.

———. 1992. "Some alternative scenarios for the South African city in the era of late apartheid." In *Urban and Regional Change in Southern Africa*, ed. D. Drakakis-Smith, 66–99. London: Routledge.

———. 1997. "Johannesburg: a city and metropolitan area in transformation." In *The Urban Challenge in Africa: Growth and Management of Its Large Cities*, ed. C. Rakodi, 150–91. Tokyo: United Nations University.

———. 1998a. Unpublished manuscript for a book. Subsequently published in 2004 as *Johannesburg: The Making and Shaping of the City.* Pretoria: Unisa Press.

———. 1998b. "Nearer my mall to thee: the decline of the Johannesburg central business district and the emergence of the neo-apartheid city." Unpublished seminar paper no. 442, presented to the Institute for Advanced Social Research, University of the Witwatersrand, Johannesburg.

———. 1998c. "'Johannesburg': coming to grips with globalization from an abnormal base." In *Globalization and the World of Large Cities*, ed. Fu-chen Lo and Yue-man Yeung, 352–88. Tokyo: United Nations University.

———. 1999. "Johannesburg, 112 ans de division: de la ségrégation à la ville post-apartheid." In *Questions urbaines en Afrique du Sud*, ed. J.-B Onana, 9–86. Paris: L'Harmattan.

———. 2000. "Northern Johannesburg: part of the 'rainbow' or neo-apartheid city in the making?" *Mots pluriels* (Revue électronique de lettres à caractère international) 13 (April), at www.arts.uwa.edu.au/MotsPluriels/MP1300kb.html. (accessed November 7, 2005).

———. 2001. "The city that slipped." *Lifestyle*, supplement to *Sunday Times*, Johannesburg, January 7, 6–7, at www.suntimes.co.za/2001/01/07/lifestyle/life03.htm (accessed November 7, 2005).

———. 2003. "Changes in the ordering of Johannesburg's spatial domain, 1990–2002." Available as Working Paper AP53 of Ostereuropa-Instituts der Freien Universität Berlin at http://userpage.fu-berlin.de/~segbers/working_papers.html (accessed November 7, 2005).

Beavon, K. S. O., and Larsen, P. 1998. "Capital productivity." *Productivity SA* 24, no. 1: 27–30.

Benjamin, C. 2003. "Gauteng Still the hijacking capital." *Business Day* (Johannesburg), February 5.

Bernstein, A. 2003. "We are a national asset, and can't be a 'global city' without unity." *Saturday Star* (Johannesburg), August 30.

Bethlehem, L. 2002. "Some of the proposals are at odds with report's findings." *The Star* (Johannesburg), October 30.

———. 2003. "Partnerships are the key to creating a booming business sector in the city." *Saturday Star* (Johannesburg), September 6.

Carruthers, E. J. 1980. "The growth of local self-government in the peri-urban areas north of Johannesburg, 1939–1969." Unpublished master's thesis, University of South Africa, Pretoria.

———. 1981. "The growth of local self-government in the peri-urban areas north of Johannesburg, 1939–1969." *Contree* 10: 16–23.

CDE. 2002. *Johannesburg, Africa's World City: A Challenge to Action.* CDE Research Policy in the Making No. 11. Johannesburg: Centre for Development and Enterprise.

City of Johannesburg. 2001. *Spatial Development Framework.* Johannesburg: City of Johannesburg.

———. 2002. *Joburg 2030 Full Report.* Johannesburg: City of Johannesburg.

———. 2003. *Integrated Development Plan 2003/2004.* Johannesburg: City of Johannesburg.

Cox, A. 2001. "R160m loss monthly: Joburg rates payments below target." *The Star* (Johannesburg), November 17.

———. 2002a. "Welcome to blunderburg: Joburg admits to billing system chaos." *The Star* (Johannesburg), July 25.

———. 2002b. "Billing system chaos spreads." *The Star* (Johannesburg), August 17.

———. 2003. "Blood-soaked flat used as chicken abattoir." *The Star* (Johannesburg), February 7.

Douglass, M. 2000. "The rise and fall of world cities in the changing space-economy of globalization: comment on Peter J. Taylor's 'world cities and territorial states under conditions of contemporary globalization.'" *Political Geography* 19: 43–49.

Douglass, M., and Boonchuen, P. 2003. "Bangkok—cosmopolis on the edge." Unpublished paper presented at the International Studies Association Meeting, Portland, Oregon, February 25 to March 1.

Ellis, E. 2003. "Conviction rate shock in villain's paradise." *The Star* (Johannesburg), August 5.

Fair, T. J. D., and Muller, J. D. 1981. "The Johannesburg metropolitan area." In *Urban Problems and Planning in the Developed World*, ed. M. Pacione, 157–88. London: Croom Helm.

Finnie, G. 1998. "Wired cities." *Communications Week International* (May 18): 19–22.

Fraser, N. 1995. "Overview: the need to revitalise the city of Johannesburg to provide formal business opportunities." Unpublished paper presented at the Conference on Commercial Opportunities in Rejuvenating Johannesburg, AIC Conferences, Johannesburg.

———. 2003. "Measurables show there is real progress." *Saturday Star* (Johannesburg), September 6.

Friedmann, J. 1986. "The world city hypothesis." *Development and Change* 17, no. 1: 69–84.

———. 1995. "Where we stand: a decade of world city research." In *World Cities in a World System*, ed. P. L. Knox and P. J. Taylor, 21–47. Cambridge: Cambridge University Press.

Garreau, J. 1991. *Edge City: Life on the New Frontier*. New York: Anchor Books, Doubleday.

Gifford, G. 1997. "Flat dwellers suffer as sewage flows free." *The Star* (Johannesburg), March 19.

Goga, S. 2003. "Property investors and decentralization: a case of false competition?" In *Emerging Johannesburg: Perspectives on the Postapartheid City*, ed. R. Tomlinson, R. A. Beauregard, L. Bremner, and X. Mangcu, 71–84. New York: Routledge.

Hodge, J. 1998. "The midrand area: an emerging high-technology cluster." *Development Southern Africa* 15: 851–73.

Isserow, M. 2003. "Crime statistics 2001." Centre for the Study of Violence and Reconciliation, Johannesburg, at www.csvr.org.za/papers/papstats.htm (accessed November 7, 2005).

Jacobson, C. 2000. "Egoli's golden goose: amazing R3-billion splurge proves Sandton property boom just gets bigger and bigger." *Sunday Times* (Johannesburg), November 19.

Johannesburg Transitional Metropolitan Council. 1995. "Map of greater Johannesburg." Johannesburg: Metropolitan Council.

Kane-Berman, J. 1978. *Soweto: Black Revolt, White Reaction*. Johannesburg: Ravan.

Keeling, D. J. 1995. "Transportation and the world city paradigm." In *World Cities in a World System*, ed. P. L. Knox and P. J. Taylor, 115–31. Cambridge: Cambridge University Press.

Knox, P. L., and Agnew, J. 1989. *The Geography of the World Economy*. London: Arnold.

Krost, P., and Ndaba, B. 2001. "New metro police are no big deal." *Saturday Star* (Johannesburg), March 31.

Leggett, T. 2001. *Rainbow Vice: The Drugs and Sex Industries in the New South Africa*. London: Zed Books.

———. 2003. *Rainbow Tenement: Crime and Policing in Inner Johannesburg*. ISS Monograph Series 78. Pretoria: Institute for Security Studies.

Louw, A., Shaw, M., Camerer, L., and Robertshaw, R. 1998. *Victims of Crime in Johannesburg*. ISS Monograph Series 18. Pretoria: Institute for Security Studies.

Lupton, M. 1992. "Class struggle over the built environment in Johannesburg's coloured areas." In *The Apartheid City and Beyond: Urbanization and Social Change in South Africa*, ed. D. M. Smith, 65–73. London: Routledge.

MacDonald, W. 1926. "Johannesburg after forty years." In *Johannesburg's 40th Birthday: An Official Souvenir*, ed. D. Wall's Jones, 7–21. Johannesburg: The Johannesburg Publicity Association.

Mandy, N. 1984. *A City Divided: Johannesburg and Soweto.* Johannesburg: Macmillan.

Moriarty, M. 2003. "Quick win against crime essential to draw investment." *Saturday Star* (Johannesburg), August 30.

Morris, A. 1994. "The desegregation of Hillbrow, Johannesburg, 1978–82." *Urban Studies* 31: 821–34.

Moya, F. N. 1997. "No gold in Egoli for Turbine Hall dwellers: disused power station building is decrepit and lacks toilet facilities but is home for many unemployed people." *The Star* (Johannesburg), July 24.

———. 2002. "Eskom puts blame on illegal users for blackout." *The Star* (Johannesburg), June 5.

Naidoo, P. 2001. "Metro AIDS Council to be launched," at www.joburg.org.za/october/aids.stm (accessed November 7, 2005).

Oliphant, L. 2002. "Freight truck hijacks soar." *Saturday Star* (Johannesburg), December 14.

———. 2003. "Council admits: billing is a mess: problems lie in the reading of meters, but something is being done." *Saturday Star* (Johannesburg), September 6.

O'Meara, D. 1996. *Forty Lost Years: The Apartheid State and the Politics of the National Party 1948–1994.* Athens: Ohio University Press.

Petrella, R. 1995. "A global agora vs. gated city-regions." *New Perspectives Quarterly* (Winter): 21–22.

Phahlane, C. 2000. "Mbeki warns of tensions between rich, poor areas: integrated neighbourhoods will help to foster unity and stability, president suggests." *The Star* (Johannesburg), October 13.

Pickard-Cambridge, C. 1988. *The Greying of Johannesburg: Residential Desegregation in the Johannesburg Area.* Johannesburg: South African Institute of Race Relations.

Prinsloo, D. A., and Cloete, C. E. 2002. "Post-apartheid residential mobility patterns in two South African cities." *Property Management* 20, no. 4: 264–77.

Robinson, S. 2000. "Back to the future." *Time* 155, no. 18 (May 8): 34–35.

Rogerson, C. M. 1996. "Urban poverty and the informal economy in South Africa's economic heartland." *Environment and Urbanization* 8: 167–81.

———. 2001. "Knowledge-based or smart regions in South Africa." *South African Geographical Journal* 83: 34–47.

Schönteich, M., and Louw, A. 2001. *Crime in South Africa: A Country and Three Cities Profile.* Pretoria: Institute for Security Studies.

Shiceka, S. 1995. "The future of Johannesburg CBD: a Gauteng government perspective." Unpublished paper presented at the Conference on Commercial Opportunities in Rejuvenating Johannesburg, AIC Conferences, Johannesburg.

Short, J. R., Kim, Y., Kuus, M., and Wells, H. 1996. "The dirty little secret of world cities research: data problems in comparative analysis." *International Journal or Urban and Regional Research* 20: 697–717.

Soja, E. W. 1996. "Los Angeles 1965–1992: from crisis-generated restructuring to restructuring-generated crisis." In *The City: Los Angeles and Urban Theory at the End of the Twentieth Century,* ed. A. J. Scott and E. W. Soja, 426–62. Berkeley: University of California Press.

———. 2000a. *Postmetropolis: Critical Studies of Cities and Regions.* Malden, MA: Blackwell.

———. 2000b. "Postmodern urbanization: the six restructurings of Los Angeles." In *Postmodern Cities and Spaces*, ed. S. Watson and K. Gibson, 125–37. Malden, MA: Blackwell.

South African Council of Shopping Centres. 2002. *South African Shopping Centre Directory 2002*. Auckland Park: Malnor.

Tabane, R. 2000. "Cops bust illegal jo'burg slaughterhouse." *The Star* (Johannesburg), February 16.

Taylor, P. J. 2000. "World cities and territorial states under conditions of contemporary globalization." *Political Geography* 19: 5–32.

Urban and Regional Research Unit. 1973. *The Witwatersrand: A Study in Metropolitan Research and Analysis Undertaken for Metrocom to Assist the Central Guideplan Committees for the East and West Rand 1972–1973, Second Report, Part 1, The Economy*. Johannesburg: Urban and Regional Research Unit, University of the Witwatersrand.

West, B. 1997. "Squalor and filth, but for some its home: once-sedate Harley Chambers is little more than a 10-storey cesspool." *The Star* (Johannesburg), July 24.

Whitlow, R., and Brooker, C. 1995. "The historical context of urban hydrology in Johannesburg. Part I: Johannesburg, 1900–1990." *Journal of the South African Institution of Civil Engineering* 27, no. 3: 7–12.

4

Bangkok: Intentional World City

Mike Douglass and Pornpan Boonchuen

CITIES AND THE GLOBALIZATION OF CAPITAL

Contemporary globalization is a highly uneven process of intensifying inter-action and interdependence among localities within the capitalist world system. Produced and reproduced over time through attachments to a diversity of territorial sites, it is a variegated process of engagement with localized constellations of power that emanate from real histories and socially constructed spaces. Contextually rich rather than uniform or linear, globalization processes are actively contested, as well as embraced at all scales of engagement. Experiences in Pacific Asia across the sweep of time, from the period of high imperialism of the nineteenth century to the economic and political crisis at the end of the twentieth century, reveal these great variations in processes and outcomes (ADB 2000; UNCTAD 2000; UNDP 1999).

In each local setting, key transformative episodes can be linked to the moments at which globalizing circuits of capital—commodity trade, production, and finance (Palloix 1973)—each reached local sites of accumulation. For most societies in this region, the first circuit of commodity trade made its most pronounced impact with the arrival of European colonialism, which actively suppressed the industrialization of colonized areas.

The postcolonial world witnessed political as well as economic changes, including the construction of authoritarian "developmental state" regimes that stayed in power by linking with local and international corporate elites while suppressing civil society through police and military force (Douglass 1994). These regimes were sustained by shifts in the global circuit of production summarized as the "new international division of labor," namely, the globalization of the production of urban-industrial commodities from the late

1960s (Fröbel, Heinrichs, and Kreye 1980) that began to see the relocation of labor-intensive manufacturing and assembly line operations to "newly industrializing economies." The transformations produced a small number of miracle economies, almost all of which were in Pacific Asia. Korea, Taiwan, Hong Kong, and Singapore were the first generation. Thailand, Malaysia, Indonesia, and the Philippines would begin a second generation of industrializing economies a decade later under quite different circumstances and with a generally shallower imprint.

In the case of the second-generation industrializing economies, including Thailand, incorporation into the new international division of labor, bringing accelerated export-oriented industrialization, was compressed into a time frame of a decade from the mid-1980s to late 1990s that also saw the intrusion of the third circuit of capital—global finance—into their economies. Suddenly infused with massive levels of speculative finance, these economies also became subject to rapid geographical switching of finance capital, and the stage was set for a massive economic free fall, which occurred at the end of 1997 when global finance capital fled these economies almost overnight as currency alignments with the U.S. dollar suddenly began to collapse.

The principal geographical components of globalization have not been national territories but rather a handful of very large city-regions, and the polarization of national economies in one or a few megaurban regions is one of the most prominent features of globalization over the past few decades (Friedmann 2002). From relatively small population sizes in the 1960s and 1970s, core city-regions in Pacific Asia now range from ten to nearly forty million in population, with some accounting for one-third to almost one-half of their national populations (Douglass 2000). Bangkok remains a principal example of this trend.

BANGKOK: FROM CENTER OF A SOUTHEAST ASIAN EMPIRE TO GLOBAL OUTPOST

Established in 1782, Bangkok was a city centered on the royal palace and a number of extraordinary temples. The social hierarchy of king, aristocracy, and religious leaders was sustained from Bangkok's ceremonial complexes, which sanctified the social order by connecting the population to deities through the position and ascribed powers of the elites (Jumsai Na Ayutthaya 1988; Kriengkaipetch 1985; Evers and Korff 2000). The building of this impressive royal city revitalized the Thai kingdom, and Bangkok quickly became a significant center of power with tributary areas and influence reaching into all of its present-day neighbors, Burma, Laos, Cambodia, and Malaysia (Saksri et al. 1989).

Its position as a regional power came to an abrupt end, however, with the signing of the Bowring Treaty of Trade and Commerce with Britain in 1855, which, while avoiding outright colonization, radically opened Thailand to external political and economic landscapes. The impacts of these changes on Bangkok were at least threefold. First, the fortification of the city with walled zones and compounds was no longer necessary as potential military confrontations moved from the city to internationally recognized national borders. Bangkok could now become an open city. Second, Bangkok, like the other colonial cities of Southeast Asia, turned to China as a source of cheap urban labor. Chinese people also came as merchants, and over the next century, they began to dominate the business world of Thailand. By the turn of the twentieth century, half the population of Bangkok was of Chinese descent (Askew 2002, 29). Third, cultural and political influences from the West were visible in clothing, architecture, food, and other aspects of urban life (Korff 1986; Askew 2002). Of singular importance was the bloodless coup of 1932, transforming Thailand into a constitutional monarchy.

Together, all of these changes propelled a shift from a precapitalist to a capitalist economy through the use of money as a medium of exchange, the commodification of land, and the development of a legal system enshrining private property, which, together with land markets, would move the development of Bangkok from royal prerogative to the hands of for-profit land developers (Potter 1976; Limtanakul 1994; Mekvichai 1998; Korff 1986; Ingram 1971). They also promoted an extreme spatial polarization of the Thai economy in a single city, Bangkok. While the kingdom's dependence on the export of rice from Bangkok's adjacent Central Plains region kept Thailand at a level of about 15 percent urban up to the end of the 1950s, which was among the lowest in Asia at that time, Bangkok's location at the mouth of the nation's arteries of river transportation made it the site of the country's main international port and added to its political and economic capacity to appropriate rural surpluses, making it also one of the most primate cities in the world. From 1900 to the 1950s, Bangkok increased from ten to twenty-three times the size of Chiang Mai, then the country's second largest city, and the capital city became the center of almost all major nonagricultural sectors and functions—commercial, financial, educational, public administration, urban culture—of the nation.

Yet, with a population of one million in 1950, Bangkok remained relatively small in comparison to what was about to happen in the coming decades.[1] The 1950s can be seen as the beginning of a new era initiating a substantial repositioning of Bangkok and the Thai economy from primary product exporter to emergent provider of low-wage, assembled and manufactured goods for world markets. The impetus for this shift was partly found in the advent of national economic planning and the establishment of the National Economic Development Board, which, under international tutelage, began to pursue foreign direct investment for urban-industrial, export-led, economic growth. New towns integrated with industrial estates, and megainfrastructure projects related to transportation—international airport, highways, container port development—became central features of this pursuit (Parnwell and Wongsuphasawat 1997; Askew 2002).

Although Thailand lagged behind the first generation of Asian "Tiger" economies, from the 1960s growth in textiles and garments and limited car-assembly and small-scale machinery industries added to the increasing dominance of Bangkok. For the first time, the Thai peasantry, now experiencing the rapid dissolution of communal support systems, the destruction of their natural environment by the demand for timber and other raw materials to build and sustain cities, and land loss through the commercialization of agriculture, began to migrate to Bangkok by the hundreds of thousands per year (Douglass 1984). Bangkok quickly tripled its population from a 1960 level of around one million to more than three million by 1980.[2] By 1980, Bangkok, with about 10 percent of the national population, accounted for more than one-quarter of the GDP, 70 percent of the nation's manufacturing employment, almost half of the nation's motor vehicles, two-thirds of the doctors, 92 percent of the university students, and 100 percent of bank headquarters (Bronger 1985, 86). Few cities in Asia had nearly such high levels of concentration (McGee and Robinson 1995).

By the 1980s, the combination of dramatic population growth, the expansion of an urban middle class, and the focus on large-scale infrastructure to service the car industry and private enterprise marked the beginning of the "Los Angelization" of the metropolis through massive suburbanization of an emerging urban middle class. The automobile arrived in ever-increasing numbers to jam streets that hardly had any traffic in the early 1960s. The network of *klong* (canals) that had been the transportation life of the city disappeared as each was paved to make way for the automobile. The middle class moved further and further away from the center, which, in switching from the palace to commerce as its dominant organizing force, began to see the construction of tall buildings.

Bangkok was also increasingly cosmopolitan in its openness to foreign residents and smaller-scale foreign entrepreneurs in the restaurant and service industries. Various quarters of the city became known for different foreign ethnic groups. Few cities in Southeast Asia were able to match Bangkok's variety of cultural sites, cuisines, entertainment, and living possibilities largely free of government surveillance. A freewheeling city that contrasted greatly with tightly controlled cities under the authoritarian regimes overseeing other industrializing economies in Pacific Asia (Douglass 1994), Bangkok enjoyed a conviviality of daily life in its small shop-lined streets and urban communities, despite its increasingly degraded environment and imbalanced priorities. In the mid-1980s, this conviviality would experience great duress as the enchanted world of global finance (Lipietz 1983) and franchise capital arrived to propel Bangkok into a new pursuit of world city formation.

1985 TO 1997: FROM ENDAKA TO THE
PACIFIC ASIA ECONOMIC CRISIS

In the early 1980s, the Thai economy was flagging. Commodity prices for its agricultural exports were falling, and its urban industrial structure seemed to have reached a plateau at a relatively low level of labor-intensive assembly operations. In the later half of the decade, however, a seemingly magical event occurred that changed the moribund economy into one of the most rapidly growing economies in the world. The Japanese yen, which had been heavily undervalued through massive intervention of the Bank of Japan, was suddenly revalued against the U.S. dollar in 1985. Labor-intensive production in Japan was no longer viable, and within a few short years, Japanese corporations began in earnest to put low value-added production offshore. Korea, Taiwan, Hong Kong, and Singapore faced similar circumstances and also began moving production into the Southeast Asia economies of Thailand, Malaysia, Indonesia, and, to a lesser extent, the Philippines.

For the first time in history, Bangkok and the Thai nation faced the possibility of becoming a manufacturing powerhouse similar to the first-generation industrializing economies of Korea, Hong Kong, Singapore, and Taiwan. From 1985 to the early 1990s, foreign investment in manufacturing increased sevenfold. Despite national policies to encourage foreign direct investment (FDI) in order to decentralize to the provinces, three-quarters of all FDI went to Bangkok (Douglass 1995). Migration to Bangkok accelerated, pushing it to the global megacity population threshold of ten million (figure 4.1).

Although the GDP growth rate jumped to over 10 percent per year for most of this period, income inequalities also increased as migration suppressed the wage of unskilled labor, and those with capital experienced miraculous increases in income not from the expansion of manufacturing but from the bubble economy of land and stock market investment that came with the opening of the Thai banking system to international finance. Thus, while Bangkok entered a globally induced boom unlike any it had experienced before, benefits were highly skewed to the rich. By 1997, the World Bank (1997, 2001) estimated that Thailand had the fifth worst income distribution in the world. These disparities were readily reflected in urban space through the appearance of new slums and the expansion of older ones (see "Persistence of Slums" below for more detail). The contrasts in living conditions became more visibly extreme. As figure 4.2 shows, the ninety-story Baiyoke Tower II, completed in 1997 as the world's tallest hotel (and

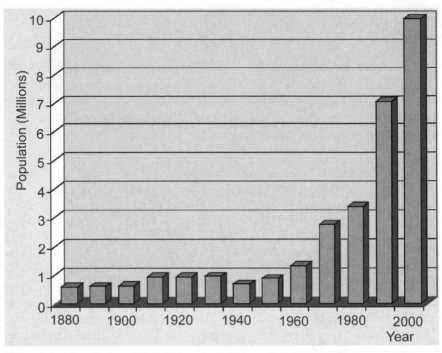

Figure 4.1.   Population of Bangkok metropolitan region, 1880–2000.

Figure 4.2.   Baijoke Tower II above, squatters below.

sixteenth tallest building), rises above squatter houses along the railroad tracks linking the core of Bangkok to the provinces.[3]

With housing making up almost 60 percent of all the built-up area of the metropolis and with land prices exponentially rising, a major pattern of urban restructuring during this period was a vast expansion of middle-class housing in ever-more-distant suburbs (Askew 2002). As the metropolitan region extended into a daily field of vehicular flows reaching more than 50 km (figure 4.3) from its center, housing estates and vast new towns on scales beyond even the most ambitious in the West were planned and built. The most pronounced increases in land prices occurred at the metropolitan fringe, where they rose by over 5,000 percent from 1987 to 1995 (Sheng and Kirinpanu 1999, table 3).

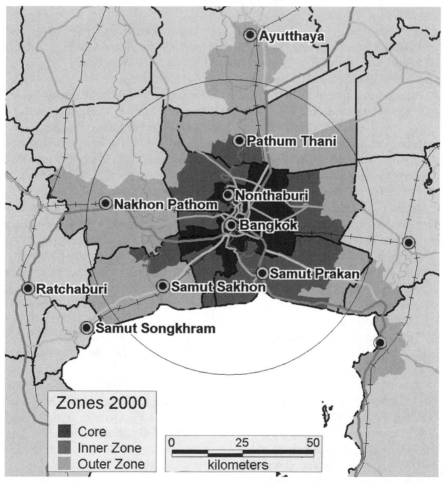

Figure 4.3. The Bangkok extended metropolitan region, 2000.

Pushed by an East Asia bubble economy emanating from Japan and the opening of the Thai banking system to short-term investment from the West, the heady pace of new housing construction in the 1990s far exceeded demand in the greater Bangkok city-region.[4]

The deluge of foreign investment was quickly funneled into speculative land purchases and development schemes:

> These funds zeroed in on those parts of the domestic economy that promised a high rate of return with a quick turnaround time, and invariably this was the real estate sector. Manufacturing and agriculture were dismissed as low-yield sectors. . . . Not surprisingly, the property sector soon became overheated in Bangkok, Manila, and Kuala Lumpur. By 1995 the inevitable glut came to Bangkok, with the consequent domino effect of developers with unsold new residential and commercial units dragging their financiers into bankruptcy with their non-performing loans. (Bello 1997, 1)

All this investment in real estate development occurred while exports of agricultural and manufactured goods were actually declining, which added to the pressure to devalue the baht (Lewis 1996). In 1997, the Thai government was finally compelled to let the baht float, immediately signaling short-term investors to shift to other economies. Short-term investment fled Thailand and several other Asian economies, creating a downward spiral of bad debts, falling land prices, and failed projects. The resulting economic collapse was registered in 1998, with the shrinking of the Thai economy by 8 percent. In terms of investment in land-development projects, assets worth $100 in June 1997 were worth $25 by September 1998 (Sachs 1999).

Up to the collapse, Bangkok continued to be subjected to a "slash and burn" style of property development (Sopon 2002) with few zoning or other restrictions. Massive housing construction was paralleled by the appearance of privately owned new towns. From 1990 to 1997, at least sixty-five buildings higher than thirty stories were completed, an average of almost ten per year (SFD 2002). The skyline of Bangkok changed dramatically in less than a decade, and the metropolitan region extended massively into its surrounding, rural hinterland.

With the economic collapse, land development came to a standstill. By the end of 1997, some 350,000 housing units in the greater Bangkok region were unoccupied and have remained so since (Sopon 2002). Annual housing construction fell from 180,000 units in the mid-1990s to fewer than 40,000 after 1997 (Sopon 2002). In every direction across the horizon of the city, large buildings stood half-completed, and due to rapid corrosion, most could never be rescued or completed. In 2001, at least 230 tall buildings remained uncompleted in the metropolis (Herron 2001). Most were simply abandoned by bankrupt owners and developers.

Among many fiascos, Muang Thong Thani stands out as one of the greatest planning disasters of the twentieth century. Borrowing $2.5 billion internationally, including from the Illinois State Pension Fund, the developers of the new city of Muang Thong Thani planned eventually to house and provide work for as many as 1 million people. According to its chief architects, NFA, "This enormous project [was] not based on imposed social relocation but on Thailand's changing societal demands and the ability of developers to recognize and market this opportunity" (Boonchuen 2002). By 1996, this "edge city" 40 km from the heart of Bangkok had completed construction of housing for 250,000 people and had built towers with 8 million square feet of offices, shops, and factories in an area "bigger than Ghent, Salzburg or Cork" in "the largest ever construction contract in the Southern Hemisphere." In the words of its visionary developer, Sino-Thai Anant Kanjanapas, "We have all intentions to develop Muang Thong Thani as a city, a complete city run by private-sector people (figure 4.4). It was not a stroke of genius. It was logic" (Kristof and Sanger 1999, 1). With the crisis, the project immediately came to a halt. Today, these buildings and housing units built at the cost of $1 billion remain empty (figure 4.5, *New York Times* 1999). Its sports complex and convention facilities are the only principal components in use.

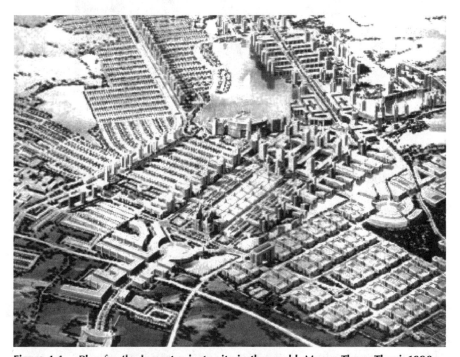

Figure 4.4.   Plan for the largest private city in the world, Muang Thong Thani, 1990.

Figure 4.5. MTT: billion-dollar ghost town, 2001.

While observers might say that the failure was due to the unforeseen financial crisis, the opposite is also true: since housing supplies for the middle class in Bangkok were already well known to far exceed demand, land-development schemes like Muang Thong Thani were the houses of cards that brought down the Thai economy.

INTENTIONAL WORLD CITY FORMATION

The heightening hypermobility of global finance fed into an equally powerful public policy drive to transform principal metropolitan regions into "world cities" intentionally (Friedmann 1986, 1998; Ito 1999; Taylor 2000). The imperatives for this effort emanate from intensifying intercity competition across national boundaries, pitting major city-regions against each other in the pursuit of global investment (Douglass 2001b; Douglass, Ho, and Ooi, 2002). The successes of reforms in opening Pacific Asian economies to all circuits of capital, a process occurring in all regions of the world, has pitted city against city to reposition economies from lower-level global manufacturing platforms to decision-making centers at the top of a perceived global hierarchy of cities. Whereas, for example, only 19 developing countries had policies favorable to FDI in 1980, in 2001 a total of 194 countries had liberalized national policies to host FDI (UNCTAD 2002). Opening a single country to direct competition for FDI translates into the compulsion of all cities in that country to engage in competition for global investment around the world.

With the rise of China and rising wages in their own economies, cities in Southeast Asia in particular began to lose their comparative advantage in labor-intensive global assembly operations.[5] Risking a regression toward a more peripheral position in the world economy, governments by the early 1990s became heavily invested in a new form of competition—not for manufacturing, but for higher order functions serving TNC networks. By the 1990s, approximately two-thirds of world trade was contained within TNC networks rather than being freely traded among national economies (UNCTAD 2002). World city formation was seen as a means of capturing both information and knowledge-intensive producer services and the regional headquarter functions of these TNC networks. In this sense, intentionally transforming a city into world city seeks to invert Friedmann's (1986, 70) hypothesis that "the form and extent of a city's integration with the world economy, and the functions assigned to the city in the new spatial division of labour, will be decisive for any structural changes" by initiating such structural changes in advance of global stimuli's doing so. More specifically, the intention is to escape being trapped in lower-level global assembly line status by reconstructing the urban landscape to become a "basing point" for the "concentration and accumulation of global capital" for corporate headquarters and global finance, transportation, and communications atop the world capitalist hierarchy of cities (Friedmann 1986, 71).

The very fuzziness of the world city concept (Short et al. 1996) lends itself to public relations programs and self-proclamations of world city status that rest more on imagery than on empirical verification. In addition to web pages and magazine advertisements extolling the world city attributes of would-be world cities, public funds are being increasingly devoted to reconstructing cities through fantastic urban designs and supporting megaprojects (Douglass 2000, 2001a). Examples include intercity competition to build the world's tallest buildings and fastest trains, huge sports and elegant convention centers to host world spectacles, world hub airports, wired high-technology corridors, upscale shopping malls and trade centers, and "Disneyland" simulations of cosmopolitan life from all corners of the globe.[6]

Bangkok has joined the fray of intercity competition. During Thailand's economic boom, the central government launched a host of megaprojects in Bangkok. Public investment and the privatization of public infrastructure for a Skytrain, subway, large-scale telecommunications infrastructure, and the new, international Nong Ngu Hao Airport aimed at rivaling the plethora of new airports in the region are all in various stages of implementation (Rüland and Ladavalya 1996). Figure 4.6 shows the location of currently prominent public land-development schemes for Bangkok.

Together, the six projects listed in the figure occupy approximately 1,500 ha., or 15 km², of the metropolitan core. When originally planned before the 1997 crisis, the Rama III Project itself was to cover an area of 12 km² with a budget of $2.2 billion. This turnkey project under the Bangkok Metropolitan Administration (BMA) and part of the Eighth National Economic and Social Development Plan (NESDB) (1997–2001) has been given the purpose of "rejuvenating" the city by creating a new global financial and commercial heart in Bangkok by 2012. The conceptual plan (figure 4.7) presents a vista of tall skyscrapers and heroic architecture that dwarfs nearby community structures.

The proposed Bangkok Metropolitan Transportation Hub at Pahon Yothin has an equally ambitious agenda. Designed to be the transportation hub for the Bangkok Metropolitan Region, its is intended not only to be an intermodal transportation center but also to serve as a new urban core, or CBD II, for northern Bangkok (figure 4.8). Owned by the State Railway of Thailand (SRT), the area covers 3.8 km². The design includes a large SRT terminal, an international business center with skyscrapers for business offices, hotels, services apartments, and a regional park. Together, they are expected to maximize "economic benefits as a complete international standard business center in today's serious rivalries—a pilot project to activate a chain reaction in economic development" (SRT 2002, 1).

Another plan focuses on the original heart of Bangkok, Rattanakosin Island, site of the royal palace, revered temples, universities, and community spaces of long standing. Its major boulevard, Rajdamnoen, is being prepared for a 15-year, $350 million reconstruction that will be accomplished by not renewing the leases of existing shops, most of which are on crown land, as they expire. A tourist shopping area offering "brand-name products and Thai handicrafts," complete with an underground road system, car park, and monorail service, will take their place. Upon completion, its ambience will "not be different from famous Champs Elysées in downtown Paris" (*Nation* 2002). The development committee, composed of government officials and private developers, states that "buildings without 'architectural value' that are obstructing the area's view will be torn down." What constitutes "architectural value" is not certain, but the stated intention to tear down the traditional Tha Tien Market to create a "visual space and a new walkway for tourists" has been among the controversies over the plan. For its part, the Crown

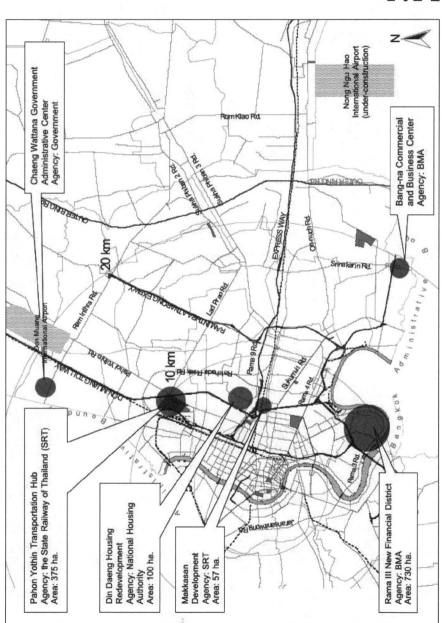

Figure 4.6. Major, currently planned, land-development projects.

Chaeng Wattana Government
Administrative Center
Agency: Government

Nong Ngu Hao
International Airport
(under construction)

Bang-na Commercial
and Business Center
Agency: BMA

Rom Klao Rd.

Srinakarin Rd.

Don Muang
International Airport

Ram Inthra Rd.

Paholyothin Rd.

20 km

10 km

RAMINTHRA-ATNARONG EXPWY

Lad Prao Rd.

Ratchada Pisek Rd.

Pahon Yothin Transportation Hub
Agency: the State Railway of Thailand (SRT)
Area: 375 ha.

Din Daeng Housing
Redevelopment
Agency: National Housing
Authority
Area: 100 ha.

Makkasan
Development
Agency: SRT
Area: 57 ha.

Rama III New Financial District
Agency: BMA
Area: 730 ha.

EXPRESS WAY

Ohnuchi Rd.

OUTER RING RD.

Rama 9 Rd.

Sukumvit Rd.

Rama 4 Rd.

Rama 3 Rd.

Jaransanitwong Rd.

Sukha Pibarn 2 Rd.

Sukha Pibarn 3 Rd.

DON MUANG TOLLWAY

N

Figure 4.7. Rama III Global Finance and Commercial Center.

Figure 4.8. Bangkok Metropolitan Transport Hub, Pahon Yotkin, 2003.

Property Bureau has registered the market as a conservation site (*Bangkok Post* 2002).

On a project-by-project basis, aspects of these and many other large-scale projects might contribute in some ways to the longer-term repositioning of Bangkok in a globalizing world system of cities. Yet, they also inherently have a number of well-known pitfalls. They absorb huge amounts of capital that might be used with far less risk for smaller scale, more flexible projects. The Muang Thong Thani fiasco is a sobering reminder of these risks. In addition, such projects prove difficult to manage and call for expertise in maintenance that is often not made available to them over the long term, resulting in serious deterioration in a few years, especially in monsoonal zones of the world. Environmental impacts of megaprojects can also be very severe and impossible to anticipate fully (Snowy Mountains Engineering Corporation 2003).

While each project could possibly be modified to respond to these issues, the total picture shows a continuing, lopsided reconstruction of the city-region, even if at a more muted magnitude than in days of the bubble economy. Transnational corporate shopping and tourist spaces are being constructed at the expense of improving local communities, upgrading slums, and developing a convivial city life for the majority of its residents. The key dimensions not receiving the scale of attention given to world city projects, include severe environmental degradation, lack of public amenities, erosion of community and civic spaces, and persistence of slums.

SEVERE ENVIRONMENTAL DEGRADATION

There is no evidence that intercity competition or intentional world city formation aids environmental management. To the contrary, abundant circumstantial evidence exists to show how short-term competition for global investment leads to neglect of longer-term environmental-management needs. This happens both through a lack of political will to adopt and enforce environmental regulations and, equally importantly, through chronic public financial deficits in environmental management because greater priority is given to winning competition for world city status. While, for example, governments are exhorted to spend the equivalent of at least 1 percent of GDP on environmental services just to meet annual incremental needs, not one in Pacific Asia has reached that level, and all face huge backlogs (Douglass and Ooi 2000). After the crisis of 1997, budgets for environmental management seriously decreased (Angel and Rock 2000).

Bangkok is among the most environmentally degraded cities in the world. In the early 1990s, the World Bank (1992) estimated that the annual cost of its air pollution was $3 billion. Sewerage covers only about 2 percent of households, piped water is not suitable to drink, and the air is considered "dangerous" to breathe, with air pollution being responsible for 1,000 to 2,000 deaths and 25,000 to 100,000 doctor's visits or hospitalizations per year (Brandon 1994). The grand Chao Phrya River running through Bangkok no longer supports life, once lively canals are extremely polluted, and ground-water extraction rates from aquifers under the city are unsustainable. Land subsidence has resulted from overpumping, and the city is highly vulnerable to flooding (BMA 2001). Wastewater from households and businesses is responsible for about 75 percent of water pollution (Douglass 1996). The economic cost of traffic congestion is estimated to be as much as $1 billion per year, with the average motorist spending the equivalent of 44 work days per year stuck in traffic. More than five hundred new cars are added to the city's road system every day (BMA 2001).

LACK OF PUBLIC AMENITIES AND LOSS OF COMMUNITY AND CIVIC SPACES

The commodification, privatization, and fragmentation of space into guarded buildings and gated communities, combined with large-scale urban design projects creating huge spaces with no local community content, have become the cutting edge of urban restructuring. All have the palpable impact of diminishing the types of urban experience so cherished by urban theorists concerned with the spontaneity and conviviality of human encounters in the city (Jacobs 1961; Peattie 1998; Friedmann 2002). Even temples have sold off land to commercial developers or have otherwise diminished their role in social life (Potter 1976; Laird 2000; Boonchuen 2002).

Concerning public spaces, at much less than 1 m² per capita, Bangkok has among the lowest ratios of park space to population in the world (Boonchuen 2002; Laird 2000). Soaring land prices during the 1985–1997 boom also left government facing insurmountable financial difficulties in purchasing land for public use (Mekvichai 1998). At the same time, the commodification of urban spaces in the form of privately owned shopping malls, together with the city's expansion into the suburbs, has limited use of and access to civic spaces (Douglass, Ho, and Ooi 2002). Being privately owned and regulated, these malls discourage activities such as free seating in open areas or people gathering in ways that are perceived to diminish shopping. Free speech is not allowed, and in Bangkok, even taking pictures is prohibited in many shopping malls (Boonchuen 2002). Deceptively "public" in design, they are not the equivalent of free spaces, such as public sidewalks fronting shopping streets, offering a place for civic interactions. The recent appearance of transnational "big box" superstores provides an even more striking absence of amenities other than vast parking lots.[7]

Traditional community spaces are also being transformed in a manner that diminishes their social and civic character. Gated communities and fragmented urban spaces have replaced open neighborhoods. Office towers with guards inhibiting popular access have replaced the small-shop ambience of the city. The loud noise and pollution of vehicular traffic inhibit conversations between people walking on public sidewalks. The more casual, daily, social encounters common when the city was a maze of waterways are impossible on roads filled with private cars. Homogeneous, suburban "bedtowns," with land divided into housing areas by income class and with few other functions nearby except industrial estates, add to the sociospatial fragmentation (Mekvichai 1998, 240).

PERSISTENCE OF SLUMS

The increasing scale of new condominium and housing-estate development has not resulted in a significant filtering of housing stock down to the poor. Thousands of houses in the huge new towns in the periphery and condominiums in the core remain empty rather than being made accessible to the poor (Rimmer and Dick 1998; ACHR 2000). This parallels the maldistribution of the benefits of globalization, resulting in widening income inequality in Bangkok (Phongpaichit and Sarntisart 2000; Boonchuen 2002). By the 1980s, slums in Bangkok already numbered over 1,000 with a combined population of 1.5 million (Kaothien and Rachatatanun 1991).

During the 1985–1997 period of hypereconomic growth, the number of slums and slum dwellers actually increased, with middle- and upper-income households enjoying unprecedented increases in income and wealth. Yet, at the same time, as they proliferated in some parts of the city, they were being cleared for commercial development in others. The Asian Coalition for Housing Rights (ACHR 2000), in its survey of slums in Bangkok in 1988, found that almost one-third of existing slum communities were in various stages of eviction, and many more were expecting threats of eviction as land prices soared with the influx of global finance. With more than 20 percent of the Bangkok population now living in environmentally degraded communities, the need for vastly improved access to good housing and environmentally healthy neighborhoods is self-evident (ACHR 2000).

The government has responded to many issues related to environmental management, open space, public amenities, and slums. Park spaces are being included in the new developments, regulating the expansion of big box stores is being considered, and the National Housing Authority (NHA) has announced the provision of four hundred thousand housing units for middle-class and low-income households (Assavanonda 2002). As worthy as these initiatives seem, they fall far short of what is needed in order to rebalance the city. Improving the environment requires massive public- and private-sector investments in all areas of air, water, and land pollution, as well as flooding and traffic congestion. Bangkok's $6 billion transportation plan, which includes the Skytrain ($1.7 billion) and new subway lines ($3.2 billion), covers an extremely limited area of the core of the metropolis, and although projected to have 600,000 passengers a day, due in part to high ticket costs and limited coverage of the city, it had only 170,000 by 2002 (Into Asia 2002).[8]

Similarly, park space remains below the very modest official target of 0.8 m² per capita, despite prioritization in the 1997–2002 Bangkok development plan.[9] Malls and big box stores proliferate while community spaces and open markets disappear. As in most countries, subsidized housing in Bangkok in the past has gone almost exclusively to government workers and the middle class (Askew 2002), and there is no solid evidence showing that the new additions of publicly subsidized new housing are actually going to slum dwellers.

More deeply rooted in the logic of globalization is the problem of how to revitalize communities that have lost or have never had ownership and control over land, urban spaces, enterprises, or the public discourse concerning the design of their cities. This is one of the great paradoxes of globalization: while it can be said that the rise of civil society and the push for democratization is promoted by flows of information associated with processes of globalization, these same processes diminish community and the urban spaces for social organization and social capital formation needed to sustain an economy in a global age effectively. Having had its own major moment of political reform toward democratic governance in 1992 in which citizen movements pushed the military out of government leadership, Bangkok also confronts this paradox. More specifically, it confronts the question of how to engage in a process of local-global interaction that can be translated into a clean environment, lower income disparities, good housing for all, and convivial community and civic life.

CONCLUSION

Over the course of the 150 years following the Bowring Treaty of 1855, Bangkok has been transformed from a walled royal city commanding a modest agrarian empire in Southeast Asia to a megaurban region integrated into a global network of cities articulating the capitalist world economy. During the first one hundred years, the economy became highly specialized in the export of agricultural commodities, notably rice, and natural resources, such as teak. Its agrarian base kept the city compact and its population size relatively stable.

By the 1960s, the physical and institutional template was in place for Bangkok to become a platform for a new order of global accumulation based on accelerated export-oriented manufacturing. Textile production began in earnest, initiating a massive proletarianization of Thai labor realized through rural migration to Bangkok. The metropolis soared in population and began spilling beyond its official administrative boundaries. As the new, urban middle class began to fill suburban housing and new towns, slums for low-wage migrants proliferated in the core. By the end of the 1970s, Bangkok had emerged as a seriously polluted and congested city-region that was the nation's engine of economic growth.

None of these periods of change prepared Bangkok for what was to occur in the mid-1980s with the confluence of a new round of foreign investment in manufacturing—this time emanating from Northeast Asia—and the opening of the Thai banking system to massive injections of speculative short-term financial capital. New waves of rural migrants and transnational industries alike gravitated to the metropolitan region. By the 1990s, Bangkok accounted for half of the nation's GDP and almost all manufacturing outside of agroprocessing, much of which was also located near Bangkok (Boonchuen 2002). Scores of tall buildings were under construction on any given day in the urban core while huge new town developments intended for hundreds of thousands of people converted agricultural land for urban uses on the metropolitan fringe. The simultaneous intensive implanting of global food, clothing, and entertainment franchises and chain stores, upscale international hotels, and big box shopping outlets placed the city's communities, public land, and open market places under siege.

The collapse of the Thai and several other Pacific Asian economies in 1997 left postapocalyptic, urban landscapes made up of the shells of hundreds of unfinished buildings and hundreds of thousands of unsold homes. Sudden pauperization reached into the new middle class, and rates of poverty soared, with more than one million people falling below the poverty line based on minimum calories needed to sustain life (*Bangkok Post* 1999). Bangkok experienced a jump in open unemployment that officially amounted to half a million people with no social safety nets.[10] Migrant workers tried to return to family support systems in the countryside, but these proved inadequate for those without sufficient agricultural land or other entitlements to basic needs (Douglass 2001a).

Requirements for receiving a $17 billion bailout fund via the International Monetary Fund pushed the country to further privatize all aspects of the economy and society, from land development to public universities, to open its doors even wider to the outside world by dismantling trade barriers, and to reduce public expenditures on the environment, community development, and public amenities. Instead of retrenching after its ill-fated global projects of the past or trying to rebalance the city toward supporting community and civic life, the government responded to the post-1997 realities by initiating yet another round of intentional world city formation dedicated to fostering globally linked economic growth through a host of large-scale urban-renewal projects on public land. Such imbalanced actions point to the concerns raised by several world city theorists (Friedmann 1986, 1998; Sassen 1991; Solomon 2003). Writing on the future of world cities in Pacific Asia on the eve of the massive economic crisis, Friedmann (1998, 22) observes that, driven by intercity competition for investment,

> The steady deterioration of life spaces in many Asian cities is a result of the single-minded pursuit of economic growth to the exclusion of other considerations and reflects, at least partly, a failure of political will to make urban development "sustainable."

Despite such assessments, policymakers throughout Pacific Asia continue to pin national economic-development hopes on megaprojects to create world cities as the only means of reestablishing the past decades of economic growth that suddenly evaporated at the end of the twentieth century. In a new century that has begun with more global crises and more countries and cities competing for investment through such ventures, the social, political, and economic risks of putting immense amounts of public resources into pursuing such a strategy are even greater now than they were a decade ago. These risks not only entail the possibility that many of these projects will fall short of their expectations (Kamol 2003) but equally involve their longer-term impacts on the environmental and community foundations for living in the city.

NOTES

1. The entire population of Thailand in 1855 was estimated to be five million, and over the next century to 1950, it increased to only nineteen million. By 2000, the population had rapidly increased to sixty-two million.

2. The government ban on further immigration of Chinese to Thailand, adopted in 1947, contributed to the labor demand for Thai workers in Bangkok (Askew 2002).

3. A peculiar feature of Bangkok is that a great number of streets connected to major thoroughfares in the city are privately owned. These landowners, who rent out property along the streets, resist both street widening and the connecting of streets. The result is "superblocks" through which automobile traffic cannot easily pass. They can be several square kilometers in size and are major contributors to traffic congestion.

4. By mid-1997, the estimated total short-term debt among enterprises in Thailand was $46 billion, which greatly exceeded the country's $31 billion in international reserves (ADB 1998). By the end of 1997 an estimated $274 billion in outstanding international bank loans had accumulated in five countries: Indonesia, South Korea,

Malaysia, the Philippines, and Thailand. About $175 billion was in short-term deposit with maturity under one year (Sachs 1999).

5. China (including Hong Kong), with more than 120 export processing zones of its own (*Asia Pulse* 1999), is now garnering 70 percent of all FDI in Asia (UNDP 2002). With its formal entrance into the World Trade Organization in 2002, this share is expected to increase. In the early 1990s, Southeast Asian economies were receiving one-third of the total FDI coming into all of Asia, including South Asia, but after 1997, their share of FDI dropped precipitously, except in the form of cross-border acquisitions of bankrupt companies by Western corporations. As concluded by *Finance Asia* (2002:1), "economies with export structures similar to China's will feel most of the competitive stress. Thailand . . . will face enormous competition from China."

6. Kuala Lumpur's Petronas Twin Towers was completed in 1998 as the world's tallest building, but is now being surpassed by even higher buildings in Shanghai and Taipei. Shanghai also boasts the new eighteen-mile Transrapid Maglev Line connecting the world's largest export-processing zone to downtown Shanghai in just eight minutes. Pacific Asia now has at least eight new, giant, regional hub airports completed over the past decade, including massive offshore airports in Hong Kong, Kansai, and Inchon, involving the leveling of islands, the creation of artificial islands with extensive transport links to major cities, and a host of world amenities such as the $18 billion Beijing 2008 Olympic facilities (Douglass 2000; APB 2002; SMEC 2003). Twenty-four of the world's fifty tallest buildings are now in Pacific Asia (Skyscrapers 2003). Kuala Lumpur now has a super mall covering 5 ha. of land in the urban core (Lopez 2003).

7. Tesco Lotus (Tesco, UK), Big C (Casino Group, France), Carrefour (France), Tops Supermarkets (Royal Ahold, Netherlands), and Makro (Food Lion, Belgium) are the most prominent (Jitpleechep 2001).

8. The subway is projected to have about three hundred thousand passenger trips per day, which will grow to eight hundred thousand by 2020, when the region as a whole can be expected to have a population of more than twenty million people (2bangkok.com Newsletter 2003).

9. The Fifth Bangkok Metropolitan Development Plan (1997–2001) declared its intention to turn unused public land into more community park spaces. By the end of the plan, per capita park space had increased to 0.6 m2 (Wayuparb 1999; Boonchuen 2002).

10. Nearly two years after the crisis, its impacts remained harsh: The recession is reverberating through the social fabric of the country, said the World Bank. It threatens traditional Thai values and social cohesion. The report said more children have been abandoned by suffering families, child labor and child prostitution is again rising, school dropouts have increased, and children are involved in more suicides, crimes, and drugs (*Bangkok Post* 1999).

REFERENCES

2bangkok.com Newsletter. 2003. "The Bangkok subway," at www.angkor.com/ 2bangkok/2bangkok/Subway/index.shtml#faq (accessed November 8, 2005).

Angel, D., and Rock, R., eds. 2000. *A Clean Revolution in Asia.* Sheffield, UK: Greenleaf.

Asia Development Bank (ADB). 1998. *Financial crisis in Asia* (Manila).

———. 2000. *Key Indicators of Developing Asian and Pacific Countries 2000.* Volume 31 (Manila).

Asia Pacific Bulletin (APB). 2001. "China versus Southeast Asia in the race for investment," November 2.

———. 2002. China Sets the Stage for a Mega-Project Boom, August 23.

Asia Pulse. 1999. "China to see steady growth of PC market," December 13.

Asian Coalition for Housing Rights (ACHR). 2000. "The poor of Bangkok," at www .achr. net/th_overview.htm.

Askew, M. 2002. *Bangkok—Place, Practice and Representation.* London: Routledge.

Assavanonda, A. 2002. "Housing—NHA to focus more on the needy, poor." *Bangkok Post,* October 27.

Bangkok Metropolitan Administration (BMA). 2001. "Cities 21 profile" (Bangkok).

Bangkok Post. 1999. "Week in review, 17–23 January," January 23.

———. 2002. "Tearing down Tha Tien Market," August 18.

Bello, W. 1997. "The end of the 'Southeast Asian miracle'?" In *Focus on the Global South (FOCUS)* (Bangkok), at www.focusweb.org/publications/1997/The%20End %20of%20the%20Southeast%20Asian%20Miracle.htm (accessed November 8, 2005).

Boonchuen, P. 2002. "Globalisation and urban design: transformations of civic space in Bangkok." *International Development Planning Review* 24, no. 2: 401–18.

Brandon, C. 1994. "Reversing pollution trends in Asia." *Finance and development* 31, no. 2: 21–23.

Bronger, D. 1985. "Metropolitanization as a development problem of Third World countries: a contribution towards a definition of the concept." *Applied Geography and Development* 26: 71–97.

Campbell, J. 1902. *Siam in the Twentieth Century: Being the Experiences and Impressions of a British Official.* London: Edward Arnold.

Douglass, M. 1984. *Regional Integration on the Capitalist Periphery: The Central Plains of Thailand.* RRS No. 15. The Hague: Institute of Social Studies.

———. 1994. "The 'developmental state' and the Asian newly industrialized economies." *Environment and Planning A* 26: 543–66.

———. 1995. "Global interdependence and urbanization: planning for the Bangkok mega-urban region." In *The New Southeast Asia: Managing the Mega-urban Regions,* ed. T. G. McGee and Ira Robinson, 45–79. Vancouver: University of British Columbia Press.

———. 1996. "Urban environmental management in Thailand—a strategic planning process." Bangkok: NESDB/DANCED.

———. 2000. "Mega-urban regions and world city formation: globalisation, the economic crisis and urban policy issues in Pacific Asia." *Urban Studies* 17, no. 12: 2317–37.

———. 2001a. "Urban and regional policy after the era of naïve globalism." In *Globalization and the New Regional Development,* Volume 1 of *New Regional Development Paradigms (NRDP),* ed. A. Kumssa and T. G. McGee, 33–56. Westport, CT: Greenwood Publishing Group.

———. 2001b. "Inter-city competition and the question of economic resilience—globalization and the Asian crisis." In *Global City-Regions—Trends, Theory, Policy,* ed. A. J. Scott, 236–62. Oxford: Oxford University Press.

Douglass, M., Ho, K. C., and Ooi, G. L. 2002. "Civic spaces, globalisation and Pacific Asia cities." *International Development and Planning Review* 24, no. 4: 345–61.

Douglass, M., and Ooi, G. L. 2000. "Industrializing cities and the environment in Pacific Asia: toward a policy framework and agenda for action." In *A Clean Revolution in Asia*, ed. D. Angel and M. Rock, 104–27. Sheffield, UK: Greenleaf.

Evers, H. D., and Korff, R. 2000. *Southeast Asian Urbanism: The Meaning and Power of Social Space*. New York: St. Martin's Press.

Finance Asia. 2002. "China's FDI strength is good for Asia," April 18, at www .financeasia.com/articles/198B9FD3-B20E-11D5 81D20090277E174B.cfm.

Friedmann, J. 1986. "The world city hypothesis." *Development and Change* 17: 69–83.

———. 1998. "World city futures: the role of urban and regional policies in the Asia-Pacific region." In *Urban Development in Asia*, ed. Y. Yeung, 25–34. Hong Kong: Hong Kong Institute of Asia-Pacific Studies, Chinese University of Hong Kong.

———. 2002. *The Prospect of Cities*. Minneapolis: University of Minnesota Press.

Friend, T. 1998. "The Asian miracle, the Asian contagion, and the U.S.A." *Wire* 6: 6.

Fröbel, F., Heinrichs, J., and Kreye, O. 1980. *The New International Division of Labor*. Cambridge: Cambridge University Press.

Herron, S. 2001. "Ghosts of the past." *Bangkok Post,* January 30.

Ingram, J. 1971. *Economic Change in Thailand, 1850–1970*. Palo Alto, CA: Stanford University Press.

Into Asia. 2002. "The Skytrain," at www.into-asia.com/bangkok/skytrain (accessed November 8, 2005).

Ito, T. 1999. "Making world cities in Japan." Presented at the Sixteenth Pacific Regional Science Conference, Seoul, Korea, July 12–16.

Jacobs, J. 1961. *The Death and Life of Great American Cities*. New York: Doubleday.

———. 1971. *Modernization without Development: Thailand as an Asian Case Study*. New York: Praeger.

Japan International Cooperation Agency (JICA) and the National Housing Authority of Thailand (NHA). 2002. *The Study for Urban Development Plan and Case Study in Bangkok Metropolitan Area in the Kingdom of Thailand, Final Report, Volume II* (main report). Prepared by Nippon Koei Co., LTD. and Urban Dynamics Institution, Takaha.

Jitpleechep, S. 2001. "Retailing: thinking even bigger." *Bangkok Post 2000 Year-end Economic Review,* at www.bangkokpost.net/yereview2000/retailing.html (accessed November 8, 2005).

Jumsai Na Ayutthaya, S. 1988. *Naga: Cultural Origins in Siam and the West Pacific*. Singapore: Oxford University Press.

Kamol, H. 2003. "Too many projects gone bust." *Bangkok Post,* April 20.

Kaothien, U., and Rachatatanun, W. 1991. *Urban Poverty in Thailand: Review of Past Trends and Policy Formation, Bangkok*. Bangkok: NESDB.

Korff, R. 1986. *Bangkok: Urban System and Everyday Life*. Saarbrucken: Breitenbach.

Kriengkaipetch, S. 1985. *Bangkok: The Symbol of Thailand* [Krung Thep: Eakarak Thai] (in Thai). Bangkok: Sumpun Publishing.

Kristof, N., with Sanger, D. 1999. "How the U.S. wooed Asia to let cash flow in." *New York Times*, February 16.

Laird, J. 2000. *Money Politics, Globalisation, and Crisis: The Case of Thailand*. Singapore: Graham Brash.

Lewis, P. 1996. "Export growth slows for Asia's tiger economies." *New York Times*, August 3.

Limtanakul, W. 1994. *The Effects of Modernization to the Neighborhood (Yaan) System of Communities in Bangkok*. Master's thesis, Department of Sociology and Anthropology, Thammasat University, Bangkok.

Lipietz, A. 1983. *The Enchanted World—Inflation, Credit and the World Crisis*. London: Verso.

Lopez, L. 2003. "Malaysia's monster mall." *Far Eastern Economic Review*, July 24.

McGee, T. G., and Robinson, I., eds. 1995. *The New Southeast Asia: Managing the Mega-urban Regions*. Vancouver: University of British Columbia Press.

Mekvichai, B. 1998. "A review of urban land management in Thailand." In *Urban Land Management: Improving Policies and Practices in Developing Countries of Asia*, ed. J. H. Ansari and N. von Einsiedel. New Delhi: Oxford and IBH Publishing Co.

Nation. 2002. "Local Champs Elysées: transforming Rajdamnoen," October 5.

New York Times. 1999. "High-rise ghost town—Muang Thong Thani rises up above barren fields on the edge of Bangkok," February 16, A10.

Palloix, C. 1973. "The internationalization of capital and the circuit of social capital." Excerpts from *Les firmes multinationales et le procès d'internationalisation* (Maspero, 1973, 137–63), in *International Firms and Modern Imperialism*, ed. H. Radice, 63–88. New York: Penguin, 1979.

Parnwell, M., and Wongsuphasawat, L. 1997. "Between the global and the local: extended metropolitanisation and industrial location decision making in Thailand." *Third World Planning Review* 19, no. 2: 119–38.

Peattie, L. 1998. "Convivial cities." In *Cities for Citizens: Planning and the Rise of Civil Society in a Global Age*, ed. M. Douglass and J. Friedmann, 247–53. London: John Wiley.

Phongpaichit, P., and Sarntisart, I. 2000. "Globalisation and inequality: the case of Thailand." OECD Conference on Poverty and Income Inequality in Developing Countries: A Policy Dialogue on the Effects of Globalization, Paris, November 30 to December 1.

Potter, J. M. 1976. *Thai Peasant Social Structure*. Chicago: University of Chicago Press.

Rimmer P. J., and Dick, H. W. 1998. "Beyond the Third World city: the new urban geography in South-east Asia." *Urban Studies* 35, no. 12: 2303.

Rüland, J., and Ladavalya, M. L. B. 1996. "Managing metropolitan Bangkok: power contest or public service?" In *The Dynamic of Metropolitan Management in Southeast Asia*, ed. J. Rüland. Singapore: Institute of Southeast Asian Studies.

Sachs, J. 1999. "Missing pieces." *Far Eastern Economic Review* 162, no. 8 (February 25).

Saksri, N., Tiptat, P., Worawan, C., Satjakun, V., Sthapitanon, L., and Chulasai, B. 1989. *An Analysis of Physical Urban Elements in Rattanakosin Area: Location and Interrelationships of Palace, Temple, Governmental Institution, Residence, Market, Canal, Bridge, and Road* (in Thai). Research presented to the Royal Highness Princess Maha Chakri's Foundation, Bangkok.

Sassen, S. 1991. *The Global City: New York, London, Tokyo*. Princeton, NJ: Princeton University.

Sharp, L., and Hanks, L. 1978. *Bang Chan: Social History of a Rural Community in Thailand.* Ithaca, NY: Cornell University Press.

Sheng, Y. K., and Kirinpanu, S. 1999. "Bangkok's housing boom and the financial crisis in Thailand: only the sky was the limit." *UMP-Asia Occasional Papers* 43, at www.serd.ait.ac.th/ump/Microsoft%20Word%20-%20OP43.pdf (accessed November 8, 2005).

Short, J. R., Kim, K., Kuus, M., and Wells, H. 1996. "The dirty little secret of world cities research: data problems in comparative analysis." *International Journal of Urban and Regional Research* 20, no. 4: 697–717.

Siam Future Development (SFD). 2002. "Bangkok highrises," at http://atlas.spaceports .com/~bkksky/ranking30-39.htm.

Skyscrapers. 2003. "World's tallest skyscrapers," at www.skyscrapers.com/re/en/bu/ sk/st/tp/al/2.

SMEC. 2003. *Developing a National Strategy for Soil Conservation, People's Republic of China.* Report to TA PRC 3548. Asian Development Bank and PRC Ministry of Water Resources. SMEC Consulting.

Smithies, M. 1986. *Old Bangkok.* Singapore: Oxford University Press.

Snowy Mountains Engineering Corporation. 2003. "The management of megaprojects in international development," at www.smec.com.au/development/mega_project .htm.

Solomon, D. 2003. *Global City Blues.* Washington, D.C.: Island Press.

Sopon, P. 2002. "Bangkok housing market's booms and busts, what do we learn?" Paper presented at the PRRES 2002, Christchurch, New Zealand, January 21–23, 2002.

State Railway of Thailand (SRT). 2002. "Bangkok metropolitan transportation hub— feasibility study, preliminary design and environmental impact study" Bangkok.

Taylor, P. 2000. "World cities and territorial states under conditions of contemporary globalization." *Political Geography* 19: 3–42.

United Nations Conference on Trade and Development (UNCTAD). 2000. "Unbalanced globalization process destabilizes world economy, UNCTAD warns policymakers at World Bank/IMF meeting." New York: TAD/INF/2846, April 15.

———. 2002. *World Investment Report 2001.* New York: UNCTAD.

United Nations Development Program (UNDP). 1999. *Human Development Report.* New York: UNCTAD.

Wayuparb, N. 1999. "Planning for green space and recreational areas in Bangkok." Graduate School of the Environment, Macquirie University, November, at www .gse.mq.edu.au/post_grad/Natarika_files/Abstract1.html.

World Bank. 1992. *World Development Report.* Washington, D.C.: World Bank.

———. 1997. "Unequal growth: what explains Thailand's rising inequality (1981–1996)." World Bank Press Release, Washington, D.C.

———. 2001. "Thailand social monitor: poverty programs must target the poorest," World Bank Press Release, Washington, D.C.

5

Laboring in the Periphery: The Place of Manila in the Global Economy

James A. Tyner

Current processes of economic globalization, according to Sassen (1994), have contributed to two distinct geographies, one of centrality and the other of marginality. She argues that the combination of the global dispersal of economic activities and global integration "under conditions of continued concentration of economic ownership and control" has contributed to a strategic role for certain major cities termed "global cities" (Sassen 1994, 4). This system of global cities, including New York, London, and Tokyo, constitutes a geography of centrality. Conversely, other cities and regions are considered peripheral to the major economic processes, forming a geography of marginality.

Whereas geographies of centrality have dominated research on globalization in general and global cities in particular, there currently exists a ground swell of interest in the geographies of marginality (Friedmann 1995; Knox 1995; Robinson 2002). Robinson forthrightly suggests that we need "to break free of the categorizing imperative, and to reconsider approaches which are at best irrelevant and at worst harmful to poor cities around the world" (2002, 549). Indeed, she argues that we should discard Eurocentric concepts and models "including the nomenclature of 'global cities'" and instead embark on a project of understanding ordinary cities (Robinson 2002, 549). While I largely agree with her proposed project, I resist the complete dismissal of the global city concept and of globalization discourses for the simple reason that these are now utilized as political resources throughout the world.

A second trend in research on global cities has been to position global cities in terms of functions rather than the construction of refined hierarchies of cities (Knox 1995; Robinson 2002). Knox (1995), for example, suggests that we must theorize global cities in terms of specific functions and their relations to global economic processes rather than refined classification and ranking schemes of cities. More challenging is Robinson's suggestion, in line with her statements above, that "simply mobilizing evidence of difference and possibly deviation within the frame of the dominant theory is not enough" (2002, 549).

This current research project forwards a number of questions that revolve around the position of global city formation in the periphery. What, for example, are the processes and strategies by which newly aspiring global cities are hoping and planning to evolve from regional centers to transnational market spaces? Likewise, following Sassen, what are cities in the periphery doing to become part of the "growth of the cross-border network of cities that constitutes a transnational space for the management and servicing of the global economy?" (1994, xiii). One understudied function-process nexus that addresses the "formation" of global cities in the periphery is that of the management and regulation of contract labor migration within the global economy. Cox (1997, 126), accordingly, identifies that, within studies of world systems in general and world cities specifically, there exists a dominant conception of capital as continually shifting locations from one point of production to another, whereas labor is perceived as generally immobile. The positing of labor as immobile, however, discounts the estimated 125 million workers residing outside their countries of origin. Consider the Philippines, with approximately eight hundred thousand government-sponsored contract workers deployed yearly. Other substantial labor-exporting countries include Indonesia, Sri Lanka, Pakistan, and India. This has significant implications, I contend, for our understanding of global city formation within the periphery. As Ball and Piper (2002, 1014) assert, the role of international labor migration and the large-scale movement of workers from less-developed countries to rapidly expanding economies are significant components of globalization.

The purpose of this chapter is twofold. First, through a case study of the Philippines, I highlight the imbrication of overseas employment policies, urbanization, and global city formation. In particular, I suggest that the actualization of overseas employment, predicated on a discourse of globalization, is manifest at the local level, as indicated by the increased concentration of administrative functions and institutional apparatuses. Concurrently, these spatial agglomerations materialize in the production of Manila as a global city. Second, I contribute to the reworking of the concept of globalization and global cities by arguing that researchers should resist classifying cities and focus instead on the social and discursive processes that contribute to the *concept* of global cities rather than the a priori *existence* of global cities.

GLOBAL CITIES AND CIRCUITS OF LABOR

When international flows consist of raw materials, agricultural products, or mining goods, the geography of transactions is determined in part by the location of natural resources (Sassen 1994, 10). More recently, however, a new geography of international transactions has appeared, one that is evident in foreign direct investment, the emergence of offshore banking centers, and the development of export processing zones. Summarizing these trends, Sassen (1994, 11–14) contends that while in the 1950s the major international flow was world trade concentrated in raw materials, other primary products, and resource-based manufacturing, by the 1980s the gap between the growth rate of exports and that of financial flows widened sharply.

In response to these shifts in international trade, the emergence of global markets for finance and specialized services has contributed to the expansion in, and centralization of, command functions (Sassen 1994, 19–20). Sassen (1994, 20) further notes that global cities are transnational marketplaces where firms and governments can buy financial instruments and specialized services. One of these services, I argue, is labor. Clearly, there exists a substantial global market for labor; concomitantly, there exists a definite expansion and concentration of command functions. In Manila, alone, for example, over four thousand workers are literally bought and sold via contracts on a daily basis.

Labor, however, does not figure prominently in research on global cities. Herod (1997, 167), for example, contends that the geographic literature on the emergence of the global economy is marked by a curious omission, an almost total neglect of the international activities of workers and labor organizations (e.g., unions). I suggest that global city research with regard to labor migration has been diverted by three false leads. First, as Cox (1997, 116) identifies, the dominant themes in the contemporary politics of globalization rest on certain quite basic assumptions as to the spatiality of globalization and contends that these refer to the mobility of productive capital and the mobility of labor power. Accordingly, researchers have devoted considerable attention to the firms that regulate the mobility of capital while downplaying similar functions vis-à-vis labor. Ironically enough, incipient interest in the formation of global cities and processes of globalization did give prominence to the circulation of labor. Sassen's (1988, 1991, 1993) work, in particular, stands out. However, despite this initial interest, Samers (2002, 389) argues that an initial linkage between capital and labor and the role of global cities was transformed (sidetracked?). He notes, for example, that a now leading group of researchers (e.g., participants of the Globalization and World Cities Network) has been preoccupied with identifying how putatively global cities are networked in terms of law, accountancy, consultancy, and other financial firms. Consequently, I agree completely with Cox's (1997, 126) pronouncement that the immobility of workers is flawed as a fundamental assumption, and this must be figured into a reconstituted understanding of global cities.

Second, while Samers' attempts to reposition immigration within the literature on global cities are laudable, he unwittingly perpetuates a related bias when he speaks principally of *immigrants* and not also of *emigrants*. This is more than semantics, even given that, technically, the words "emigrant" and "immigrant" refer to the same migrant. I contend that the continued emphasis in the literature on "immigrants" implies a destination focus and, hence, excludes a priori many cities, most of which are located on the periphery. Thus, both Sassen and Samers in this respect consider only sites of destination for immigrants and neglect sites of origin. In an attempt to revise the global cities literature, for example, Samers (2002, 395) suggests that one must be attentive to the relationship between changes in *immigration policy* and the growth of global cities (my emphasis). But, as this chapter argues, as does some of my earlier work (Tyner 2000a), migration is not unidirectional; indeed, there is a substantial circulation of temporary labor (including both skilled and unskilled migrants). Moreover, this circulation of labor is considerably well organized and regulated (whether these regulations are always legally followed is a separate question), and cities on the periphery typically assume a large share of this organization (cf. Shah and Arnold 1986; Abella 1992, 1993). Therefore, we must acknowledge not only *immigration* policies but also *emigration* policies to gain a more accurate portrayal of labor migration and global cities.

A third misperception is that labor, when it is considered mobile, simply moves in response to globalization, that migrants simply respond to regional inequalities and, accordingly, gravitate toward sites of capital accumulation. In contrast, I follow Sassen's thinking that "migrations do not just happen; they are produced. And migrations do not involve just any possible combination of countries; they are patterned" (1993, 73). Accordingly, I forward the argument that various state apparatuses and private agencies combine to produce global patterns of contract labor migration (Tyner 2004). In short, migrants must be made; they must be incorporated within the global circulation of labor. Moreover, the making of migration is part and parcel of the discursive production of globalization. In this sense, globalization is not a natural process; rather, it is a practice derived from economic decisions and political contestations. The fact that these decisions, policies, and regulations must *take place* is what generates our concept of global cities.

Having discussed three false leads and, consequently, three reasons for the inclusion of the circulation of capital, let us now revisit the standard criteria used in assessing global cities. Sassen (1994, 19), for example, defines global cities as key sites for the organization and management of a global production system and a global marketplace. Friedmann likewise suggests that these cities "serve as centers through which flow money, workers, information, commodities, and other economically relevant variables" (1995, 22). A commonality, certainly, is the assemblage of firms within a particular city and the fact that, through the combination of these firms, a disproportionate share of decision making for a particular system of circulation is exercised. Note also, following Friedmann (1995, 22), that we are talking about cities as spatially organized socioeconomic systems; we are talking about "global cities" as places and sites rather than as actors. New York, in other words, is a city with no agency per se; rather, it is through the control of particular functions by institutions within New York that power is exercised.

More recently, another aspect has been identified, one that is decidedly less material though no less significant. Short and Kim (1999), in particular, identify that globalism (and I would add global cities) has two interrelated parts. On one hand, globalization denotes the "stretching of similar economic, cultural and political activities across the globe," whereas, on the other hand, the term signifies a particular discourse that "portrays the process as a force beyond political control" (Short and Kim 1999, 3–5). In particular, these practices are not uncommonly explained, or rationalized, through allusion to a particular discursive formation of globalization. Hence, in the Philippines, the expansion of overseas employment as an economic strategy designed to accumulate capital is defended through reference to globalization.

My theoretical stance vis-à-vis global cities and labor is straightforward. Following Robinson (2002) and Knox (1995), among others, I begin with the ontological supposition that global cities "as material entities" do not exist. Rather, global cities are discursive creations and serve a multitude of functions, including acting as a heuristic device, as well as a political resource. My principal concern lies in the articulation of policies couched within discourses of globalization and the manifestation of these policies in the urban landscape. In short, my attention is directed toward the social, political, and economic processes that produce global cities as discourses rather than locating them within a static hierarchical ranking. To this end, stronger focus on process than categories could lead one to think about how global processes affect all cities (Robinson 2002, 539).

THE PLACE OF MANILA

Metro Manila, or the National Capital Region (NCR), is composed of seventeen local government units: twelve cities and five municipalities. Initially, the Greater Manila Area was composed of four cities: Manila, Pasay, Quezon, and Kalookan. In the mid- to late 1990s, eight of the former municipalities assumed city status.

While only occupying an area of 636 km², or approximately 0.21 percent of the country's aggregate land area, the economic, political, and social dominance of Manila is not in question. With a population of just under 10 million, Metro Manila contains approximately 13 percent of the country's total population. This translates to a population density of over 15,617 people per square kilometer, three times the density of Singapore. Densities are even greater for specific cities and municipalities within the NCR. The city of Manila, for example, registers a population density of over 41,000 people per square kilometer, whereas the municipality of Navotas has a density of 88,617 people.

Large size may qualify a city as a megacity but not a global city. Accordingly, the primacy of Manila must not be measured by population alone. Economically, the NCR accounts for approximately 30 percent of the country's gross domestic product. Moreover, of the top fifty corporations in the country, based on 1998 gross revenues, forty-one were located within Metro Manila. Makati accounted for the largest share. The relative strength of Metro Manila is further revealed by the fact that following the 1997 Asian financial crisis, the NCR maintained a growth rate of 0.1 percent compared to an overall decline of 0.5 percent for the country. The NCR accounts for approximately 90 percent of all private businesses, as well as a majority of cultural, educational, and medical establishments. In 2000, for instance, the NCR accounted for 179 of the country's 1,712 hospitals (10 percent). Likewise, in the late 1990s, the Metro Manila region accounted for just under 17 percent of the total number of higher educational institutions. For the 2000–2001 school year, 256 out of 1,603 higher educational facilities were in the NCR.

The Metro Manila region is a focal point of transportation and communication technologies, a fact that contributes to the concentration of business activities. Two rail systems service the NCR, including the Light Rail Transit and the Metro Rail Transit. With respect to communications, an estimated 70 percent of all households in the NCR are exposed to newspapers compared to a national average of just 29.8 percent. Also, in 2000, the National Telecommunications Commission reported a total of just over 6.9 million telephone lines in the country; of these, 43.8 percent were in the NCR. Moreover, the telephone density (lines for every 100 of the population) of the NCR stood at 29.07 compared to a national average of just 9.05.

The overurbanization of the NCR has, however, contributed to a notably declining quality of life for many of its residents. This is seen in rising levels of pollution, traffic congestion, morbidity, and more proximate indicators, such as lack of access to sanitary facilities, clean water, and housing. In the NCR during the 1990s, for example, nearly 5 percent of all households were forced to obtain their drinking water via itinerant peddlers compared to a national average of 1.8 percent. In addition, over 9 percent of all households rely on pits, pails, or some other primitive system as toilet facilities in the city (the national average is, however, a staggering 42 percent). Lastly, an estimated eleven thousand households were illegally occupying dwellings on land without the consent of the owner.

In response to the acknowledged overconcentration of activities within the NCR, as well as regional disparities between Metro Manila and the rest of the country, the Philippine government has proposed a number of strategies. Specifically, the past three decades have witnessed numerous attempts to deconcentrate both political power and economic activities; all attempts, however, have either failed or met with only limited success. These include the development of urban centers outside of Metro Manila, particularly the Cavite-Laguna-Batangas-Rizal-Quezon, or Calabarzon, Corridor of southern Luzon and the Cagayan de Oro-Iligan Corridor, or CIC, of Mindanao, and the development of transportation networks linking major industrial centers such as the Subic-Clark Toll Road and the Southern Tagalog Arterial Road (NEDA 2001, 238). Kelly (2000, 64) notes also that certain legislative acts, such as the Local Government Code of 1991, were intended to encourage industrial zones and to attract investment within their jurisdictions. However, given the requirement of adequate infrastructure and accessibility to transportation and communication facilities (which, as indicated above, are concentrated in the NCR), those municipalities closest to Manila have been most successful (Kelly 2000, 65).

More significantly, however, *national* policies formed in the context of globalization continue to augment the (over)urbanization of Metro Manila. As Sassen (1995, 63) writes, a key dynamic explaining the place of major cities in the world economy is that they concentrate the infrastructure and servicing that produce a capability for global control. The martial law period (1972–1981) of the Philippines witnessed significant economic transformations in that country as it was more fully incorporated into the global economy (see, for example, Hawes 1987; Wurfel 1988). The declaration of martial law, moreover, produced a sharp increase in the concentration of political power within the government as President Ferdinand Marcos centralized his control through a series of administrative changes (Timberman 1991). New economic policies were designed primarily to attract foreign direct investment as the Philippines' development policy became increasingly oriented toward export production (Kelly 2000, 33). Hence, this political period set the stage for what Sassen identifies as a defining feature of the contemporary era of globalization, namely, a global dispersal of economic activities combined with a concentration of regulatory control over these activities. Specific national economic policies, therefore, continue to congregate business activities within a few key locations, most especially Manila. To this day, investment and production activities continue to be concentrated in the Manila region (Kelly 2000, 64).

MANILA'S COMPARATIVE ADVANTAGE

Since the 1970s, the Philippines have pursued an aggressive campaign to increase foreign investment through the promotion of export-oriented industrialization. This is consonant with other less developed countries in that a key component of globalization for indebted states is the drive for export-oriented, hard-currency earnings; in the case of the Philippines, however, this has been augmented and, indeed, largely generated by labor export (Ball and Piper 2002, 1014). In this section, I consider, first, the *institutional* spatial concentration of overseas employment within the NCR and, second, how this *nationally conceived* program of overseas employment contributes to the making of Manila as a global city.

Sassen (1991, 3) identifies the massive trends toward the spatial dispersal of economic activities at the metropolitan, national, and global levels that we associate with globalization as contributing to a demand for new forms of territorial centralization of top-level management and control functions. Given the centralization of bureaucratic functions within the NCR of the Philippines, Manila emerges as a key node in the larger circulation of contract labor. Geographically, for example, it is evident that the Philippines' overseas employment program constitutes a spatially diverse economic function. Consider that the 800,000 contract workers departing the Philippines are employed in over 160 countries and territories.

In "Global Cities and Circuits of Global Labor: The Case of Manila, Philippines," (Tyner 2000a), I document the social organization of global circuits of labor and examine how this social organization is spatially concentrated in Manila. Empirically, it is evident that the day-to-day operations of the Philippines' overseas employment program are highly concentrated within the NCR. The majority of government institutions tasked with overseas employment, including the Philippine Overseas Employment Administration (POEA), the Department of Labor and Employment (DOLE), the Department of Foreign Affairs, the Overseas Workers' Welfare Administration, and Technical Education and Skills Development Authority (TESDA) are all located in Metro Manila. And while these agencies, such as the POEA, do maintain regional offices, the principle decision making and regulatory functions remain concentrated in the NCR (see Tyner 2000c). Aside from government institutions, the overseas employment program is dependent upon the machinations of private recruitment agencies. These remain overwhelmingly concentrated within the NCR.

Patterns of out-migration also reflect the preeminence of the Metro Manila region as the focal point of overseas employment. In 2001, for example, a total of 866,590 contract workers were deployed from the Philippines. Of these, 855,701 (98.7 percent) departed through the Labor Assistance Center at Ninoy Aquino International Airport in Manila. Hence, even if these workers did not originate in the Manila region, they were still required to pass through the city prior to departure. Even if only on a temporary basis, and not counting any family or friends accompanying them, this translates to over twenty-three hundred migrants per day entering the city.

Limited information is available on migrant origins. In 1997, for example, over 37 percent of all overseas Filipino workers claimed to originate from the NCR (Tyner 2001). Admittedly, it is not known how many of these migrants truly originated from the NCR or simply listed this as their last address following an internal migration from other parts of the country. In either case, again, we are detailing a substantial increase, even if temporary, of people into the NCR as a result of overseas employment.

Given the concentration of activities within the NCR, we must next consider how a policy of overseas employment contributes to the making of Manila as a global city. I have indicated that economic policies formulated during the martial law years and afterward spatially favored the NCR at the expense of the rural areas of the country. These policies were formulated as part of Marcos's *development diplomacy*, a policy perspective predicated on the observation that less developed countries contained large population bases as well as vital natural resources that could be used at the global level. In the case of the Philippines, the Marcos regime attempted to utilize the country's surplus labor to demonstrate the feasibility of "interdependent" development (Gonzalez 1998, 34). It was more pressing, however, that the reorganization of the Philippine political economy under the Marcos administration was predicated on a discursive formation that emphasized individual and national discipline and, concurrently, the sacrifice of personal liberties for economic development (Timberman 1991; Tyner 2004). This approach conforms with Armitage and Roberts' (2003) notion of total mobilization in that the government attempted to mobilize (in some cases literally) all segments of society to facilitate capital accumulation.

Aside from attracting capital into the country, the martial law government sought to utilize migrant labor as a source of capital earnings. In 1974, Marcos signed Presidential Decree No. 442, the Labor Code of the Philippines, which entailed the realignment of all labor policies and programs with overall development goals (Khan 1988, 4). The labor code created the Overseas Employment Development Board (OEDB) and the National Seaman Board (NSB) to facilitate, with the assistance of the Bureau of Employment Services (BES), the recruitment and deployment of land-based and sea-based workers. The perceived benefits of overseas employment were identified early on, as indicated in a 1976 speech by Marcos:

We have provided jobs for our people not only in our new and expanding industries but also in the world labour market. Filipino talents and skills are becoming ubiquitous in many parts of the world. Returning Filipino workers have helped improve our skills and technological standards (quoted in Catholic Institute for International Relations 1987, 120).

Consistent with the increasingly centralized dictatorial regime of Marcos, the Philippines' overseas employment program was initially envisioned to be a government monopoly, a factor which contributed to the concentration of institutional actors within the NCR (for more complete discussion, see Ople 1979; Asis 1992; Gonzalez 1998). Mirroring the expression "all roads lead from Rome," Manila emerged as the central focal point for the recruitment and deployment of overseas contract labor (Tyner 2000a, 2000c). Subsequent institutional transformations of the program solidified this centralization. In 1982, through Executive Order No. 797, the OEDB, NSB, and BES were merged to form the POEA. An attached agency to the DOLE, the POEA remains the principal government agency involved with overseas employment.

An examination of the discursive formation undergirding the concrete rules and regulations of overseas employment is crucial to explicate fully the formation of Manila as a global city. I contend that initiating and forwarding a discourse of globalization contributed to the materialization of specific policies that favored the concentration of overseas employment functions within Manila. In this manner, the discursive construction of overseas employment and the concomitant policies that facilitated the movement of workers conjoined in the centralization of decision-making operations.

The POEA's philosophy was to adopt a "discriminating marketing approach" in the "development of labor markets for Filipino overseas contract workers" (1987, 5). This was to be accomplished through the penetration of "non-traditional markets," defined as either skills based or geographically based, in search of "high-benefit, high-growth areas suited for grooming [the] premium international image for the Filipino workers" (POEA 1987, 5). Moreover, it was the POEA's mission to "equip itself with suitable surplus labor to fill demand trends" and to "ensure that no one market spoil[ed the Philippines'] overall market image and/or block[ed] . . . entry to newly emerging opportunities" (POEA 1987, 5). Accordingly, these state apparatuses worked to expand the deployment of labor power to all parts of the world.

Despite presidential changes, as well as institutional transformations of the POEA, the government's advancement of overseas employment has changed very little. There currently exists a discourse of globalization that underlines the legitimation of overseas employment as a development strategy. In October 1997, for example, the POEA disseminated a white paper on overseas employment. Entitled "Managing International Labor Migration and the Framework for the Deregulation of the POEA," this paper articulates the perceived impact of globalization on the continuation of overseas employment (for a broader discussion of this globalization discourse, see Tyner 2000b,

2001, 2004). The white paper asserts, "Managing a global phenomenon starts with understanding the philosophy of humankind, dynamics of migration, history and natural laws which cannot be repealed" (Casco 1997, 2). Moreover, the document continues,

> The economic law of supply and demand is an irrepressible force in the global labour market, what more now with the globalization era. Unfortunately, this reality seems overshadowed by the application of national labour laws and administrative systems that perpetuate a pathological fallacy that labour migration is a program creation or innovation of government to address employment gaps (Casco 1997, 2–3).

As is apparent in this document, globalization is discursively identified as a natural, irrepressible force, one that the Philippine government is powerless to combat. International labor migration is likewise represented as a natural by-product of globalization, an intrinsic search on behalf of individuals to find better opportunities elsewhere. The POEA, however, is clearly concerned with doing more than just managing a natural phenomenon. It is actively producing migration through specific policies designed to exploit new labor markets, maintain existing markets, or eliminate nonprofitable markets (Tyner 2004, 45).

Although these sentiments seem, at face value, discordant with the nearly three decades of active government involvement in overseas labor, the context of the statements must be acknowledged. Following a series of highly publicized cases in 1995, including the execution of a Filipina domestic worker in Singapore and the near execution of another in the United Arab Emirates, the POEA was threatened with its institutional elimination. Republic Act 8042, the Migrant Workers and Overseas Filipino Act of 1995, called for the deregulation of the POEA and a gradual phaseout of all regulatory functions within five years (see also Gonzalez 1998; Tyner 2000b; Ball and Piper 2002).

Of most significance in the white paper, especially as pertains to the place of Manila in the global economy, is its positioning of the country in an era of globalization:

> What is the Philippine standing in the global imbalance of human resources? Media sensationalism tends to overshadow the fact that the global presence of Filipino labour is our strategic contribution to the global development, from which we reap net rewards central to the goals of our social economy. Managing means being able to objectively recognize and subsequently dominate our niche and comparative advantage (Casco 1997, 4).

A surplus of labor is posited as the Philippines' natural, comparative advantage within the global economy. Although the author(s) of the white paper apparently lament this fact, they also insist that the government and the country as a whole objectively recognize this position and attempt to make the best of the situation. Hence, a continuation, indeed an augmentation, of overseas employment as a development strategy is deemed the best (albeit natural) course of policy. Accordingly, a continuation of policies that facilitate the export of labor, it is believed, will likewise intensify the growth of the NCR through the continued centrality of relevant institutional functions in Manila. Just as certain key corporations concentrated in a few sites (e.g., London, New York, and Tokyo) are presumed to dominate the circulation of capital, so, too, does Manila function as the dominant mode of regulation in the circulation of labor. Indeed, it is this function, clearly, that the Philippines have advocated for nearly three decades. As Secretary of Labor Patricia A. Santo Tomas explains,

> We are looking at the world where competition is so much keener between and among nations not just for goods but for services as well. We are facing globalization and its effects, both within the country as well as relative to the movement of our people. The way we do things, our procedures, really ought to be reexamined in the light of the changes that [are] happening in the world (POEA 2001, 2).

She continues,

> I think you also have to redefine just exactly what you are in business for. . . . What we probably need now is a greater focus on marketing and how to ensure that the deployment of our workers can be done faster, better, and at the least cost to them. We probably also ought to set the ground rules for being able to meet market demands very quickly (POEA 2001, 2).

In summary, let me be absolutely clear on my position regarding the salience of overseas employment to the process of global city formation. The policy of overseas employment is most decidedly not a deliberate strategy on behalf of Philippine officials to promote Manila as a global city. Indeed, there is apparently no explicit recognition on the part of relevant state apparatuses (e.g., those tasked with regulating overseas employment and those tasked with managing the NCR) that overseas employment may affect the urbanization of Manila, either positively or negatively. This, in and of itself, I suggest, is a fundamental omission in the regulation of both labor market functions and urban problems. Nevertheless, the perpetuation of overseas employment as a development strategy intensifies the urbanization of Manila through the spatial agglomeration of institutional apparatuses and the inmigration of peoples in search of overseas employment. It is significant also that discourses of globalization are used to legitimate and justify the continuation of a controversial program such as overseas employment (see Tyner

2004) while simultaneously contributing to the discursive construction of Manila as a global city.

My discourse-privileging argument is not intended to suggest, however, that geographical questions do not materialize in any real sense on the landscape. Indeed, the Philippine government did propose measures to decentralize political power, including some measures associated with overseas employment (see Tyner 2000c). However, the motivating factor behind these decentralization proposals was not to lessen any agglomeration tendencies that contribute to overurbanization but rather to incorporate peripheral regions of the country more fully into the global circuit of labor. This was to be accomplished through a more efficient and spatially extensive dissemination of overseas employment opportunities beyond the NCR.

(BE)LABORING THE GLOBAL CITY CONCEPT

Robinson (2002, 536) caustically writes that "the discursive effectiveness of the global city hypothesis depends on the pithy identification of the 'global city'—a category of cities which are claimed to be powerful in terms of the global economy." She further asserts, "If the 'global city' were labeled as just another example of an 'industrial' district . . . it might not have attracted the attention it did." Her comments speak more broadly to the ontological and epistemological basis of global city research. What exactly is the object of study? And how are we to acquire our knowledge of this object? In short, what is the referent that the label "global city" denotes? Friedmann (1995, 25–6), for example, enunciates five traits that define a world (or global) city: (1) world cities serve as organizing nodes of a global economic system, (2) a space of global capital accumulation exists, but not all places are connected, (3) world cities are large urbanized spaces, (4) these cities may be arranged hierarchically in accord with economic power they command, and (5) the culture of these cities is cosmopolitan, and their ideology is consumerist. Friedmann (1995, 26) concludes by suggesting that if no a priori agreement is reached on these five points, then we must part company.

In my work on Manila, I take seriously these concerns. If, as Robinson (2002, 539) suggests, we are trying to fit "structurally irrelevant" cities of the periphery into a Eurocentric-based paradigm (à la Friedmann's five points), then the less developed regions of the world will remain marginal both literally and metaphorically. Consider, for example, Friedmann's position on the categorization of global cities. He notes, "A city's ability to attract global investment ultimately determines its rank in the order of world cities" (Friedmann 1995, 26). World cities thus become "end-points" (or receptors that *receive* both capital and immigrants), more reminiscent of a production line, rather than nodes in a circular system. Given the malleability of supposedly rigid definitions, therefore, perhaps we are asking the wrong questions. I forward the argument that global cities are simply whatever we as researchers define global cities to be. There is no natural or essential global city. My focus of study, therefore, is the *process of becoming a global city*. This is most decidedly not a clarion call to jettison all research on globalization and global cities. Instead, we should examine particular scaled processes and, concomitantly, the manifestation of these processes at particular (and interrelated) sites. In some circumstances, these sites may reflect an agglomeration of functions. However, rather than assigning a ranking (and, by implication, a sense of superiority), we should consider both the material and discursive consequences of this agglomeration.

Based on my work on Manila, I agree that there is something "happening" that we discursively label "globalization." However, I also agree with Parnreiter (2002, 147–48) that globalization does not simply "happen" but rather results from a deliberate reshaping of relations of capital, state, labor, and space. As such, and stemming from a study of Manila, I also forward the argument that the agglomeration of firms is certainly not necessarily a deliberate attempt to produce a global city. Instead, it is a post facto rationalization of this agglomeration that researchers such as Friedmann and Sassen have identified as a process of global city formation. To be sure, certain urban planners and managers, as well as marketing agencies, have since jumped on the global city bandwagon and attempted to produce (or, more simply, to promote) cities as global. Nevertheless, we should hold in abeyance any notion of a "natural" process of globalization and global city formation; rather, we should direct attention to specific policies and programs and their respective consequences, irrespective of intent. In the Philippines, for example, the decades-long promotion of overseas employment as a national development strategy has, unintentionally, contributed to the spatial agglomeration of both government and private businesses associated with the global circulation of labor. In line with this reasoning, one suspects that the concentration of particular firms engaged in the circulation of capital likewise clustered there because of other perceived benefits, or even because of a particular set of conditions that were conducive to business transactions. Accordingly, we need to focus on actual transactions in a multitude of forms.

REFERENCES

Abella, Manolo. 1992. "Contemporary labour migration from Asia: policies and perspectives of sending countries." In *International Migration Systems: A Global Approach*, ed. M. M. Kritz, L. L. Lim, and H. Zlotnik, 263–78. Oxford: Clarendon.
———. 1993. "Role of formal labour schemes in the development of Third World countries." *International Migration* 31, nos. 2/3: 389–402.

Armitage, John, and Roberts, Joanne. 2003. "From the hypermodern city to the gray zone of total mobilization in the Philippines." In *Postcolonial Urbanism: Southeast Asian Cities and Global Processes*, ed. R. Bishop, J. Phillips, and W.-W. Yeo, 87–101. New York: Routledge.

Asis, Maruja M. B. 1992. "The overseas employment program policy." In *Philippine Labor Migration: Impact and Policy*, ed. G. Battistella and A. Paganoni, 68–112. Quezon City, Philippines: Scalabrini Migration Center.

Ball, Rochelle. 1997. "The role of the state in the globalisation of labour markets: the case of the Philippines." *Environment and Planning A* 29: 1603, 1628.

Ball, Rochelle, and Piper, Nicola. 2002. "Globalisation and regulation of citizenship: Filipino migrant workers in Japan." *Political Geography* 21: 1013–34.

Casco, Richard R., ed. 1997. *Managing International Labour Migration and the Framework for the Deregulation of the POEA*. Manila: Philippine Overseas Employment Administration.

Cox, Kevin. 1997. "Globalization and the politics of distribution: a critical assessment." In *Spaces of Globalization: Reasserting the Power of the Local*, ed. Kevin R. Cox, 115–36. New York: Guilford Press.

Friedmann, John. 1995. "Where we stand: a decade of world city research." In *World Cities in a World-System*, ed. Paul L. Knox and Peter J. Taylor, 21–47. London: Cambridge University Press.

Gonzalcz, Joaquin L., III. 1998. *Philippine Labour Migration: Critical Dimensions of Public Policy*. Singapore: Institute of Southeast Asian Studies.

Hawes, Gary. 1987. *The Philippine State and the Marcos Regime: The Politics of Export*. Ithaca, NY: Cornell University Press.

Herod, Andrew. 1997. "Labor as an agent of globalization and as a global agent." In *Spaces of Globalization: Reasserting the Power of the Local*, ed. Kevin R. Cox, 167–200. New York: Guilford Press.

Hugo, Graeme. 2001. "Women's international labour migration." In *Women in Indonesia: Gender, Equity and Development*, ed. Kathryn Robinson and Sharon Bessell, 158–78. Singapore: Institute of Southeast Asian Studies.

Kelly, Phillip F. 2000. *Landscapes of Globalization: Human Geographies of Economic Change in the Philippines*. London: Routledge.

Khan, M. 1988. *Labour Administration: Profile on the Philippines*. Bangkok: International Labour Organization, Asian and Pacific Regional Centre for Labour Administration.

Knox, Paul L. 1995. "World cities in a world-system." In *World Cities in a World-System*, ed. Paul L. Knox and Peter J. Taylor, 3–20. London: Cambridge University Press.

National Economic and Development Authority (NEDA). 2001. *The Medium-Term Philippine Development Plan, 2001–2004*. Manila: NEDA.

Ople, Blas. 1979. "The Philippines overseas employment program." *Philippine Labour Review* 4: 11–25.

Parnreiter, C. 2002. "Mexico: the making of a global city." In *Global Networks: Linked Cities*, ed. S. Sassen, 145–82. New York: Routledge.

Philippine Overseas Employment Administration (POEA). 1987. "Market development: seeking purpose and promise for Filipino skills." *Overseas Employment Info Series* 1, no. 1: 5–9.

——. 2001. "Directions from Secretary Patrica A. Sto. Tomas." Annual Report.

Robinson, Jennifer. 2002. "Global and world cities: a view from off the map." *International Journal of Urban and Regional Research* 26, no. 3: 531–54.

Samers, Michael. 2002. "Immigration and the global city hypothesis: towards an alternative research agenda." *International Journal of Urban and Regional Research* 26, no. 2: 389–402.

Sassen, Saskia. 1988. *The Mobility of Labour and Capital: A Study of International Investment and Labour Flow*. Cambridge: Cambridge University Press.

——. 1991. *The Global City: New York, London, Tokyo*. Princeton, NJ: Princeton University Press.

——. 1993. "Economic internationalization: the new migration in Japan and the United States." *International Migration* 31, no. 1: 73–99.

——. 1994. *Cities in a World Economy*. Thousand Oaks, CA: Pine Forge Press.

——. 1995. "On concentration and centrality in the global city." In *World Cities in a World-System*, ed. Paul L. Knox and Peter J. Taylor, 63–75. London: Cambridge University Press.

Shah, Nasra, and Arnold, Fred. 1986. "Government policies and programs regulating labor migration." In *Asian Labor Migration: Pipeline to the Middle East*, ed. F. Arnold and N. Shah. Boulder, CO: Westview Press.

Short, J., and Kim, Y. 1999. *Globalization and the City*. Edinburgh Gate, UK: Addison Wesley Longman Limited.

Timberman, David G. 1991. *A Changeless Land: Continuity and Change in Philippine Politics*. New York: M. E. Sharpe.

Tyner, James A. 2000a. "Global cities and circuits of global labor: the case of Manila, Philippines." *The Professional Geographer* 52, no. 1: 61–74.

——. 2000b. "Migrant labour and the politics of scale: gendering the Philippine state." *Asia Pacific Viewpoint* 41, no. 2: 131–54.

——. 2000c. "The spatial structure of the Philippines' overseas employment program." *Asian Geographer* 19: 139–56.

——. 2001. "Regional origins of Philippine overseas contract workers." *International Journal of Population Geography* 7: 173–88.

——. 2004. *Made in the Philippines: Gendered Discourses and the Making of Migrants*. London: Routledge Curzon.

Tyner, James A., and Donaldson, Daniel. 1999. "The geography of Philippine international labour migration fields." *Asia Pacific Viewpoint* 40, no. 3: 217–34.

Wurfel, David. 1988. *Filipino Politics: Development and Decay*. Ithaca, NY: Cornell University Press.

6

Place-Imaging Tampa in the Age of Globalization

M. Mark Amen and M. Martin Bosman

Tampa Bay, located in west central Florida, is among a growing number of urban areas in the United States that are wrestling with the contested relationship between globalizing economic processes and decentralizing state capacities. The area also represents a growing number of metropolitan regions throughout the world that have turned their attention to place-imaging through attempts at rescaling and transforming urban governance for the purposes of local economic growth and economic competition. The particular impetus for these changes is the growing number of people living in the four-county region that identify Tampa Bay as their home. The perception of Tampa Bay as a self-evident metropolitan region has become a staple of policy discourses and is steadily taking hold in the consciousness of its residents, albeit in the shape of an integrated consumer market. This is a relatively recent occurrence. Fifty years ago, the cities of St. Petersburg, Tampa, and Clearwater were mutually exclusive reference points for people living outside the area. Each city was understood and portrayed as relatively independent of the others, represented by a distinct social history, and based on a different geoeconomic infrastructure. While the U.S. Bureau of the Budget identified Tampa–St. Petersburg and their respective counties as a standard metropolitan area (SMA) when SMAs were adopted in 1950, many communities even today continue to identify themselves as residents of one of the three cities (i.e., Tampa, St. Petersburg, or Clearwater) or two counties (i.e., Hillsborough or Pinellas) rather than of Tampa Bay. The current metropolitan statistical area (MSA), with a population of over 2.5 million, now includes two more counties to the north (i.e., Pasco and Hernando). However, electoral politics and municipal structures, taxation policies, school systems, health care, police and fire protection, and the region's aviation authorities (including the Tampa International Airport and Clearwater–St. Petersburg Airport) still identify with the geopolitical boundaries established when Pinellas County was carved from Hillsborough County in 1911. More recently, however, the image of Tampa Bay has steadily emerged as the nodal point for business recruitment (e.g., Tampa Bay Partnership), metropolitan politics (e.g., Hillsborough-Pinellas Planning Council), cultural entertainment (e.g., Tampa Bay Performing Arts Center), and professional sports (e.g., the Tampa Bay Buccaneers, Devil Rays, and Lightning).

While image-based urban-planning efforts to produce an attractive place-identity for Tampa Bay for potential inward investors and tourists are intensifying throughout the MSA, we limit our analysis to those in the city of Tampa and Hillsborough County. Our focus on place-imaging addresses the cultural manifestations of the area's power relations. While we realize that the entire metropolitan community of Tampa Bay contributes to its culture, social power is unevenly distributed within and between communities (e.g., Dahl 1961; Domhoff 1978). Urban government and the business community, alone or in partnership (e.g., Amin and Malmberg 1992; Ward 2000; Davies 2003), have exerted significant pressure in shaping Tampa Bay's place-image because both command considerable institutional resources (i.e., statutory authority and investment capital) that severally restrain the ability of citizens and other urban stakeholders to "talk truth to power" (Benveniste 1989). For this reason, we give exclusive attention to the efforts of the business and political sectors in Hillsborough County and the city of Tampa.

We combine this focus with an approach to culture advocated by Geertz (1973), which Tomlinson (1999) has linked to globalization. Tomlinson takes culture to be "the order of life in which human beings construct meaning through practices of symbolic representation [whereby] people make their lives, individually and collectively, meaningful by communicating with each other" (1999, 18). People create and participate in culture by engaging in a range of seamless rather than discrete and disconnected practices in their everyday lives. All practices, including language itself, are symbols that convey meaning to life and together constitute a "way of life," approximating what Pierre Bourdieu (1984) referred to as "habitus." Since many everyday practices are symbolized (Kristeva 1986), our concern is with those symbol(ization)s that are intended to convey meaning as an end (e.g., what it means to live in Tampa Bay, who and what is Tampa Bay, how the community imagines itself, and for what ways of living is it known) rather than those that are intended to facilitate functioning in everyday life (e.g., how to reach a destination, operate a computer, or vote in an election).

Although we consider only the activities and practices of the political and business sectors in this chapter, there have been other recent grassroots initiatives to unify the community around a particular image and preferred future of Tampa Bay. Two of these are the Hillsborough Tomorrow civic movement (1994–2000), which sought to create a communitywide strategy and vision, and Speak Up Tampa Bay (1995–), which was launched as a civic journalism initiative (Amen 2001). The former ended when its leader decided to run for governor; the latter now runs the public-access television network. More recently, after Richard Florida (2002) presented his work during meetings in Tampa in 2003, Creative Tampa Bay was founded as a nonprofit organization to rebuild and reconstruct the image of the regional economy to make it more attractive to "creative workers." Other less visible place-imaging initiatives and events have contributed to Tampa Bay's self-representation: the controversial proposal to create a "piracy" museum in Tampa that would house the eighteenth-century slave ship the *Wydah Galley* (Yelvington, Goslin, and Arriaga 2002), the initiative to privatize Tampa General, the relocation of people living in public housing, and debates about naming professional sports venues for football, baseball, and hockey or providing public funds to support centers for the performing and visual arts.

We begin by describing the Tampa Bay MSA's potential to be a global player, despite a history that is marked by an enduring pattern of local fragmentation and place-competition. We then turn to a consideration of the complex geometry of spatial struggles that the administrative and business elites of Hillsborough County and Tampa have engaged in during this globalizing effort through the various contested local and regional development projects to define a regional brand image for Tampa Bay. We follow Leslie Sklair (2001, 85), who notes that "global brands are at the center of the culture-ideology of consumerism that drives the capitalist system, giving the system as a whole a meaning and, in a real sense, providing a universal substitute for moral and spiritual values." We are interested in identifying how the efforts at regional place-imaging and global branding have fared and what they may reflect about the influence of globalization on Tampa Bay's political and economic cultures. We conclude with how the competing place-imaging strategies within Tampa and Hillsborough County have reconfigured power relations within the MSA and influenced Tampa Bay's image as an aspiring global city. Finally, we consider why more in-depth research of the "real social economy" of Tampa Bay is needed to determine how its globalizing efforts have altered the area's asymmetrical power geometries.

THE TAMPA BAY MSA

When the neoliberal policy prescriptions in the United States created opportunities for cities and metropolitan regions to participate in an increasingly globally networked economy (e.g., Hodos 2002; Clarke and Gaile 1998; Clark 2000), most cities and metropolitan regions were compelled to initiate "regional development coalitions" (Keating 1997; Clarke and Gaile 1998) with the private sector that relied on "global cities" discourses and strategies. Of course, all MSAs need dynamic political leaders and competent institutions (Fainstein 1990; Fitzsimons 1995; Clarke and Gaile 1998, 13) that are able to position and steer them effectively in the evolving and competing international divisions of economic and political power by presenting strategic place-images that can mobilize economic and political actors, develop new strategic capacities, access and utilize resources, and unify the population in a common, broader effort. The indicators compiled in table 6.1 illustrate that the Tampa Bay MSA has significant market potential to be a major player in a globalizing world. Since 1999, its economic ranking among U.S. MSAs has risen from 104 to 50, and as of 2000, it has a population ranking of fiftieth largest in the United States.

Clearly, the Tampa Bay MSA has the population size, natural resources, and strategic location to be a key regional node in the global network of cities. But, in order to realize its potential, the global economic-development agenda of the region will require strategic leadership capacity and competent governance structures that can establish creative policies across different and competing economic sectors and interests, on the one hand, and establish effective institutional mechanisms for organizing and mobilizing public opinion or will-formation, on the other hand. Apropos of Tampa Bay, Joel Kotkin (2000, 160) notes that "cultural events, by their nature, make for weekend places; they cannot sustain a constant flow of people. Securing a long-term role for a geographic place depends upon the recognition by local merchants, developers, and property owners, as well as by the citizenry, that the success of many areas depends precisely on maintaining and cultivating a place's unique characteristics as a *marketplace*" (original emphasis).

The Tampa Bay MSA, especially Pinellas County, relies on tourism for its economic vitality. As shown by the loss of revenue in the wake of September 11, 2001, and the subsequent drop in air travel, the area is heavily dependent upon the entertainment and tax revenues brought in by tourism (State of Florida 2005). Public revenues dropped by over a billion dollars, prompting a special session of the Florida state legislature, which, by reducing the state budget, also reduced those of local governments. Although other industries thrive in the Tampa Bay region, notably agriculture and mining (e.g., the phosphate industry), economic diversity is not the region's strong point (Florida Statewide Strategic Plan 2004). Although high-technology initiatives have been launched in the last ten years to address this issue, the MSA's growth has been primarily in the service sector (e.g., tourism, retail, back-office operations) and real estate development.

Despite its obvious potential, Tampa Bay is a diverse metropolitan region with a history that has proven a structural obstacle to creating a competitive place-imaging strategy in the global economy. Experimental efforts at re-

Table 6.1. Tampa Bay Metropolitan Statistical Area

	MSA	Hillsborough	Pinellas	Pasco	Hernando
Year established	1981	1834	1911	1861	1843
Square miles	2,631	1,061	309	772	488
National MSA ranking	50 (2002)*	N/A	N/A	N/A	N/A
Total 2002 population	2,486,472	1,054,560	933,972	361,456	136,484
Year county chartered	N/A	1983	1980	None	None
County gov't type:					
Commissioners	None	7	7	5	5
Other	None	Administrator	Administrator	None	None
Incorporated cities	35	3	24	6	2
Largest incorporated city	N/A	Tampa	St. Petersburg	New Port Richey	Brooksville
2002 population	585,687	311,880	250,354	16,193	7,260
Mayoral System	N/A	Strong	Strong	CM+	CM+
Population of other 31 incorporated cities	471,922				

Sources: Florida Department of Revenue, "Adjusted 2002 Population Estimates for Florida Counties and Municipalities"; Florida Association of Counties, "County Information," April 2003, at www.fl-counties.com/CountyInfo/counties_ab.htm (accessed November 10, 2005); Policom Corporation, "Economic Strength Ranking," at www.policom.com/ranknum.htm (accessed May 2003); Hillsborough County City-County Planning Commission, "Census 2000 Report: Initial Data Release," at www.theplanningcommission.org (accessed November 10, 2005).

Notes:
*MSA economic strength ranking is based on eighteen categories, including per capita personal income and earnings and employment for several types of workers (wage and salaried, nonfarm proprietors, and retail trade).
+Council manager.

gional governance and "metropolitics" (Harrison 1998) have created a confusing geometry of policy initiatives driven by the various purposes for which key regional institutions were established. To make matters worse, none of Tampa Bay's regional agencies has more than advisory power. Members of the Tampa Bay Regional Planning Council (TBRPC), for instance, are required by law to engage in economic cooperation, and Tampa Bay Water has adopted a regional governance format, but without any statutory authority.

The current Tampa Bay MSA, established in 1981, is composed of several autonomous and independent political jurisdictions that were carved into the territory over two centuries. In this respect, and as the indicators in table 6.1 show, the territorial extent of the MSA includes several distinct geopolitical boundaries: four counties and thirty-five incorporated cities, two of which (Tampa and St. Petersburg) are significantly larger than the others. Further, 43 percent of the MSA population and over 69 percent of the population in Pinellas County reside in incorporated cities. Population density per square mile and travel distance to work vary among the four counties: from 3,216 people in Pinellas to 280 people in Hernando with considerable automobile-based travel across the four counties to Tampa or St. Petersburg for both work and urban entertainment. Work commute times in the MSA are among the highest in the United States. Furthermore, some counties are chartered while others are run by county commissions. Some incorporated cities are run by strong mayors, and others have a council manager system. Many of these jurisdictions were established in the nineteenth century and have entrenched political traditions.

Furthermore, the establishment of the Port of Tampa and the emergence of the Cuban cigar industry in Tampa's Ybor City in the nineteenth century brought an early international flavor to the city's daily life. The port has since grown into Florida's largest port and is one of the fastest-growing cruise ship ports in the United States, as well as a major export hub for bulk cargo like fertilizer and phosphate products. Tampa's international networks were bolstered further by labor migrations from Spain and Cuba. The new immigrants established themselves in Tampa as distinctive political constituencies whose voices continue to influence city politics (Deitche 2004). In recent years, the population has become even more diverse as new immigrants from across Latin America, the Caribbean, and Asia have moved to Tampa Bay. In Pinellas, Hillsborough, and Pasco counties, the foreign-born population has grown far faster than the general population. A 2002 U.S. Census Bureau survey found that the percentage of foreign-born residents in the tri-county area has grown significantly since 1990: Hillsborough, 13 percent; Pinellas, 10.1 percent; and Pasco, 6.2 percent (Waite 2003). Internal migrations within the United States from the Northeast and Midwest have also contributed to what has become a culturally heterogeneous population with an increasingly marginal indigenous population. Moreover, as the headquarters for the Gulf States Accord between the United States and the Mexican states bordering the Gulf of Mexico, the city of Tampa is a frequent participant in trade missions sponsored by Florida's development officials and export firms. The city has also established an active International Visiting Professionals Program, which is sponsored by the U.S. State Department. Together with St. Petersburg and Clearwater, the city also recently launched a failed bid for the 2012 Olympics as a strategy to secure and enhance Tampa Bay's global position, both materially and symbolically.

POLITICAL PLACE-IMAGES OF THE MSA

Political leaders in Tampa and Hillsborough have not fared too well in their attempts to unify the public will around a common set of goals and images of Tampa Bay's position in the emerging "transnational urban system" (Sassen 2000b, 49–55). County officials, both elected and appointed, have often frustrated the ability of city leaders to redefine the territorial scope of policy initiatives as a way to forge a new unifying place-image for the Tampa Bay city-region as a seamless economic and cultural space. The articulation of such a place-image is a matter of intense "place wars" (Haider 1992) and spatial representational politics. As the most dominant political jurisdiction in the region, Hillsborough County has a long history of divisiveness within its own institutions, as well as with the city of Tampa (Kerstein 2001). The resulting failure to metropolitanize government across the city-county divide has had serious negative consequences for Tampa because population growth across the county has taken place at the expense of the city. For instance, the county's population has more than doubled over the last 30 years, from 490,265 in 1970 to 1,054,560 in 2002, whereas the population of Tampa (279,913 in 1970) has grown by less than 10 percent during the same period.

However, the county is marred by a tradition of political intrigue, infighting, and lack of transparency that has undermined its political function of crystallizing the weakly organized regional public interest. Consequently, prosperous suburban communities in Hillsborough have not looked to county commissioners or the county administrator for vision or leadership. Residents' low regard for the commissioners was confirmed when, in the early 1980s, four commissioners either pleaded or were found guilty to accepting bribes in exchange for supporting rezoning decisions in favor of suburban land developers (Kerstein 2001, 216). More recently, in November 2003, the county administrator, Dan Kleiman, was forced to resign after an unofficial vote of the commission indicated that he would have been fired. He was the tenth person to serve in that position and did so for ten of the thirty years since it had been created. Ostensibly, his resignation was precipitated when four of the seven commissioners claimed he had failed to manage his staff effectively. Others claim he was the victim of infighting among commissioners, some of whom were heavily influenced by a small but powerful lobby of pro-development Republican businessmen (Melone 2003).

Fragmentation across the multiple jurisdictions of Tampa Bay has proven to be an organizational impediment to creating a coherent system of regional governance, which is necessary for successful regional place-imaging (Clarke and Gaile 1998). Indeed, as Judith Innes and Judith Gruber note, "One of the greatest challenges for urban and regional policy today is to develop constructive and coordinated action across the fragmented and often warring jurisdictions" (2001, 2). The political fragmentation in Tampa Bay between the county and the city is mutual. For their part, city leaders have not conducted themselves as a unifying force on behalf of the Tampa Bay metropolitan region either. Tampa, like St. Petersburg, has a strong mayoral system of government. Accordingly, mayors control the policy agenda and, by virtue of their executive powers, have considerable potential to shape their respective cities' place-images. However, Tampa's mayoral system has created a tradition of political networking based on nepotism, political opportunism, and patronage, particularly favoring family and ethnic ties and corporate connections; a lack of citizen participation in the political process; and weak neighborhood involvement in policymaking. Successive mayors have either embraced this tradition or spent their political capital trying to overcome it. Thus far, neither approach has done much to advance a spatially more coherent or inclusive metropolitics of development, either as "global city" or under some other economic-development rhetoric.

Regrettably, Tampa politics remains captive to the longstanding competition between downtown and suburban interests about the scope and content of urban social policies. Of Tampa's five mayors over the past thirty years, William Poe (1974–1979), Bob Martinez (1979–1986), and Dick Greco (1995–2003) promoted an overt pro-growth, pro-business image of economic expansion and downtown development, rather than one of managed growth and neighborhood preservation and revitalization. None of these mayors' administrations championed an image of Tampa as a gateway or global city, and none promoted Tampa as a key node within the regional economy linked to the world. While Kerstein (2001) provides a detailed account of the key differences among these mayors, all of them appealed to local images of economic development within the city and did so primarily to win support from the local business elites.

The business community has been the decisive source of organizational and political power in the city. While its own power structure may have changed since the 1980s from one made up of a close-knit core of old-money patricians, namely, Ye Mystic Krewe, to one reflecting a new business culture with figures who have moved into the community from elsewhere in the United States, corporate business interests continue to be the driving force behind Tampa politics (Kerstein 2001, 195). With the exception of Sandy Freedman (1986–1995), Tampa's mayors have not projected an image of the city that relied on support from neighborhood groups and nonbusiness interests. Even Martinez's support for the construction of the Tampa Bay Performing Arts Center during his 1979 campaign for reelection was principally linked to how the center would enhance the city's competitive image among inward investors.

The two nonconsecutive administrations of Mayor Dick Greco personify the "growth machine" politics (Molotch 1976) and "mendicant entrepreneurial culture" (Teague 1994, 289) that have characterized the city of Tampa in the current era. Like so many of his predecessors, Greco established his power base by rhetorically appealing to the multiple stakeholders of Tampa. But in practice, unlike his predecessors, Greco became an unabashed tool of the city's commercial elites and provided them with unprecedented access to the major's office. He actively promoted and subsidized the local business community's development projects both in the historic downtown and through annexation of more land into the city limits (Kerstein 2001, 275–78). He was mayor of Tampa twice, first from 1967 to 1974, when he resigned to take a position as governmental affairs liaison for indoor shopping mall development with DeBartolo Development, one of the largest privately held real estate development companies in the United States. Greco became mayor once more from 1995 to 2003. He would have run for a third term had voters not rejected, by nearly 66 percent, a referendum in November 2000 to eliminate term limits. During his two terms in office, which amounted to a total of 14.5 years, Greco developed extensive networks with the commercial interests and the various law-enforcement agencies of Tampa. Under his less-than-transparent leadership, Greco focused almost exclusively on big-ticket, aspirational, commercial redevelopment projects adjacent to downtown (i.e., Channelside near the Port of Tampa and Ybor City, where migrants from Cuba had located the cigar-making industry during the nineteenth century). He guaranteed federal loans to Centro Ybor, an opulent shopping and entertainment complex that was suppose to spearhead and anchor the revitalization of Ybor City. When the project's owners could not pay the remaining $16 million in loans, the current mayor, Pam Iorio, was obligated to cover them with city tax funds (Karp and Albright 2004).

Iorio campaigned and won the 2003 city mayoral election on a platform that promised to make Tampa more livable and government more accountable. She had a long history of public service at both the county and city levels, including a stint as commissioner of elections for Hillsborough County during the controversial 2000 presidential election. Her main opponent, a former member of the Clinton administration, campaigned on a global economic-development platform. In an unusual move for a Tampa public official, Iorio spoke of "an earth without boundaries. Many times in politics, there is more focus on boundaries—on turf—than on solving problems. I pledge to you an administration that looks beyond lines on a map and focuses on people" (Iorio 2003). Yet, Iorio's policy actions during her first year as mayor conformed to the traditional politics of "city limits" (Peterson 1981) established by her predecessors.

Despite her earlier campaign support for metropolitanism related to a host of regional public goods, Iorio has focused on more prosaic matters, such as neighborhood problem solving, rather than taking on challenges like championing a borderless vision for Tampa Bay. Consistent with her focus on civic capital formation, such as improving public-service provisions across the city's neighborhoods, Iorio created three top-level positions for the Public Works and Utility Services Department, Economic Development, and Neighborhood Issues (Varian 2003). Her first budget proposal for $648 million in August 2003 did not request an increase in property taxes and was packaged as an investment "in neighborhoods" rather than in the big downtown commercial and entertainment projects of the Dick Greco era. Iorio also planned to redistribute funds across several areas of the city, mainly to improve roads, intersections, parks, and signage, to upgrade city buildings, and to increase the number of city employees. The success of this local human-capital strategy has now been jeopardized by Iorio's recent decision to honor the city's obligation to bail out a major downtown redevelopment project (Centro Ybor) that Greco began and by her endorsement of an ill-fated public-private partnership, ironically named Civitas, which was later flatly rejected by the Hillsborough County Commission. Civitas was presented to city officials and the residents of Tampa as a residential and commercial redevelopment project for Central Park, an impoverished 157 acres in the northeast downtown area of the city (Karp and Varian 2004).

BUSINESS PLACE-IMAGES OF THE MSA

The political leaders in Tampa and Hillsborough County have been either unable or unwilling to champion a compelling image of Tampa Bay as an emerging nodal region in the transterritorial network of global connectivity. That various organized business interests in the metropolitan region would attempt to forge such a place-image is, therefore, not surprising since, at least in Tampa and Hillsborough, they are the dominant players and the instrumental force in scripting the politics of local economic development. However, for all their dominance and influence, the major economic power elite within the region has not been able to offer a regionally conceived and inclusive vision that could appeal to the preexisting and often competing organized interests of key economic sectors (e.g., tourism, real estate development, the utilities). A key reason why such a vision has not been forthcoming is that the respective business communities of the two largest cities (Tampa and St. Petersburg) and counties (Hillsborough and Pinellas) within the MSA are politically fragmented, lack institutional and strategic leadership capacities, and continue to promote separate economic-development strategies.

For example, the individual chambers of commerce in Pinellas and Hillsborough counties have resisted efforts to create a common chamber because of concerns over the potential loss of brand equity. Furthermore, the members of the Greater Tampa Bay Chamber of Commerce, which serves Hillsborough, have struggled for years over internal control of the organization and its agenda. Chamber leadership positions are highly coveted as a symbol of status and influence within the business culture of the metropolitan area. And yet, the political leadership of the chamber has not been an organizing and unifying force for the business community. In October 2000, the Donovan-Wadley Group (DWG), a management-consulting firm specializing in economic development and image-based planning, which had been retained by the chamber to conduct a locational audit and recommend a business recruiting strategy, reported that Hillsborough County lacked a coherent agenda and strategy and that rampant growth in the area was raising serious questions about place-identity and land use. The study noted that there were tensions among groups advocating development, agriculture, and open space. Furthermore, it found that the area had a confusing platform of regional economic-development structures and strategies and that its members did not agree about the proper relationship between regional and county or local economic-development programs (Wadley-Donovan Group 2000). In the aftermath of the report, the chamber fired its executive director, whom they had brought in from Asheville, North Carolina, in May 2000. The chair of the chamber rotates annually, thereby contributing to the lack of institutional capacity and policy continuity in chamber programs and the use of the position to promote the partisan interests of its occupant. The chamber also has a "Committee of 100," which has inserted itself into the policy landscape as the official economic-development arm of Hillsborough County and its three incorporated cities. Its members include representatives of major public and private organizations in the county.

Since the Greater Tampa Bay Chamber of Commerce has not been a visionary force within the business community, other private-sector initiatives have emerged in the last ten years to promote a new hegemonic image for the metropolitan region and its preferred future. One of these, the Tampa Bay Partnership (TBP), was formed in 1993 as a private, independent, not-for-profit, marketing organization to serve Tampa Bay. The impetus to establish the TBP came from a few utilities companies (Tampa Electric, Florida Progress), the banking sector (NationsBank, Barnett, First Union, Sun Trust, and AmSouth), and some economic-development councils within the seven-county region of west central Florida that has defined the boundaries of the partnership since its creation. These counties constitute the largest consumer market in Florida and the second largest, after Atlanta, in the Southeast. While the founding sectoral members agreed to market Tampa Bay as "one cohesive region," their respective spatial and sectoral interests were defined almost exclusively in local terms (e.g., creating a seamless delivery system for utilities customers, developing local workforce skills for the financial sector, and stimulating economic growth at the county level). These sectors have remained the driving forces in the development of the TBP; some (e.g., the technology growth coalition) have only recently become visible players, and others (e.g., the tourism industry, which is the backbone of the region's economy) have never had an association with it.

Initially, the TBP declared its mission to be "a regional organization that works with its partners to market the region nationally and internationally, to conduct regional research and to coordinate efforts to influence business and government issues that impact economic growth and development" (TBP 1998, 4). Its stated goal is to increase Tampa Bay's market visibility and investment potential by streamlining the site-selection process for relocating and expanding companies. Using the imagery of globalization, the TBP wants to redefine Tampa Bay's image as a national and regional connector node in the network of global interaction and exchange. The TBP became a legitimate regional marketing organization and place-image entrepreneur in its first five years by adopting a conventional, neoliberal brand identity: "Tampa Bay—The Climate Is Right."

It entered phase II (1999–2003) with the singular goal of promoting economic growth in the region. During this period, as membership grew, the partnership identified "competing effectively on the world stage" as the best vehicle for regional growth. "Brand management as priority one" was the window to a "global market" that would secure the region's strategic position (TBP 1998, 1). The partnership called for and received some financial investment, primarily from economic-development organizations and a few large companies, to create a "superfund" to market the region to corporations from other countries that were considering relocation. The partnership used its budget to focus on the usual capital-development strategies, such as workforce training and development and large public-private infrastructure projects. Its marketing focus was directed almost exclusively at the national business community, in the hope that U.S. companies would see the region as an attractive place to relocate and invest. Ascribing to itself an entrepreneurial role, the TBP promoted itself as a key initiator and facilitator in solving critical fixed-investment, infrastructure, growth-management, and strategic-planning issues, such as water, transportation, and education.

The TBP made a critical decision in its third strategic plan (2004–2009) to move from its declared position as the region's dominant place-image entrepreneur and marketer to the region's public-policy advocate. By 2009,

$625,000 (compared to an average of $25,000 in past years) of the new annual budget of $2.6 million in the first 2 years and $3.1 in the last 3 years was to be used to hire lobbyists in Tallahassee, Florida's state capital, and in Washington, D.C. The steering committee and staff were determined to impose, if not create, a new political order in the region by increasing the business sector's power and influence over both state and federal policy coordination and growth-management strategies. Of the four priorities in the TBP's Phase III plan, the steering committee put singular emphasis on building a new policy framework for coherent regional governance at the state and federal levels. The TBP believed that a new political culture and governance structures were needed to respond to the growing complexity of the problems created by economic restructuring and global competition. Moreover, in this new political and policy landscape, it wanted to ensure that market priorities shaped the policy solutions to regional collective-action problems, such as transportation, water, growth management, workforce training, and technology development. Since the region represents 25 percent of the state legislature's votes, the TBP could move its pro-market agenda forward by developing a unified voice for their collective interests. The steering committee felt that the TBP had already become recognized for its regional policy entrepreneurship. It cited two examples: the TBP brought about a regional governance arrangement for water-supply planning and delivery, and "its successful efforts to recommend candidates for the USF [University of South Florida] Board of Trustees" indicated "that business influence can weigh heavily in public policy" (Tampa Bay Regional Planning Council 2002, 5).

The international business sector was never a TBP priority. The partnership paid lip service to that sector by creating an international advisory committee (IAC) and an international directory of regional businesses. This lukewarm approach came to a head at the 2002 annual meeting when representatives of the international business community expressed their frustration that the TBP was only using rhetoric when, in the past, it claimed that the region would become competitive in the "global market." The TBP's steering committee for the meeting responded by relegating the matter to the partnership's staff. Ensuing exchanges between the staff and the IAC revealed that visions differed as to what globalizing the local economy meant. The staff was committed to attracting foreign direct investment (FDI), primarily from Europe and Latin America, while the IAC wanted to expand trade with Latin America. It wanted the TBP to act as a clearinghouse that would coordinate trade-policy advocacy on behalf of the various regional mayors with political representatives in the state legislature and the U.S. Congress; support the export efforts of midsize and small companies, which generated 80 percent of Florida's export business; identifying new global markets; and merge the partnership's marketing and international committees into a single unit.

The final strategic plan was changed to accommodate most of the IAC's requests, including "global brand management," and the TBP agreed to increase global awareness among its constituents and to leverage the marketing efforts of its development partners to increase overall focus on the global marketplace. An additional $200,000 of the TBP's annual budget was allocated to an international outreach effort to foster links with target industries outside the United States as a means to increase their awareness of the existence of the Tampa Bay region. But, no clear decision or strategy has yet been developed for how to brand the region as an exporter or an emerging FDI destination, or both.

A second business initiative, the Florida High Technology Corridor Council (hereafter, the council), was formed in February 1994 by the then presidents of two of Florida's leading universities, namely, the University of Central Florida (UCF) and the University of South Florida (USF). It is jointly funded by the Florida legislature and participating technology companies. The idea to establish the council was the brainchild of USF's president, Betty Castor, and UCF's president, John Hitt. They teamed up with Enterprise Florida, the public-private partnership that replaced Florida's Department of Commerce, to lobby and influence corporate decision makers to opt for inward investment as opposed to foreign investment. This particular vision and the growth coalition had their genesis in the early part of 1994. At that time, the giant telecommunications company, AT&T, announced a major round of corporate restructuring and divisional reorganization and consolidation. In spite of cutbacks and consolidations in virtually all other AT&T divisions, the company's microelectronic division in the city of Orlando made national and international news when it announced that it was considering expanding its computer chip facility.

This news immediately triggered a fierce international battle for the new facility between Florida and other cities and regions across the world. Ultimately, AT&T spun off its microelectronic division into Lucent Technologies, entered into a strategic alliance with the Silicon Valley–based Cirrus Logic, and invested more than $600 million in a new joint venture, Cirent Semiconductors. Florida's economic-development officials eventually fended off a $90 million bid from the city of Madrid, Spain, and the new chip plant was located in Orlando, Florida. Significantly, the incentive package included a commitment by USF and UCF to provide collaborative research and nearly $1 million in training for Cirent's 600 employees.

The Cirent case prompted the two university presidents to consider "a very simple—yet utterly visionary—question: If this can be done to avoid losing a company in Florida, what can be done to help attract companies to Florida?" (Reich 1999, 21). Betty Castor noted, "We recognized that if we could bring high-tech, high paying jobs to any part of the corridor, the whole region would benefit" (Reich 1999, 21). Thus began the strategy to lure other chip and high-tech manufacturers to Florida. Recognizing the strategic importance of ideas and institutional leadership, Castor and Hitt directed their attention to the formation of a problem-oriented policy community. They began meeting regularly and creating channels of dialog and decision making, as well as establishing the grounds for collective action, among diverse interests, including local- and state-level government officials, a series of horizontal networks of nongovernmental actors, such as economic-development organizations, and local leaders in the high-tech industry.

The council, which now resembles a full-blown regional-growth coalition, is composed of academic, business, and government leaders from the twenty-one counties that make up the service area of UCF and USF. Its primary focus is to attract and capitalize on six high-tech industrial sectors, namely, aviation and aerospace; information technology; medical technology; microelectronics; modeling, simulation, and training; and optics and photonics. The council acts as a policy innovator and mediator that actively lobbies state and local economic-development commissions, the state legislature, local governments, and local businesses to offer innovative incentives intended to promote Florida's I-4 Corridor as one of the leading high-tech regions in the United States to inward investors from across the world.

CONCLUSION

Political elites at both the county and city levels have yet to agree on a more broadly based growth coalition and physical development strategy for Tampa Bay. County government continues to offer no unified or inclusive vision for the region. In the city, mayoral candidates advocate images to either developers or neighborhoods that reinforce the wider social and spatial realities of economic and political power between these two general constituencies rather than offer a vision that would unite or forge a pragmatic accommodation between these two contending sides. Once elected, mayoral priorities and agendas usually address a combination of traditional urban physical development problems, such as transportation, utilities, property taxes, and zoning, that appeal to longstanding, partisan electoral and growth coalitions. In Tampa, real estate and commercial land developers have had a longstanding and disproportionate influence over the political process, particularly the city's physical development apparatuses, than have those interested in managed growth, neighborhood revitalization and infill, regional integration, or high technology. Greco, Martinez, and Poe were preoccupied with the continued viability of downtown Tampa and its fixed investments and rarely referred to the benefits of regional development across the MSA.

Moreover, as the 2000 WDG report found, business leaders also do not share a common vision and image of Tampa Bay. Traditional business interests and divisions continue to be the driving force within the chamber of commerce and within the international business community. Ironically, leadership there does not seem to reflect the type of aggressive, neoliberal, market-oriented economic model of municipal entrepreneurialism that has become associated with globalization. At the same time, there are new growth strategies that may yet capitalize on the MSA's regional potential and global linkages. Both the TBP and the I-4 High Technology Initiative represent emerging efforts to unite the region as a single consumer market or as a high-technology industrial entertainment corridor. Both movements have organized a new, private-sector power base across metropolitan Tampa Bay that does reflect a neoliberal, competitive, cutthroat, urban-based entrepreneurialism. The TBP annual budget has grown over the last 10 years from $250,000 to $2.6 million. While its focus is emphatically regional rather than local, the TBP nonetheless has promoted itself as a place marketer and, more recently, as a regional political-advocacy organization. Its marketing strategy has been focused nationally and, as mentioned earlier, only recently modified to accommodate traditional international business interests in either FDI or trade. Although the TBP has not integrated the tourism sector into its strategic planning, it has relied on good climate and sunshine, neither of which is recognized as a signifier of globalization.

The I-4 Corridor High Technology Initiative continues to operate as inwardly focused as it was when it was formed to entice AT&T's microelectronics division to locate in Orlando rather than Madrid. This regional initiative was led by higher-education institutions, which promoted technology as a way to diversify and globalize the region's economy. Recently, the I-4 initiative has developed partnerships with other local, high-technology initiatives, including the TBP, as a way of broadening its territorial scope of action. Like the TBP, and despite the focus on high-technology as a signifier of globalization, the I-4 initiative has not yet established a compelling image of the region as a platform for global exchange and interaction. This has not, however, deterred the I-4 leadership from marketing the region as a high-technology destination. The belief is that this marketing strategy will eventually become a self-fulfilling prophecy when the region better defines its key technology cluster or niche (e.g., medical, microelectronics, information).

For now, no regional development coalition has achieved the necessary degree of economic and political coherence across Tampa Bay that "both establishes legitimacy and nourishes relations of trust" (Amin and Thrift 1995, 102) in and for the region. The formation of a broadly shared vision and strategy for Tampa Bay to prosper within the emerging global web of city-regions must accommodate the particularities of place, local governing traditions, and the unique economic circumstances across the multiple political jurisdictions that make up Tampa Bay. For the metropolitan area to develop as a legitimate "regional actor," the historical legacy of rampant economic development, municipal localism, and antiregionalism that has defined much of the political and economic history of Hillsborough and Pinellas counties must be put to an end. Regional development coalitions and other regional stakeholders must develop the innovative institutional networks and strategic local leadership capacities (Fainstein 1990) necessary to build a viable regional place-identity for Tampa Bay. Existing global city-regions like London, New York, and Tokyo have all built distinctive niche identities for themselves in the financial-services sector. Indeed, all globalizing cities require a niche (Paddison 1993; Fretter 1993; Watson 1991). The evidence suggests that the political and business elites of Tampa and Hillsborough have yet to develop a shared vision and unified voice in political and economic terms that would give the Tampa Bay region a stronger presence in the emerging global division of power. In the meantime, the competing place-images discussed in this chapter reflect the inability of the region's power brokers to leverage the unique comparative advantages of the region and blend the capacities of a range of actors and stakeholders to develop strategic regional economic-policy capacity.

Tampa Bay's economic and political elites will have to broker the tensions and contradictions between preexisting "city" and "county" issues, which have become one of the key institutional obstacles in the process of regionalization and place-imaging. Effective leadership on this issue will require what Amin and Thrift refer to as "institutional thickness," meaning in-depth understanding of the "social and cultural factors [that] lie at the heart of success" (1995, 101). In the context of Tampa Bay, this notion will encompass, among other things, in-depth knowledge of the local, regional, and global conditions that continue to affect the region. What is the depth of knowledge in the political and business sectors in Tampa and Hillsborough County about these conditions? This unknown requires further research. How representative of the region are the policies and projects of Hillsborough County and Tampa mayors? The MSA profile we offer in table 6.1 demonstrates complex differences that call for further in-depth study of the geoeconomic and geopolitical realities of Pinellas, Pasco, and Hernando counties.

We suspect that a more complete picture of the region's role in globalizing processes will only be complete after further study of both the formal and informal economic and other activities of the Tampa Bay MSA. Beyond the formal economy lies an arena of activity that may well be more indicative of how globalization has already influenced Tampa Bay. How much do the political and business leaders we have identified know about these developments? Therein lies our future research agenda, the outcome of which will allow us to develop a more grounded account of how the structures of power are changing in Tampa Bay and what role globalizing processes have played in moving it into a new transnational network of cities.

REFERENCES

Amen, M. M. 2001. "The power of institutions and agents: sources of failed university-community collaboration." *Metropolitan Universities* 12, no. 4: 30–49.

Amin, A., and Malmberg, A. 1992. "Competing structural and institutional influences on the geography of production in Europe." *Environmental and Planning A* 24, no. 3: 401–16.

Amin, A., and Thrift, N. 1995. "Living in the global." In *Globalization, Institutions, and Regional Development in Europe*, ed. A. Amin and N. Thrift, 1–22. Oxford: Oxford University Press.

A. T. Kearney, Inc., and the Carnegie Endowment for International Peace. 2002. "Globalization's last hurrah?" *Foreign Policy* (January/February): 38–51.

Barkin, D. 2000. "Urban management in the global economy." In *Global City Regions: Their Emerging Forms*, ed. R. Simmonds and G. Hack, 207–13. New York: SPON Press.

Bassett, K. 1996. "Partnerships, business elites and urban politics: new forms of governance in an English city?" *Urban Studies* 33, no. 3: 539–55.

Benveniste, G. 1989. *Mastering the Politics of Planning*. San Francisco: Jossey-Bass Publishers.

Bourdieu, P. 1984. *Distinction: A Social Critique of the Judgement of Taste*. Cambridge, MA: Harvard University Press.

Clark, T. 2000. "Old and new paradigms for urban research—globalization and the fiscal austerity and urban innovation project." *Urban Affairs Review* 36, no. 1: 3–45.

Clarke, S., and Gaile, G. 1998. *The Work of Cities*. Minneapolis: University of Minnesota Press.

Dahl, R. 1961. *Who Governs? Democracy and Power in an American City*. New Haven, CT: Yale University Press.

Davies, J. S. 2003. "Partnerships versus regimes: why regime theory cannot explain urban coalitions in the UK." *Journal of Urban Affairs* 25, no. 3: 253–69.

Deitche, S. M. 2004. *Cigar City Mafia: A Complete History of the Tampa Underworld*. Fort Lee, NJ: Barricade Books.

Domhoff, G. W. 1978. *Who Really Governs? New Haven and Community Power Reexamined*. New Brunswick, NJ: Transaction Books.

Fainstein, S. 1990. "The changing world economy and urban restructuring." In *Leadership and Urban Regeneration*, ed. M. Parkinson and D. Judd, 31–47. London: Sage.

Fitzsimons, D. S. 1995. "Planning and promotion: city reimaging in the 1980s and 1990s." In *Reimaging the Pariah City: Urban Development in Belfast and Detroit*, ed. W. J. V. Neill, D. S. Fitzsimons, and B. Murtagh, 1–49. Brookfield, VT: Avebury.

Florida High Tech Corridor, at www.floridahightech.com (accessed April 2002).

Florida, R. 2002. *The Rise of the Creative Class: And How It's Transforming Work, Leisure, Community and Everyday Life*. New York: Basic Books.

Fretter, A. 1993. "Place marketing: a local authority perspective." In *Selling Places: The City as Cultural Capital, Past and Present*, ed. G. Kearns and C. Philo, 163–74. Oxford: Pergamon Press.

Geertz, C. 1973. *The Interpretation of Cultures*. New York: Basic Books.

Gilb, C. 1989. "Third World cities: their role in the global economy." In *Cities in a Global Society*, ed. P. Knight and G. Gappert, 96–107. Urban Affairs Annual Reviews 35. Beverly Hills, CA: Sage Publications.

Gottman, J. 1989. "What are cities becoming the centers of? Sorting out the possibilities." In *Cities in a Global Society*, ed. P. Knight and G. Gappert, 58–67. Urban Affairs Annual Reviews 35. Beverly Hills, CA: Sage Publications.

Graham, S. 2000. "Planning cyberspaces." In *Global City Regions: Their Emerging Forms*, ed. R. Simmonds and G. Hack, 236–43. New York: SPON Press.

Haider, D. 1992. "Place wars: new realities of the 1990s." *Economic Development Quarterly* 6: 127–34.

Hall, P. 1998. *Cities in Civilization*. New York: Pantheon Books.

Harrison, B. 1998. *It Takes a Region (or Does It?): The Material Basis for Metropolitanism and Metropolitics*. Cambridge, MA: Lincoln Land Institute.

Hodos, J. 2002. "Globalization, regionalism, and urban restructuring: the case of Philadelphia." *Urban Affairs Review* 37, no. 3: 358–79.

Hueber, D. 2001. "Drought management at the local government level in the Southwest Florida water management district." Unpublished report, July 2000.

Innes, J., and Gruber, J. 2001. *Bay Area Transportation Decision Making in the Wake of ISTEA: Planning Styles in Conflict at MTC*. Berkeley: University of California Transportation Center.

Iorio, P. 2003. "Remarks of Mayor Pam Iorio," Office of the Mayor, Tampa, Florida, April 1.

Karp, D., and Albright, M. 2004. "Tampa must absorb Centro Ybor loan." *St. Petersburg Times*, January 8, A1, A10.

Karp, D., and Varian, B. 2004. "Time runs out on Civitas Project." *St. Petersburg Times*, January 16, A1, A6.

Keating, M. 1997. "The political economy of regionalism." In *The Political Economy of Regionalism*, ed. M. Keating and J. Loughlin, 17–40. London: Frank Cass.

Kerstein, R. 2001. *Politics and Growth in Twentieth-Century Tampa*. Gainesville: University Press of Florida.

Knight, R. 1989. "Introduction: redefining cities." In *Cities in a Global Society*, ed. R. Knight and G. Gappert, 15–20. Urban Affairs Annual Reviews 25. Beverley Hills, CA: Sage Publications.

Knox, P. 1996. "World cities and the organization of global space." In *Geographies of Global Change*, ed. R. J. Johnston, P. T. Taylor, and M. J. Watts, 232–47. Cambridge, MA: Blackwell Publishers.

Kotkin, J. 2000. *The New Geography: How the Digital Revolution Is Reshaping the American Landscape*. New York: Random House.

Kristeva, J. 1986. "Word, dialogue, and the novel." In *The Kristeva Reader*, ed. T. Moi, 35–61. New York: Columbia University Press.

Melone, M. J. 2003. "Hillsborough government swallows its latest meal." *St. Petersburg Times*, November 23, B1.

Molotch, H. 1976. "The city as a growth machine: toward a political economy of place." *American Journal of Sociology* 82: 309–30.

Noponen, H., Graham, J., and Markusen, A. R., eds. 1993. *Trading Industries, Trading Regions: International Trade, American Industry, and Regional Economic Development*. New York: Guilford Press.

Ohmae, K. 1995. *The End of the Nation State: The Rise of Regional Economies.* New York: Free Press.

Paddison, R. 1993. "City marketing: image reconstruction and urban regeneration." *Urban Studies* 30, no. 2: 339–50.

Peterson, P. 1981. *City Limits.* Chicago: University of Chicago Press.

Pierce, N. 1993. *Citistates: How Urban America Can Prosper in a Competitive World.* Washington, D.C.: Seven Locks Press.

Prudhomme, R. 1989. "New trends in the cities of the world." In *Cities in a Global Society,* ed. R. Knight and G. Gappert, 44–57. Urban Affairs Annual Reviews 35. Beverly Hills, CA: Sage Publications.

Reich, M. 1999. "Sunny skies and silicon dreams." *USF Magazine* 1, no. 4: 19–23.

Rosenau, J. N., and Czempiel, E. O., eds. 1993. *Governance without Government: Order and Change in World Politics.* Cambridge, MA: Cambridge University Press.

Sassen, S. 1997. "Saskia Sassen on the 21st century city." *Government Technology* (June), at www.interlog.com/~blake/sassen.htm (accessed January 2, 2002).

———. 1998. *Globalization and Its Discontents.* New York: The New Press.

———. 1999. "Urban economies and fading distances." Megacities lectures, at www.megacities.org.

———. 2000a. "Cities in the global economy." In *Global City Regions: Their Emerging Forms,* ed. R. Simmonds and G. Hack, 267–76. New York: SPON Press.

———. 2000b. *Cities in a World Economy.* 2nd ed. Thousand Oaks, CA: Pine Forge Press.

Scanlon, R. 1989. "New York City as global capital in the 1980s." In *Cities in a Global Society,* ed. R. Knight and G. Gappert, 83–95. Urban Affairs Annual Reviews 35. Beverly Hills, CA: Sage Publications.

Sklair, L. 2001. *The Transnational Capitalist Class.* London: Blackwell.

Stanley, B. 2003. "Going 'global' and wannabee world cities: (re)conceptualizing regionalism in the Middle East." In *Crisis and Resistance in the 21st Century World Systems,* ed. W. A. Dunaway, 151–70. Westport, CT: Praeger.

State of Florida. 2005. "Statewide Strategic Plan 2004," at www.eflorida.com/strate gicplan/2005/?sectionid=&print=p.

Storper, M. 1997. *The Regional World: Territorial Development in a Global Economy.* New York: Guilford Press.

Tampa Bay Partnership (TBP). 1998. *The Tampa Bay Partnership Phase II, Through 2003.*

———. 2000. "Tampa Bay Partnership PowerPoint presentation1," December 12, 2000, at www.tampabay.org (accessed April 2002).

———. 2000. "Tampa Bay Partnership PowerPoint presentation2," December 12, 2000, at www.tampabay.org (accessed April 2002).

Tampa Bay Regional Planning Council. 2002. "Goals of future of the region," at www.tbrpc.org (accessed April 2002).

Taylor, P. T. 2001. "Urban hinterworlds: geographies of corporate service provision under conditions of contemporary globalization." *Geography* 86, no. 1: 51–60.

Teague, P. 1994. "Governance structures and economic performance: the case of Northern Ireland." *International Journal of Urban and Regional Research* 18, no. 2: 275–92.

Tomlinson, J. 1999. *Globalization and Culture*. Chicago: University of Chicago Press.

Trigaux, R. 2002. "Tampa Bay area, meet your neighbors in South Tampa Bay." *St. Petersburg Times*, March 11.

Tyner, J. A. 2000. "Global cities and circuits of global labor: the case of Manila, Philippines." *Professional Geographer* 52, no. 1: 61–74.

Van Vielt, W., ed. 2001. *Cities in a Globalizing World (Global Report on Human Settlements 2001)*. United Nations Centre for Human Settlements (Habitat). Sterling, VA: Earthscan Publications Ltd.

Varian, B. 2003. "Iorio appoints city administrator for public works." *St. Petersburg Times*, December 31, 3B.

Wadley-Donovan Group/Garnet Consulting Services. 2000. *Executive Summary: Locational Audit and Business Recruiting Strategy*. Prepared for the Greater Tampa Chamber of Commerce, October.

Waite, M. 2003. "Born in U.S.A.? Not in Miami." *St. Petersburg Times*, September 3, A1, A6.

Wallace, H. 1996. "Politics and policy in the EU: the challenge of governance." In *The European Union*, ed. H. Wallace and W. Wallace, 3–36. Oxford: Oxford University Press.

Ward, K. G. 2000. "A critique in search of a corpus: revisiting governance and reinterpreting urban politics." *Transactions of the Institute of British Geographers* 25, no. 2: 169–85.

Watson, S. 1991. "Gilding the smokestacks: the new symbolic representations of deindustrialized regions." *Environment and Planning D: Society and Space* 9: 59–70.

Yelvington, K., Goslin, N., and Arriaga, W. 2002. "Whose history? Museum-making and struggles over ethnicity and representation in the Sunbelt." *Critique of Anthropology* 22, no. 3: 343–79.

7

Gentrification, Globalization, and Governance: The Reterritorialization of Sydney's City-State

Scott Salmon

In what is now a voluminous literature on globalization, one recurrent theme is the apparent disembedding of political, economic, and social relations from their local place-based contexts. Despite the variety in emphasis, research object, and orientation, one common thread in the diversity of globalization analyses is a focus on the increasing circulation of commodities, capital, identities, and images through global space. These accelerating global flows are said to embody processes of deterritorialization through which human social relations are increasingly being disembedded from places and territories (Appadurai 1996). However, there are at least two significant problems with this emphasis on flows, circulation, and deterritorialization. First, it tends to overlook the relatively fixed and immobile forms of territorial organization that characterize much of contemporary capitalist life: cities and the regulatory institutions that govern them. Second, it neglects the ways in which the current round of neoliberal globalization has been both dependent on and expressed through transformations of territorial organization on multiple scales (Brenner 1999).

Recent rounds of globalization have reconfigured the scalar organization of capital's endemic cycle of de- and reterritorialization, which has been dubbed *glocalization*, "the combined process of globalization and local-territorial reconfiguration" (Swyngedouw 1992, 61; 1997). In the case of global cities, this rescaling of urbanization has been fairly thoroughly analyzed, but the concomitant processes of state rescaling have received far less attention. It is this process of state rescaling and reterritorialization that I want to focus on in this chapter.

Much of the work on the politics of globalization has employed what is essentially a zero-sum conception of state power in relation to the global economy, such as the now familiar "hollowing out" of the state thesis, which presumes that the state declines in power and strategic significance as the process of globalization intensifies. Where these ideas have been employed in the study of cities, they have often led urbanists, like many other globalization researchers, to assume that economic globalization is leading to an erosion of state territoriality. At the risk of gross oversimplification, it is possible to identify two related positions that flow from this assumption (following Brenner 1999), depending on the reading of globalization employed. The first suggests that capital's purportedly greater mobility and increasing scales of operation irreversibly weaken the state's ability to regulate economic activity within its boundaries. The second posits that states are reacting to intensified global economic interdependence by constructing new forms of national socioeconomic policy but are not themselves qualitatively transformed through these new global-national interactions.

I want to argue here, in contrast to these positions (and, again, following Brenner 1999), that the state's role as a form of territorialization for capital should be understood as logically distinct from the structural significance of the national spatial scale in demarcating capital flows, economic transactions, urban hierarchies, and social relations. From this viewpoint, it is possible to acknowledge the ongoing decentering of the national scale of political-economic regulation but not necessarily to interpret this as evidence of a contraction, retreat, or dissolution of state territoriality. Likewise, it is possible to recognize the importance of state territoriality but not necessary to assume that this role remains tied inextricably to the national scale of state institutions and policies. In other words, both positions tend to obscure the various (and ongoing) transformations of state territorial organization through which, qualitatively, new institutions and regulatory forms are being produced on both sub- and supranational scales.

The central thesis of this chapter is that the process of reterritorialization and, specifically, the reconfiguration and rescaling of the city and the local state should be understood as a constitutive, enabling moment in the process of globalization and global city formation. This reterritorialization is a highly contested and conflictual process, mediated through a range of political struggles for control over urban space that are in turn articulated upon multiple scales. As such, the outcome of these struggles over reterritorialization has significant implications for democracy and citizenship in the global city. In order to illustrate this argument, this chapter focuses on the ongoing globalization of Sydney, Australia, and, in particular, on the struggle over the restructuring—and reterritorialization—of governance in the city.

URBAN GOVERNANCE AND THE RISE OF "GLOBAL SYDNEY"

Australia has a three-tiered political system—federal, state, and municipal—and, although there has been some antagonism between these levels, fairly stable coalitions have been in power since 1995. At the federal level, John Howard's Liberal/National coalition has been in power since 1996 while Bob Carr's Labor government has ruled the state of New South Wales since 1995. At the symbolic center of "Global Sydney," the City of Sydney Council has been led throughout most of the period by the electoral coalition of independent, but Labor-aligned, Mayor Frank Sartor. However, although Sydney is usually characterized as a single unit, the Sydney metropolitan area, and the 4.2 million Sydney-siders who inhabit the metropolitan area certainly conceptualize the city as a single entity, the city is not a singular political unit. Rather, Sydney is a conglomeration of thirty-nine separate councils, each with its own elected representatives and mayor. In central Sydney alone, there are eight distinct municipal jurisdictions. In the discussion that follows, I focus primarily on three, the cities of Sydney, Leichardt, and South Sydney.

Sydney has always been Australia's largest city, but only relatively recently has it decisively surpassed Melbourne as the nation's undisputed seat of financial, corporate, and political power. During the 1990s and into the 2000s, Australia enjoyed a decade of prosperity, but nowhere were the gains more pronounced than in Sydney (O'Neill and McGuirk 2002). In this period, the growing global integration of the Australian economy and the deregulation of its financial markets enabled the city to become Australia's leading switching point into a globalized financial capitalism (Fagan 2000; O'Neill and McGuirk 2002). As O'Neill and McGuirk (2002) argue, Sydney has effectively become the locus of Australia's accumulation strategy. It now produces 30 percent of the nation's GDP and houses the regional headquarters of 500 global corporations operating in the Asia-Pacific (City of Sydney, n.d.). Between 1986 and 1997, the floor space in the city of Sydney dedicated to property and business services increased by 72 percent while finance and insurance floor space increased by 36 percent. In other words, finance and business services based overwhelmingly in Sydney have been the major drivers of Australia's economic growth and prosperity. And the city has reaped the rewards: by the end of the 1990s, the 240,000 workers in inner-city Sydney earned, on average, 40 percent more income than equivalent workers in the other regional capitals of Australia. High and rapidly rising Sydney real estate prices reflected the demand for quality housing by these well-remunerated households. Between 1987 and 1999, the average Sydney house increased in value an incredible three times. Likewise, the unemployment rate for the entire Sydney metropolitan area at the end of 1999 was 4.7 percent, 50 percent below the national average—the largest differential in Australian history (Council of the City of Sydney 2000).

Sydney is also very aware of how important it has become to the NSW state economy and, indeed, the national economy as a whole. Through groups like the Committee for Sydney and the Property Council of Australia, Sydney's business community projects the city's economy as an exemplar of new economy growth based on high value-added, technology-intensive, professional service activities (O'Neill and McGuirk 2002). Similarly, Sydney has come to dominate the production and transmission of news and entertainment media within Australia. As a result, Sydney has increasingly become the national arbiter of news, style, architecture, food, fashion, and lifestyle. Sydney's strategic significance has also become an explicit feature of the prevailing neoliberal policy discourse at the state level where it has been actively constituted as a key terrain in the project of forging a successful state strategy. At the same time, there has been a much greater emphasis, at all levels of government, on enhancing Sydney's international competitiveness and global city status (Connell 2000). Perhaps the most notable recent example is the unprecedented exposure (and economic opportunity) generated by Sydney's hosting of the 2000 Olympic Games.

Despite this self-conscious dominance, until relatively recently Sydney has lacked a stable governing coalition with the ability to exercise preemptive power in setting policy agendas and shaping governance goals (McGuirk 2003). Private-sector associations have long been present in Sydney's urban political landscape, and many have exerted political influence over particular legislative and regulatory issues; as political actors, however, these groups are perhaps best characterized by their fluid and disparate nature rather than by their coalescence into identifiable and enduring coalitions with a common agenda and approach. Rather, a changing network of political influence has circulated around government institutions, driven by the distinctive and contested agendas of differentiated fractions of capital (McGuirk 2003). Different economic interests have apparently been able to benefit from Sydney's economic buoyancy without needing to forge active and ongoing cross-sectoral coalitions to exercise power. More commonly, it seems that conflicting fractions of capital, often with quite divergent priorities, have engaged in transient bargaining arrangements with government, sometimes formalized into public-private partnerships. These partnerships have typically been specifically targeted at the development of large-scale, "global" consumption, entertainment, and infrastructure facilities (Searle and Bounds 1999). In the case of these site-specific governance collaborations, state government has played a crucial role as the animateur, but beyond these, cross-sectoral collaborations in urban governance have characteristically been contingent and disjointed rather than systematic (McGuirk 2003).

Sydney's changing scalar context has, however, witnessed the discursive construction of the city as a crucial site and scale for governance, as part of a strategic state project integrating Sydney, hence, the national economy, into global accumulation circuits. The emergence of this strategic scalar agenda has been accompanied by the rise of a particular political configuration. In fact, the discursive construction that emerged around governing Sydney facilitated the emergence of a coalition of interests aligned around the shared agenda of producing a globally competitive Sydney. At the heart of this coalition was an unlikely, but mutually beneficial, alliance between the independent mayor of Sydney, Frank Sartor (and his dominant electoral coalition on the Sydney City Council) and key figures in Bob Carr's (NSW) state Labor government.

Sartor is a populist politician who proudly compares himself to New York's former mayor Rudy Giuliani. Under his stewardship, the city of Sydney was transformed into an almost entirely privatized, pro-development, local state that is (like the city's business community, which it represents) self-consciously global in its ambitions. In 2000, for example, Sartor established the Global Sydney Committee with an invited membership of prominent figures from key CBD business sectors and leading state and local government bureaucrats. The committee's stated aim is to address "issues relating to Sydney's standing and role in a global context" (City of Sydney, 1999). However, although Sartor eagerly claimed the world stage as the official host of the 2000 Sydney Olympics, few viewers outside Australia would have been aware that almost all of the Olympic proceedings took place at sites outside his political jurisdiction. Indeed, at that time, the city of Sydney was relatively unusual in that it occupied the smallest territory of the eight inner-Sydney councils and contained virtually no residents. This was apparently the source of some consternation to Sartor, who believed that in order to achieve true global status, the city of Sydney should have a larger territorial and residential base. Perhaps equally revealing was his confession to a sense of embarrassment when meeting with the mayors of other global cities who presided over large populations when he controlled so little (Sartor, personal interview, 2002). Whatever the motivation, it came as little surprise to most when Sartor emerged as the leading advocate for local government reform in Sydney and, especially, when it became apparent that "reform," as he conceived it, entailed a greatly expanded empire for the city of Sydney.

RETERRITORIALIZATION AND LOCAL GOVERNMENT "REFORM"

In October 2000, the minister for local government in Carr's NSW Labor government announced his intention to reform local government in Sydney and commissioned an independent public inquiry to establish the most optimal outcome. Drawing on almost five hundred written submissions and eighty-nine oral presentations, the commission presented a wide-ranging report on the process of local government reform for the eight inner-city councils of Sydney (Sproats 2001).

In their submission to the public inquiry and the accompanying public statements, the city of Sydney and Mayor Sartor made much of the need for what they termed "good government." According to the city's submission, good local government is based on "good local councils, strong local communities and an effective partnership between the two" (City of Sydney 2000, 7). According to the city, the eight inner-city local councils failed to meet the needs of local communities in an efficient and effective manner. In the ensuing public debate, however, it appeared that Mayor Sartor's notion of good government was somewhat mechanistic, centering as it did on issues such as the length of grass in public parks, parking fees at public meters, the presence of graffiti, street cleaning, and the frequency of garbage collection. Regardless, the way forward according to both the mayor and the city lay in a greatly expanded city of Sydney and in a council structure that would ensure "that Sydney remains competitive within the global economy, for so much of the region's livelihood and prosperity depend on this" (City of Sydney 2000, 126).

The Commission of Inquiry ultimately recommended that a thorough and ongoing process of reform be activated through a partnership between state government and the local community and grounded in the formation of four entirely new councils (to replace the existing eight) defined by their functional and land-use characteristics (Sproats 2001).[1] Somewhat inexplicably, however, the commission's suggestions were almost entirely ignored by the (NSW) state government, which proposed instead a series of piecemeal changes to the current situation, the net effect of which was to deliver a greatly expanded territory to the city of Sydney at the expense of the neighboring councils of Leichardt and South Sydney.

Under the state's proposal, the Leichardt City Council would lose the residential neighborhoods of Glebe and Forest Lodge to Sydney, while South Sydney would lose a total of seven neighborhoods,[2] as well as the Royal Prince Albert Hospital and the University of Sydney. To summarize the impact of these changes, Leichardt stood to lose a considerable portion of the municipality's prime waterfront residential real estate and South Sydney would lose both affluent residential neighborhoods and thriving commercial districts. Despite the fact that the existing eight councils were to remain, the state minister for local government initially attempted to characterize the proposed changes as being in line with the recommendations of the public inquiry. Eventually, the inquiry's commissioner was forced to contradict the minister on national television. As the commissioner characterized it to me during an interview, it seemed obvious that the minister's representation of harmony between the commission's findings and the state's proposal was a cynical calculation rather than a genuine misinterpretation (Sproats, personal interview, 2002).

RESISTANCE IN LEICHARDT AND SOUTH SYDNEY: THE POWER OF PLACE?

I have suggested that the struggle over the territorial organization of urban governance in Global Sydney entailed the complex interconnection of multiple geographic scales. It has also entailed quite distinct conceptions of what constitutes the urban. Henri Lefebvre (1995) has argued that struggles over the territorial organization of the urbanization process express the dual character of spatial scales under capitalism, that is, their roles as framings for everyday social relations and as productive forces for successive rounds of global-scale capital accumulation. This tension between the spaces of everyday urban life and the spaces of capital accumulation were drawn into sharp relief in the struggle over the proposed reterritorialization of governance in Sydney. Both the Leichardt and South Sydney city councils, as well as many of their residents, mobilized in opposition to the proposed restructuring, and each in their own ways gave voice to unique, place-based conceptions of everyday urban life in Sydney.

The Leichardt City Council and a group called Residents against Glebe's Expulsion, or RAGE, centered their opposition on explicitly place-based notions of democracy and citizenship. The focal point of their campaign was a low-density neighborhood of working-class homes known as Glebe and the right of Glebe residents to control the fates of their own communities. This campaign articulated two key discursive themes, both emphasizing Glebe residents' fundamental attachment to place and their right to the city.

- The need for democracy and the right of residents to control their own future. This theme was captured in the campaign's slogan "Let the People Decide."
- The threat that the transfer presented to the unique character of Glebe and the inner-city, working-class way of life it represented. The campaign explicitly contrasted Glebe to the nearby neighborhood of Pyrmont that has been rapidly transformed in recent years into a high-density, high-rise neighborhood increasingly favored by affluent members of the managerial classes. These concerns were captured in the slogan "Save Glebe from High Rise."

The Leichardt campaign utilized traditional door-to-door organizing strategies of grassroots campaigns in concert with a fairly high-technology strategy designed to target the city's e-savvy service workers. The campaign set up a very popular website, which advocated participatory democracy through various virtual and real venues. A feature of this site, which garnered considerable media attention, was the "Where's Harry" page, a playful reference

to the well-known children's television game "Where's Waldo," which highlighted Minister of Local Government Harry Woods' refusal to meet with either the media or opponents of the proposed changes.

Similarly, neighboring South Sydney's campaign reflected the unique
character of the place that its residents have constructed. King's Cross and
the Darlinghurst neighborhoods are widely recognized as comprising Sydney's gay- and lesbian-friendly capital. Inside the borders of South Sydney lie
most of Sydney's HIV health facilities (a network of clinics that provide free
and anonymous treatment), and most of the cities gay and lesbian cultural
events occur (such as the annual Mardi Gras festivities). The South Sydney
City Council (SSCC) frequently paraded its gay and lesbian credentials. At the
time of the campaign, it had an openly gay mayor, and according to the
council, one in four of its residents was gay or lesbian. Everyone I interviewed in South Sydney interpreted the proposed merger as a direct threat
to the character and lifestyle that is South Sydney. The proposed changes
also represented a considerable threat to the area's unique commercial
character—the King's Cross neighborhood houses most of Sydney's sex
industry—and the wide range of services SSCC provides to meet the needs
of these communities. In mobilizing support to prevent the expansion of
Sydney, the SSCC appealed directly to its gay and lesbian constituents. This
is the first time in the history of Sydney, indeed, in the history of Australia,
that the gay and lesbian community has been directly enlisted to assist in a
campaign about issues pertaining to basic electoral procedures. Previous
governments had sought contributions from the gay and lesbian community
on issues concerning public space only if they were lesbian and gay specific.
To be called upon to intervene in a "mainstream" political debate in a manner that served to emphasize gay and lesbian visibility and citizenship was
seen as quite revolutionary.

At the same time, the SSCC took on the question of exactly what constitutes "good government," arguing that it provided the kind of governance
that reflected the unique needs of its community. The slogan of the SSCC
campaign was "South Sydney Council Works for Me." Apart from a series of
very large and very public parades emphasizing the unique nature of the
South Sydney community, the action was also centered on a very astute legal campaign designed to delay and derail the process of territorial restructuring through action in the courts.

GLOBAL CITY FORMATION AND RETERRITORIALIZATION

Given the vast discrepancy between the findings of the Commission of Inquiry and the changes that were actually proposed, the NSW state's motivation was the subject of much speculation within the city. Several competing
narratives enjoyed wide currency, each offering differing interpretations of

the apparently incomprehensible conclusion. One interpreted the proposed change as a simple payback to Mayor Sartor for achieving success with the 2000 Olympics, an event widely recognized, even by its critics (e.g., Lenskyj 2002), as promoting a positive image for and of Sydney throughout the world. This account, however, largely overlooked the fact that, while assuming a high public profile, Lord Mayor Sartor did not play a particularly influential role in orchestrating the city's Olympic success. Another, more complex account suggested that the mayor was taking the lead in advocating boundary reform so as to enable the NSW State Labor Party to transfer solid blocks of Labor Party support to the city of Sydney, ensuring Labor Party control over future city administrations. The reward for the mayor was reportedly a safe Labor seat in the next state election. This account was fueled by Premier Bob Carr's public admission that he would like to have Sartor "on board" and Sartor's own announcement that he would not be contesting the 2003 city election. This was a very popular interpretation but one that rested on the assumption that the districts being transferred to the city of Sydney by the proposed changes were actually safe Labor constituencies at the local government level. However, given the changing demographics (and rising incomes) of rapidly gentrifying inner-city Sydney, few former Labor strongholds could be regarded as absolute certainties in the changing currents of local government.

Both of these accounts may have contained the requisite intrigue and whiff of political patronage to satisfy the cynicism of the jaded Sydney-sider. But a remarkably explicit account of a public hearing that was published in Sydney's *Morning Herald* (Gilmore 2001) may point to another impetus for the proposed changes:

With a smirk, Sydney Lord Mayor Frank Sartor transformed himself into Napoleon Bonaparte before his new subjects yesterday.

Mr. Sartor addressed Glebe and Forest Lodge residents for the first time since the NSW Government decision to include them in the expanded City of Sydney.

At a stormy meeting, one resident shouted: "Go back to the city, you little Napoleon bastard."

In response, Mr. Sartor grabbed an Akubra hat and placed it sideways on his head. Then he dug his hand into his shirt in a parody of the diminutive French ruler.

In the front row, a new Sartor loyalist stood up before the emperor at Glebe Primary School. She said: "I have one question. When can I lodge my development application with the new Sydney Council and get it away from these f***wits at Leichhardt Council?"

Half of the room burst into loud cheers and applause at the reference to the notoriously slow development application processing time at Leichhardt.

Both the South Sydney and Leichardt city councils have more stringent development controls and much more elaborate procedures for the approval of development applications than those in place at the city of Sydney. In the city of Sydney, development applications are handled in a streamlined process through a separate development bureau within the city administration while, in Leichardt and South Sydney, applications require the approval of their respective full city councils. In the development-friendly city of Sydney, it takes an average of 35 days to process development applications compared with an average of 103 days in South Sydney and 137 days at Leichardt (Jamal and Halloran 2001). Not surprisingly, there is also a far higher rate of approval for development applications in the city of Sydney. These facts led many to suggest that the move toward local state reterritorialization was primarily driven by the desire to reap the rewards of property development enabled by the accelerating accumulation and gentrification of Global Sydney.

Yet, however much mayoral ambition, state Labor Party electoral strategizing, and the pecuniary interests of local developers may have coalesced around the issue of local government redistricting, it seemed as if the very multiplicity of regulatory institutions operating at different spatial scales might serve to thwart the reterritorialization process. In May of 2002, the SSCC's legal challenge to the proposed boundary changes bore unexpected fruit when it was upheld in the Land and Environment Court. The ruling that the very process for drawing up the boundaries (employed by the Boundaries Commission) was procedurally unfair and therefore invalid effectively halted the entire redistricting plan. However, even as redistricting opponents were celebrating the ruling, few of the major players seemed to believe this to be the end of the matter.

ANNEXATION, SACKING, AMALGAMATION, AND BACKLASH

As it turned out, the Land and Environment Court's ruling was not to be the end of the redistricting initiative. After seeking legal advice, Harry Woods, minister of local government, appealed the ruling to the Supreme Court, which subsequently overturned the prior judgment of the Land and Environment Court. This paved the way for the city of Sydney to gain areas including Kings Cross, Wooloomooloo, Glebe, and Forest Lodge, as well as the University of Sydney campus and Royal Prince Albert Hospital, from the South Sydney and Leichardt councils. South Sydney was ordered to pay the cost of both the appeal and the Land and Environment Court action— reportedly AUD$250,000 (*Sydney Morning Herald* 2002). The decision also allowed for a transitional period under which the councils would negotiate the details of the change, including asset and staff transfers. In the case of the city of South Sydney, this process proved to be particularly problematic as eight investment properties, delivering around AUD$8 million per year to the city, were located on land to be transferred to the city of Sydney. In real terms, the annexation would mean South Sydney would lose 30 percent of its area and 40 percent of its income, raising the real possibility of imminent bankruptcy.

While the fallout from the Supreme Court decision was being absorbed and contested by the affected councils, there was a leadership transition in the city of Sydney. Long-term mayor Frank Sartor stood down after twelve years to take up a position within the NSW state government as minister for energy and utilities and minister for science and medical research. He was replaced by Councilor Lucy Turnbull, who became the first female lord mayor in the city of Sydney's 160-year history. Her reign was, however, destined to be short-lived. The impending fiscal crisis in the city of South Sydney was to provoke yet more changes in the city's political landscape.

The precarious financial situation of the SSCC, in large part created by the annexation of its territory and investment properties, provided an opportunity for the NSW state government to intervene and impose its own political geography upon the city of Sydney. Faced with the loss of income from the properties and mounting legal bills, South Sydney's new Labor mayor, Tony Pooley, committed an act of apparent political suicide by proposing the amalgamation of the South Sydney and Sydney city councils. Sydney lord mayor Lucy Turnbull responded by describing South Sydney as "a very sick puppy which should not be delivered into the hands of any other local government until its problems have been sorted out" (quoted in Nicholls 2003). Shortly thereafter, Sydney dropped its legal claim to the eight lucrative properties, effectively making the merger unnecessary. Nonetheless, the Carr government instructed the Boundaries Commission to hold a public inquiry to examine the financial consequences of amalgamating the councils and the effects on services to residents. This inquiry was conducted on an abbreviated timetable with the call for submissions issued on December 26, 2003, and closing on January 27, 2004, in order to ensure that the process was completed before the March council elections, for which rolls closed on February 16.

Perhaps not surprisingly, such haste elicited considerable criticism, not least from Sydney's lord mayor, Lucy Turnbull, who publicly denounced the process variously as "rushed and ill-conceived," a "gerrymander," and a "farce" (quoted in Nicholls, Davies, and Pearlman 2003 and Delaney and Pryor 2004). Accusing the Carr government of an abuse of process designed to "get its hands on Town Hall," the Sydney lord mayor indicated that she would take the matter to court to stop a merger with South Sydney (Nicholls, Davies, and Pearlman 2003). This defiance elicited a swift response from former lord mayor Frank Sartor, who reportedly called his successor within an hour of the announcement, accusing her of "rubbing his nose in the dirt," adding, "you are just a bunch of local government pissants" and "the Government is powerful and we will destroy you and the council" (quoted in O'Rourke and McClymont 2004).

Events were, however, to overtake this colorful conflict. Early the following morning, immediately after the Boundaries Commission's recommendations, the NSW governor sacked both the South Sydney and Sydney city councils in a proclamation that caught both councils by surprise. On February 6, 2004, the governor proclaimed the merger of the former Sydney and South Sydney city councils. Councilors from both areas were replaced by three commissioners: former lord mayor Lucy Turnbull, former South Sydney mayor Tony Pooley, and director general of the Department of Local Government Garry Payne. The commissioners were to act as the interim administration until the local government elections the following month. Under the new megacouncil, there would be nine councilors and a directly elected mayor for the entire area.

Predictably, this move was widely interpreted as a power grab on the part of the NSW state Labor government (Nicholls 2003; Allen, Hepworth, and Skulley 2004). Amalgamation would greatly increase Labor's chance of gaining control of Sydney town hall and installing a Labor lord mayor, as South Sydney included strong Labor voting areas such as Redfern and Waterloo, although gentrification in other areas has boosted the independent and green vote in recent years. The Carr government's dismissal of the councils came just six weeks before council elections and seemed virtually to ensure that former federal labor minister Michael Lee would become Sydney's new lord mayor. It also seemed to guarantee that Labor-backed governments would control all property developments between the Opera House and Sydney's airport 15 km south of the CBD. Moreover, the sacking and amalgamation of the two councils by the NSW state government was a direct contradiction of its repeated promise that there would be no forced council amalgamations.

The immediate consequence of the amalgamation announcement was a surprisingly strong public backlash against the apparent abuse of power by the state government. Ironically, the depth of this reaction was in large part due to the popularity of the Labor-controlled SSCC. In the midst of the public outcry following the announcement, popular, independent, inner-city member of parliament Clover Moore announced she would stand for lord mayor, apparently blindsiding the government plan for Labor candidate Michael Lee to assume the office. Moore's maverick candidacy gave disenchanted Labor voters, elements of the area's large gay vote, and the newly emerging green vote a rallying point and a means to express their dissatisfaction. By Election Day, the strength of this emerging coalition was sufficient to secure Moore the lord mayoralty and an absolute majority on the new Sydney City Council. Thus, despite transferring over sixty thousand new Labor voters onto the expanded city of Sydney electoral roll, the NSW government's attempt to create a Labor stronghold in central Sydney went badly amiss. In a paradox of political fortune, the actions of the NSW government (and the public's perception of them) in many respects "created" Clover

Moore and the emergent urban social movement that cost it the very prize it sought. As Moore herself put it on election night, "Labor tried to take the 'local' out of local government and tried to buy Sydney Town Hall. They have rightly paid the price" (quoted in Mitchell 2004).

CONCLUSION: ACCUMULATION, RETERRITORIALIZATION, AND THE URBAN

On the basis of the evidence presented here, it is possible to suggest that, in Sydney at least, the current round of neoliberal globalization is rescaling state territory rather than eroding it. In fact, it could be argued that the rise of Global Sydney entailed not only the construction of a "new industrial space" for post-Fordist forms of industrialization (Fagan 2000) but also prompted an attempt to consolidate a "new state space" to enhance the state's capacity to mobilize urban space as a productive force. Global Sydney has been constituted as a key site within the multiscalar ensemble of institutions that is the Australian state and as a key site in the national accumulation strategy and in supplying the conditions of growth in the Australian economy and in its competitive positioning in the space-economy of neoliberal globalization. The implementation of both urban rescaling and state reterritorialization was a highly contested process, mediated through a series of sociopolitical struggles for hegemonic control of urban space and the property-led capital accumulation it enables, which was in turn articulated upon multiple spatial scales.

The emergent politics of scale regarding the territorial organization of urban governance within contemporary global cities may be animated by the imperatives of capital accumulation, but they nonetheless must confront the realities of everyday urban life. During the interviews I conducted with city councilors in both South Sydney and Leichardt in the course of conducting this research, it became apparent that they saw their constituencies as unique, residential, and, to varying degrees, working-class communities, and as they expressed it to me, they understood their political futures (and their electoral mandates) as depending on preserving and defending those communities against powerful forces of redevelopment and gentrification. Without exception, they interpreted the process of reterritorialization as a threat not simply to their own political futures but to the fundamental character of the places and communities they represented. In Sydney, a "politics of scale" emerged in which both geographical scales and the terrain of everyday urban life simultaneously operated as sites and stakes of political struggle. Ultimately, however, local, place-based conceptions of the urban proved to be the most politically persuasive to the residents of central Sydney.

NOTES

1. These were an enhanced city of Sydney, a mixed residential/industrial city, a beachside/harborside residential city, and an inner-West residential gateway city.

2. These seven neighborhoods included Woolloomooloo, Potts Point, Rushcutter's Bay, Elizabeth Bay, Darlinghurst, Chippendale, and King's Cross.

REFERENCES

Allen, L., and Hepworth, A., with Skulley, M. 2004. "ALP's council power grab." *The Financial Review* (July 2): 6.

Appadurai, A. 1996. *Modernity at Large: Cultural Dimensions of Globalization*. Minneapolis: University of Minnesota Press.

Brenner, N. 1999. "Globalisation as reterritorialisation: the rescaling of urban governance in the European Union." *Urban Studies* 36, no. 3: 431–51.

City of Sydney. 1999. "Living City." Meeting no. 1297, September 20, at www.city ofsydney.nsw.gov.au/Council/documents/meetings/excl200999.pdf (accessed November 9, 2005).

———. 2000. *Submission to the Public Inquiry into the Structure of Local Government*, at www.cityofsydney.nsw.gov.au/boundaries (accessed January 10, 2001).

———. n.d. "Global Sydney fact sheet," at www.sydneymedia.com.au/html/2291-global-sydney.asp (accessed November 9, 2005).

Connell, J., ed. 2000. *Sydney: The Emergence of a World City*. Melbourne: Oxford University Press.

Council of the City of Sydney. 2000. *City of Sydney Yearbook 1999*. Special Projects Unit. City of Sydney, available at www.cityofsydney.nsw.gov.au/citystore/item.asp?id=29 (accessed November 9, 2005).

Delaney, B., and Pryor, L. 2004. "City drops legal claim amid fight on merger." *Sydney Morning Herald*, September 1, 3.

Dunford, M., and Kafalakas, G., eds. 1992. *Cities and Regions in the New Europe*, 39–67. New York: Bellhaven Press.

Fagan, B. 2000. "Industry change in the global city: Sydney's new spaces of production." In *Sydney: The Emergence of a World City*, ed. J. Connell, 144–67. Melbourne: Oxford University Press.

Gilmore, H. 2001. "Emperor Frank looks the part." *Sydney Morning Herald*, November 25, 39.

Jamal, N., and Halloran, J. 2001. "Sartor woos with cut in parking fees." *Sydney Morning Herald*, November 17, 4.

Lefebvre, H. 1991. *The Production of Space*, trans. D. Nicholson-Smith. Cambridge, MA: Blackwell.

———. 1995. "The right to the city." In *Writings on Cities*, 63–184. Cambridge, MA: Blackwell.

Lenskyj, H. 2002. *The Best Olympics Ever? Social Impacts of Sydney 2000*. Albany: State University of New York Press.

McGuirk, P. 2003. "Producing the capacity to govern in Global Sydney: a multi-scaled account." *Journal of Urban Affairs* 25, no. 2: 201–23.

Mitchell, A. 2004. "Clover Moore is off to town hall." *Sydney Morning Herald*, March 28, 1.

Nicholls, S. 2003. "Turnbull rails at ALP 'control grab.'" *Sydney Morning Herald*, November 22, 11.

Nicholls, S., Davies, A., and Pearlman, J. 2003. "Inner-city super councils back on the drawing board." *Sydney Morning Herald*, December 9, at www.smh.com.au/cgi-bin/common/popupPrintArticle.pl?path=/articles/2003/12/08/1070732147971.html (accessed November 9, 2005).

O'Neill, P. M., and McGuirk, P. 2002. "Prosperity along Australia's eastern seaboard: Sydney and the geopolitics of urban and economic change." *Australian Geographer* 33, no. 30: 241–61.

O'Rourke, C., and McClymont K. 2004. "We'll destroy you, sacked mayor told." *Sydney Morning Herald*, July 2, 1.

Searle, G., and Bounds, M. 1999. "State powers, state sand and competition for global entertainment: the case of Sydney." *International Journal of Urban Regional Research* 23: 165–72.

Sproats, K. 2001. *Inquiry into the Structure of Local Government in Eight Council Areas in the Inner City and Eastern Suburbs of Sydney*. New South Wales Government Commission of Inquiry, at www.dlg.nsw.gov.au/dlg/dlghome/documents/information/binqrep.pdf (accessed November 8, 2005).

Swyngedouw, E. 1992. "The mammon quest: 'glocalisation,' interspatial competition and the monetary order—the construction of new scales." In *Cities and Regions in the New Europe*, ed. M. Dunford and G. Kafalakas, 39–67. New York: Bellhaven Press.

———. 1997. "Neither global nor local: 'glocalization' and the politics of scale." In *Spaces of Globalization*, ed. K. Cox, 137–66. New York: Guilford Press.

Sydney Morning Herald. 2002. "Amalgamate, don't tinker." September 9, 10.

8

Reluctant Globalizers: The Paradoxes of "Glocal" Development in Brussels

Erik Swyngedouw and Johan Moyersoen

BRUSSELS: A WORLD CITY?!

It is ironic that Brussels has received relatively little attention in recent debates on global urban change and development, when the city figures prominently in international media. In the United Kingdom or in the United States, for example, "Brussels" stands as shorthand for the European Union or the North Atlantic Treaty Organization (NATO). This alone suggests that Brussels has achieved, at least in the public imagination, the status of "World City," a notion that is confirmed by empirical research.[1] If we just take one of the standard variables that are invariably summoned to claim World City status (i.e., the presence of international organizations), Brussels clearly stands out among the "great" cities of the world (see table 8.1) (Elmhorn 1998).

Nevertheless, the globalization of Europe's capital city constitutes a paradoxical urban condition. On the one hand, the macroeconomic dynamics are undoubtedly positive in comparison with other metropolitan areas in the EU. On the other hand, problems of social disintegration, of labor markets that are out of joint, and of a generally low socioeconomic profile are manifestly present. While capital accumulation turns around quite frenetically, this strong economic performance is not paralleled by a correspondingly high socioeconomic profile. On the contrary, in Brussels, social polarization and economic exclusion go hand in glove with economic growth and competitive success. We argue in this chapter that this conundrum is the result of two main and related "battlefields," or domains of tension and competition, that hold Brussels in a paradoxical straightjacket.

155

**Table 8.1.   Presence of International Organizations
in Selected World Cities, 1960–1997**

	1960	*1972*	*1976*	*1985*	*1990*	*1997*
Brussels	148	480	500	901	981	1,466
Geneva	111	153	209	342	361	393
London	199	283	412	815	500	571
New York	85	94	273	622	231	292
Paris	374	520	666	1,102	780	874
Washington	43	80	180	47	157	215

Source: Elmhorn 1998.

The first arena is the interurban competition between Brussels and other cities. Brussels has become an important player in international markets. For example, if we consider financial flows alone, there has been a sweeping internationalization of financial markets, and Brussels has become an increasingly important player. Brussels constitutes one nexus in the nodal system that controls and manages these "spaces of flows" (Castells 1989a, 1994; Sassen 1988, 2002). The contemporary city is conceived as a spatial concentration of headquarters of political and financial institutions conducting the global economy (Castells and Hall 1994; Scott 1998). The expansion of financial and related services in the last two decades is, today, responsible for most of the direct and indirect growth in employment in metropolitan areas. This is also true for Brussels. Nevertheless, the status of world player is, obviously, not granted to every city. While interurban competition intensifies, the relative competitive success of cities depends crucially on the competitive structure of their internal economic and institutional frameworks. Therefore, the entrepreneurial elite in Brussels promotes a reliable and transparent business climate to enable Brussels to jump scales and helps the city to become one of the European, or even global, capital poles against other urban centers, such as London, Paris, and Frankfurt.

The need for a stable, institutional, urban climate for investment often conflicts with the need for mediation, fussiness, and adjustment in the fragmented reality that constitutes the local, urban social space. Therefore, the second battlefield to consider is the intraurban competition between the diverse social, political, cultural, and economic interests embodied in a highly heterogeneous and cosmopolitan city. Brussels' response to its desired role as catalyst of globalization stands in sharp contrast with the innumerable and often incompatible and divergent needs of its various users and local elites. Indeed, over the past few decades, Brussels has transformed from a national capital to an international crossroad of peoples, goods, capital, ideologies, opinions, and cultures. The resulting highly differentiated and kaleidoscopic urban social fabric has become rather fragile (Bollens 2000). Spatial density in a city forces the different and increasingly heterogeneous users of the city to encounter each other both spatially as well as functionally, not only as a result of intergroup competition between users of the city but also because of economic interdependencies (Bollens 1999).

The strong interconnection between people and spatiality defines urban space as the key arena where social, economic, and cultural configurations are contested and mediated (Harvey 1973, 1996). This intraurban fragmentation and competition results in a situation wherein each attempt to intervene in the urban fabric is experienced as an imposition on other user groups, on their social, economic, and cultural security, and invariably raises issues of sociospatial fairness and justice. Consequently, a proliferating patchwork arises comprising institutions (e.g., neighborhood groups, local councils, town managers) that attempt to mediate between these often widely heterogeneous groups that make up the urban fabric. Nevertheless, this process of mediation becomes increasingly messy and fussy as a fragmented society faces intransigent, crosscutting issues. Yet, the increasing complexity of urban interventions requires the mobilization of resources of different actors, agents, and user groups (Lowndes and Skelcher 1998). Moreover, many actors in this negotiation process are extra- or supralocal and operate at a scale where the traditional regulatory arrangements have no real grip or power.

As a result, an outspoken impasse arises between, on the one hand, the need for mediation, fussiness, and arbitrage at the "local" urban scale and, on the other, the need to forge a "boosterist" and entrepreneurial climate at the global level. The ensuing tensions and contradictions produce a fragmented polity, a disjointed form of urban governance, and a disjuncture between political and economic processes. We argue in this chapter that, while the key actors and drivers of Brussels' economy are international and global, the political and cultural elite actors are decidedly local and regional. In sum, the political scales of governance and their associated power geometries are out of joint with the scales of economic organization. It is in this context that we define Brussels as a reluctant globalizer. Nevertheless, in the cracks and fissures that the confrontation between these two battlefields generates, liminal spaces emerge in embryonic form and provide an arena for experimentation with alternative forms of urban living and practice. It is this argument that the remainder of the chapter explores in greater detail.

BATTLEFIELD 1: INTERURBAN COMPETITION

During its turbulent history, Brussels has lived through moments when active and hegemonic growth coalitions provided and constructed a vision for the city and its future. Through often unholy alliances of bundled forces, Brussels succeeded in permitting important epochal transformations. First, in the nineteenth century, under the autocratic leadership of King Leopold II, a concerted attempt was made to recreate Brussels in the image of a grand, imperial-colonial, national capital. In the mid-twentieth century, the particular Belgian "Fordist" form of urban governance and development centered on a tacit alliance between local and national political elites and local urban entrepreneurs. The Fordist form steamrolled through the city in an attempt to produce a modern and global city by eradicating its provincial and vernacular antimodern characteristics (Papadopoulos 1996). This tacit alliance between entrepreneurs and the Brussels political establishment secured a sound foundation for the implementation of ambitious, large-scale, modernist infrastructure projects. Of course, such hegemonic elite coalitions generate all manner of tensions and conflicts and lead to deeply problematic rescriptings and reengineering of the urban fabric. These modernizing projects were generally pushed through without the involvement of or concern for the inhabitants of Brussels. The proliferation of large infrastructure projects was so tangible and pervasive that the international architectural community refers to this process as *BruXellisation*, meaning that it ignored local history and permitted real estate developers to take advantage of a weak political system to shape the city in their own image, driven primarily by profit-maximization criteria. The profit maximization was, moreover, guaranteed through the state's "partnership." The first notorious infrastructure project in the twentieth century, finished in 1952, was the tunneling of the Brussels North-South railway axis; in its wake came the destruction of a vast proportion of the popular neighborhoods in Brussels.[2] As the term *BruXellisation* already suggests, the political system of Brussels is weak and fuzzy.

In 1993, Belgium reinvented itself as a federal state made up of two linguistic communities (Flemish and French, plus a small German-speaking community) and three regions (Flanders, Wallonia, and Brussels). There is still a national parliament and government, but each region has a directly elected parliament and executive. In Brussels, which is officially bilingual, the French and Flemish community councils overlap and are responsible for the so-called bodily matters in the city-region of Brussels. This refers to domains such as education, health, and cultural policy. Different policies are implemented for each of the two legally accepted language groups (or communities). The regional government for the capital city of Brussels is bilingual and is responsible for "territorial" matters that include, among others, public transport, economy, environment, urban planning, and public works. In the regional government, the Flemish-speaking group has a proportionally greater representation than the French-speaking group. Although it represents only approximately 20 percent of the population of Brussels, the Flemish group has equal representation in the regional government, with the exception of the minister-president of the capital region, who is appointed to a five-year term (see Witte and Velthoven 1999).[3]

In other words, the political rights of the linguistic minority groups are constitutionally protected by affording them equal power sharing in the executive branch of the city-region's government. In addition, there is a provincial government (ten provinces in total) with relatively restricted powers[4] (Witte and Velthoven 1999; Demey 1992; Fitzmaurice 1996; Timmerman 1991). Moreover, the recent creation of these new scales of governments did not displace the old structure of local government in the Brussels region. Indeed, in addition to the regional government, there are still nineteen municipalities, each with its elected council. This system of overlapping governments in Brussels is a result of a compromise between Flemish and French politicians seeking to maintain their power on and in the Belgian capital (Terhorst and van de Ven 1997). Needless to say, all manner of conflict and tension unfolds within and between these various scales of government and governance (Hooghe 1995), a situation which also renders the reenacting or reinvention of the hegemonic growth coalitions of the nineteenth and twentieth centuries difficult, if not impossible, to achieve.

In this context of disjointed and disarticulated governance, it is somewhat surprising that the Brussels region represents the second richest region in the European Union in term of gross regional product (GRP), just after the Parisian region (see table 8.2). In fact, it moved from third place in 1991–1993 to second in 1997–1999. Both Flanders and Wallonia perform significantly worse. Of course, these data even ignore the growing and thriving informal economy. This suggests that the economic foundations of Brussels are basically healthy and dynamic. This is not surprising given the significant presence of high-level and often international administrative and service activities, high-technology companies, and important cultural and financial

Table 8.2.   Gross Regional Product per Capita for the Top Eight Urban Regions in Europe

City	[QA: unit]
Inner London	246
Brussels region	223
Hamburg	183
Luxembourg	180
Ile de France	154
Vienna	151
Oberbayern	150
Darmstadt	148
Flanders	108
Wallonia	80

Source: European Commission.
Note: Based on per capita gross domestic product (1997–1999) for the fifteen EU member states.

activities that are all embedded in a relatively small geographical area, which possesses significant scale and agglomeration economies (without many of their classic disadvantages).

In 1998, the European Union institutions[5] alone employed approximately twenty thousand people in Brussels and generated expenditures worth €2 billion, half of which was spent directly in Belgium. Brussels is also hosting other international public institutions (e.g., NATO, Western European Union, Benelux, Eurocontrol), which significantly contribute to the regional economy (employment: 4,305; expenditures in Brussels: 345 million). Overall, employment in these international organizations rose from fifty-five thousand to sixty-two thousand between 1994 and 1998, and expenditures in Brussels grew to more than €4 billion (see table 8.3). With the expansion of the European Union eastwards, this number is expected to grow rapidly over the next few years. Of every 10 jobs in Brussels, 1 is in the international sector, while at least 13 percent of GRP is generated by the international sector. Estimates by Iris Consulting predicted that, by 2005, when the EU was expected to have twenty-one member states and NATO would have three additional members, overall employment in international institutions would rise to eighty-four thousand (Iris Consulting 1998). The impact on employment has been far greater than predicted because EU members increased to twenty-five in May 2005 and seven new members joined NATO in March 2004.

Companies such as Coca-Cola, UPS, Toyota, Daimler Chrysler, Sony IT, Hewlett Packard, Ericsson, Exxon Chemical, and Ascom have located their European headquarters in Brussels. In addition, Brussels has attracted major financial actors. The Brussels stock market is part of EURONEXT, which was formed, in September 2000, through the merger of the Amsterdam, Brussels, and Paris exchanges. NASDAQ, the world's second largest stock exchange, has become the major shareholder in the Brussels-based European Associa-

Table 8.3.   International Public Sector and Related Employment in Brussels, 1994–1998

	1994	1998
European Union[a]	16,364	20,052
European Union Dependent[b]	9,198	10,330
European Union Related[c]	28,050	27,577
Other International Public Sector[d]	1,483	4,345
TOTAL	55,095	62,304

Source: Iris Consulting 1998.
Notes:
[a] European Commission, Council of Ministers, European Parliament, Economic and Social Committee, Committee of the Regions.
[b] International organizations, international financial sector, law firms, business services, congress organizers.
[c] Permanent representatives of third countries, press, regional offices, lobby firms, Welcome Unit.
[d] NATO, West European Union, International Schools, Benelux, others.

tion of Security Dealers Automated Quotation, or EASDAQ. This new entity is now called NASDAQ Europe. The Society for Worldwide Interbank Financial Telecommunication (SWIFT) has also located its headquarters in the Brussels agglomeration. SWIFT supplies secure messaging, interface software, and 24-hour global support to over 6,000 financial institutions in more than 160 countries. In addition, the number of international law firms specializing in EU questions has increased from only 40 in 1979 to 167 in 1998 (Mens en Ruimte 1994; Iris Consulting 1998; see also Elmhorn 2001).

The international influx brought along the establishment of international schools, which employed an estimated fifteen hundred people in 1998. Brussels is also a leading city for hosting international conferences. Even without considering EU and NATO meetings, Brussels ranks fourth among cities in the world as a location for international meetings. The presence of international institutions attracts also a wide variety of lobby groups. By 1997, the European Parliament had accredited 1,842 lobbies. In 1999, the number of lobbyists around the European Commission was estimated to be ten thousand, and their number has grown rapidly with the enlargement of the EU and the increasing importance of the Committee of the Regions (Elmhorn 2001). In sum, for each EU job, another two are created in EU-dependent and EU-related sectors. For each euro spent by the EU, another three are spent in related sectors.

Elmhorn (2001) defines the economy of the Brussels city-region as a reflexive world city economy. Brussels is center stage to the building of European partnerships and lobbying of European policies and legislation. To get a grip on the specific information and contacts present in Brussels, one needs to be physically located in Brussels and to engage actively in the existing elite networks.

The presence of this rapidly expanding, "glocal" elite in the socioeconomic fabric of Brussels has far-reaching consequences. First, a significant part of the public service sector, which constitutes the pivot of the economy, is largely located in Brussels despite itself. The ten thousand jobs at the EU, NATO, and other related institutions are located in Brussels because of international geopolitical considerations. Brussels "received" these institutions because of external factors.

In addition, the administration of the Flemish community is equally located in Brussels for strategic considerations, not for the particular locational qualities of the city. Moreover, the main part of the employment effects and a significant share of the direct and indirect multiplier effects leak away to the commuting belt. This leakage effect is extremely high in the case of Brussels. Moreover, the cultural and social elites that are associated with these institutions are largely absent from the arenas of power that define and shape the governance of the city. In many cases, they deliberately remain outside the official institutional networks.

Second, the private service sector, principally the business-services sector, is now largely international. This might be unproblematic in itself; however, once again, the actors that drive these activities are in no way directly or indirectly involved in the networks of governance and management that give form to the institutional structure of the city. They show an even greater resilience to forming locally embedded coalitions with political and cultural elites. Another important economic pillar is the real estate sector. In recent years, this sector has rapidly internationalized, and foreign developers (the city builders) control and finance a sector that is driven largely by speculative motivations and strategies. The ballooning of real estate prices between 1986 and 1996, for example, has contributed to a significant transfer of income from the (local) rental sector to private owners. Moreover, the intricate relationships between real estate developers and urban governance remain implicit and operate in the shady area of the public-private interface: a rather disturbing example of this is the story of the European Parliament, in which predominantly French financial interests had a controlling stake, and the ex post legitimization of the project by the local systems of governance. The speculative carrousels of externally controlled capital and development groups frame Brussels as an easy and often receptive target for profitable ventures.

Yet, the global networks of these relatively new economic and institutional elites that emerged as an integral part of the globalization of Brussels are not well connected to the local political elite networks. In other words, the new glocal economic elites are not well articulated with the traditional local political elites. The current dysfunctionality of Brussels resides exactly in the absence of the new glocal elites in local structures of governance and government and in formal and informal local networks, while traditional elites stage insider fights to maintain their eroding power based on themes that often contradict the global dynamics of current development processes. While the socioeconomic restructuring of the last two decades or so has led to the emergence of a new global-local elite that shapes the trajectory of urban economic change (but often without any deep-seated linkage to the local institutional or cultural fabric), urban governance remains locked in an amalgamated collection of traditional elites and their internal power conflicts. Brussels is a world city despite itself.

BATTLEFIELD 2: INTRAURBAN COMPETITION

The "annihilation of space by time" and the accompanying acceleration of processes of deterritorialization and reterritorialization have propelled the mobility of capital, commodities, and, to a lesser but still significant extent, people to new heights. Undoubtedly, the ease by which people and commodities overcome the barrier of space is unprecedented. Of course, this brings growing cultural, ethnic, gender, and other forms of differentiation among the working class but also intensifies the geographical processes that are so central to current restructuring (see Harvey 1995). Cities are becoming, more than ever before, multicultural and cosmopolitan melting pots where hybrid identities are forged that connect the most intimate of spaces and relations with the most remote things and places. The exotic and the strange may appear just around the next corner.

In Brussels, 28.5 percent of the population is non-Belgian; 38 percent of families are of mixed ethnic descent. Almost 128 nationalities are represented in the Brussels capital region (14.6 percent European, 8 percent African, 3 percent Asian, and 0.7 percent American). Amid the cosmopolitan character of the city, these "foreigners" are excluded from the local, regional, or national political process (with the exception of EU citizens, who can register to vote for local elections; Belgian citizens are legally obliged to vote) and remain largely absent from the traditional political and institutional configurations that govern Brussels. In some municipalities, such as Sint-Joost Ten Node, the share of non-Europeans has risen to more than 35 percent of the population. It is in this context that the paradox of the parallel economic success, social polarization, and spreading poverty needs to be examined.

The transformation from Fordism to post-Fordism intensifies fragmentation and polarization in cities (Amin et al. 1994). In the last decades, industry took its heels out of the inner city and moved to suburban or even more exotic (less expensive) destinations. Instead of providing the manual labor for manufacturing, the city became the breeding ground for a thriving consumer and service industry. Recently, this economic restructuring caused the first Europewide strike and workers' action against the closure of the Brussels Renault factory (a closure that had, of course, everything to do with overproduction in the sector and little with globalization). During the period from 1960 to 1974, 174 industrial firms left or went bankrupt in the Brussels regional capital, and between 1975 and 1986, Brussels lost one-third of its manufacturing employment (De Beule 1994).

At the same time, Brussels experienced an out-migration of its middle classes. Despite the rising number of jobs in financial and other business services, an increase of 43 percent between 1970 and 1991, the Belgian political elite, dominated until recently by the Christian Democrats, pursued a distinct antiurban policy. By means of grants-in-aid for buying property, soft loans, and other incentives, they encouraged middle-class, inner-city families to move to the suburbs. This policy went hand in glove with the promotion of the car and infrastructure projects to make the city "accessible" to the suburbs. Today, more than half of the Brussels workforce (54 percent) retreats to Flemish and Walloon (often well-to-do) suburban areas in the region surrounding Brussels. The commuter belt around Brussels constitutes, on average, the wealthiest districts in the European Union. Concurrently, a low-skilled, often immigrant working class replaced the middle class in the inner city, despite the decline of the labor-intensive industrial sectors in Brussels. They came foremost from Spain, Italy, Portugal, Morocco, Turkey, and Tunisia.

It is not surprising that in this context, inequalities are considerable and increasing. Between 1982 and 1996, the share of the lowest income tenth in total Belgian net income after taxes fell from 2.6 to 2.4 percent, while the share of the highest income 10 percent rose from 20.4 to 23.9 percent. Half of the total income from capital assets is in the hands of the richest 10 percent, and one-fifth of capital assets are owned by the 1 percent most affluent. In Brussels, the concentration of income among the richest 10 percent is even greater (see figure 8.1).

Recently, the average per capita income for Brussels fell below not only that of Flanders but also of the historically rather poorly performing Wallonia. In 1963, average income in the Brussels region was 60 percent higher than the Belgian average. By 1995, Brussels' average income level was 7 percent below the Belgian average, while comparable levels in Halle-Vilvoorde and Nivelles (adjacent suburban districts) rose and were, respectively, 20 and 16 percent higher than the average Belgian income (National Institute of Statistics). The top 20 percent of the income hierarchy left the city during the 1980s and early 1990s (De Keersmaecker 1998). This indicates that a significant share of GRP leaked away to other regions, mainly as a result of the significant commuting flows between Brussels and the rest of the country and because of geopolitical strategies that actively encouraged this segmentation between Brussels as a space of production and Flanders and Wallonia as the eager recipients of the income flows.

Total unemployment in Brussels rose between 1985 and 1996 with 17.9 percent against just 12.5 percent for the rest of Belgium, while unemployment actually fell in the municipalities around the Brussels region (BRES 1997). Despite the powerful growth of the service sector, unemployment for both men and women affected this sector most acutely. A restructuring of the service economy began to emerge, from the early 1990s onwards, out of the intense wave of deindustrialization of the 1970s and 1980s, despite a continued period of rapidly rising unemployment and a seriously dysfunctional labor market. Over the same period, unemployment in the industrial sector rose by 19.1 percent (against 8.1 percent for the whole of the country) (see figure 8.2).

The creeping socioeconomic polarization in terms of labor and income security is further illustrated by the disturbing rise in the number of people who receive social benefits from the Public Centres for Social Work (OCMWs). Their number almost doubled between 1990 and 1998 from 6,890 to almost 14,000 (Vranken et al. 1999) (see table 8.3).

In sum, Brussels is losing part of its wealthy population and is now facing serious impoverishment in comparison to its ever-more prosperous neigh-

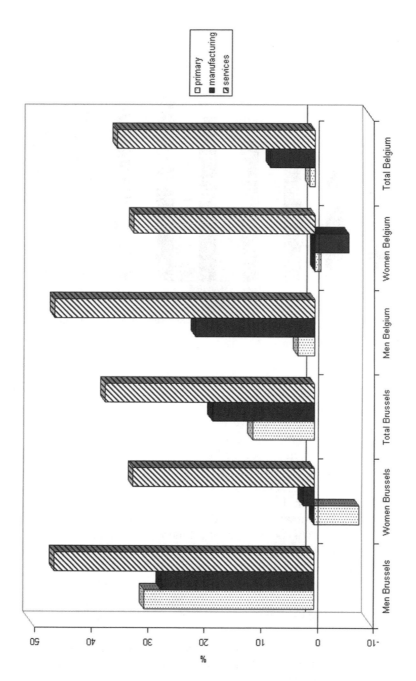

Figure 8.1.   Sectoral evolution of unemployment in Brussels and Belgium   (in percentages), 1990–1996.

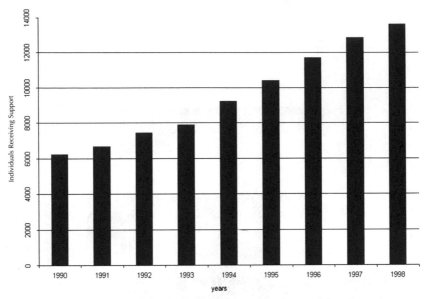

Figure 8.2. Number of individuals living in Brussels receiving income support, 1990–1998.

boring suburban districts. Personal income taxation is the main source of income for the Brussels region (57.5 percent). Consequently, the Brussels regional government is facing relative impoverishment compared to neighboring communities where most commuters reside.

The political establishment pursued three strategies to tackle the problem of falling tax revenue: (1) establishing greater interregional tax solidarity between the three regions, (2) enlarging the territory of the Brussels capital region in order to broaden the tax base by including surrounding affluent municipalities, and (3) reattracting the middle class. These three strategies were long-term solutions. The political establishment did not have a short-term strategy to alleviate the problem. As a consequence, rich private developers filled the vacuum, and the authorities welcomed them as a way to ease the public finance crunch. Therefore, Brussels became a haven for speculators. Yet, the speculative fever led ultimately to a significant oversupply of offices. In 1995, 6.3 percent of the building surface of the innercenter of Brussels was vacant.

In sum, Brussels was rapidly becoming a shrinking city. In 1968, Brussels had a population of 1,079,181. Between 1967 and 1996, approximately 250,000 Belgians, mostly the educated middle class, left the inner city for the suburbs. Over the same period, Brussels experienced a net inflow of 144,000 immigrants (De Lannoy et al. 2000). This in-migration turned Brussels into a truly diverse, globalized, and cosmopolitan city.

This differentiation and heterogeneity has generated a great number of geographical tensions, conflicts, and struggles, many of which are not even remotely emancipatory, liberating, or empowering. Notorious examples include the continuous tensions between Turkish and Kurdish groups in the neighborhood surrounding the railway station Brussels North; the riots in November 1997 in Kuregem, an area in the southern, immigrant part of the city, after the shooting of Saïd Charki by the local police force; and the rise of anti-internationalist and deeply regionalist political parties exemplified in Brussels and Flanders by the success of the extreme right-wing Vlaams Blok.

Moreover, the institutional impasse and fragmentation accentuates these tensions and intraurban struggles. Indeed, on the local scale, the existence of the "semifeudal" power bastions of the municipal power fiefdoms and their localist and parochial power networks, often based on deep-seated paternalistic and nepotistic practices, leads to fragmentation, centripetal struggle, conditions of permanent semiconflict, and a perpetual displacement of problems. The problems are not addressed; they are just moved around. The parochialism of the local "warlords" inhibits, if not prevents, the formation of alliances between global, "progressive," economic elites and an "enlightened," local, political elite. On top of this, the institutional structure of the regional forms of governance (on the scale of the Brussels region) is characterized by enduring tribal antagonisms along linguistic lines that engender contradictions and conflicts, which lead to enduring tensions, implosive forces, and a perpetual risk of disintegration and instability. This is particularly ironic in a context in which neither Flemish nor Walloon economic interests still play a pivotal role in directing the economic development of Brussels.

Moreover, the institutional structure of the capital region of Brussels remains embedded in the national Flemish-Walloon divide, whereby strictly regionalist political considerations and agendas are often played out in the arena of Brussels. Both ethnic regions regularly use Brussels as their preferred, politically "safe" battlefield for scoring political points that are cashed in, in either Flanders or Wallonia. This, of course, reinforces the perceived status (in the other regions) of Brussels as an enduring problem and as inherently troublesome. Moreover, a large part of the social, political, and administrative elite is not part of the Brussels community. This not only poses problems in terms of loyalty and commitment but reinforces and permits the perpetuation of a representation, a scripting, and a framing of the city by the elites, for themselves and the outside world, as dystopian and marginalized.

Particularly in Flanders, but also to some extent in Wallonia, Brussels is framed as an "outsider space," as a space on the margin. Indeed, the Flemish and Walloon political and economic elites embody, actively cultivate, and

perpetuate, albeit for entirely different historical reasons, an extremely ambiguous and often outright hostile attitude toward Brussels. Although the
larger part of the produced welfare for Flanders, and also for Wallonia, is realized in Brussels (but leaks away), the regional political-economic elites remain, at best, absent from potential local growth coalitions and, worse, outright hostile vis-à-vis the issues that shape Brussels' future.

Consequently, the *imagineering*, that is, the production of visions, images,
and representations of Brussels and its future, is largely constructed by external actors and elites. Both the planning documents of the various levels of
government and the imaginings of the city by a significant part of the cultural, media, and political elites are founded upon an outspoken antiurban
imagination and perception. The predominantly white, endogenous, usually
male civil servant, politician, journalist, or policy consultant is usually a suburban or semirural commuter for whom the "big" city often invokes an image of poverty, disintegration, vandalism, criminality, immigrant domination,
and a hotbed of all varieties of perversions and insecurities.

THE INTERSTITIAL SCALE

Comparative international research has demonstrated that the existence of a
close and "hegemonic" growth coalition that weaves together public and private elites plays a foundational role in generating and maintaining competitive spaces (Judge, Stoker, and Wolman 1995). The success of cities and regions as diverse as Baltimore, Los Angeles, Emilia-Romagna, Veneto,
Flanders, Manchester, Berlin, Bilbao, and Barcelona suggests that a coherent
and relatively homogeneous coalition of local, national, and international
elites is instrumental to initiate and maintain a "boosterist" climate and a
competitive growth trajectory (Cox and Mair 1989, 1991). Such coalitions
play a pivotal role in generating and mobilizing financial means, the establishment of formal or informal institutions or networks, the coordination of
key power brokers in the area, and the formulation and dissemination of a
clear and visionary image of the city or region that is capable of mobilizing
large segments of the local population while portraying an image of dynamism and success to the outside world (Zukin 1996). At the end of the day,
economic growth is carried by the economic, political, and cultural elites. It
is social power that creates growth.

The absence in Brussels' formal and informal institutions and frameworks
of governance of a dense network of new glocal elites that could generate a
hegemonic project and vision for the future is the city's greatest barrier to cohesive socioeconomic development. The rearguard actions of a semifeudal
local government and the extroverted power choreographies of regional political elites that characterize the power geographies of the contemporary

Brussels landscape intensify that malaise, reinforce the imagery of a disinte-grated urban fabric, and erode its economic vitality. The burlesque comedy around the staging of Brussels, cultural capital of Europe 2000, was a sad yet telling example. Whereas Glasgow, Scotland, was a glowing success as a re-sult of the forging, however difficult it proved to be, of a growth coalition that fused new and old economic, political, and cultural elites together around the construction of a negotiated—and not always publicly fully endorsed—hegemony of vision, the organization in Brussels was riddled with centrifugal forces that emanated from largely traditional elite forces. The internal conflicts between local elites that do not govern but stage and enact parochial, territorial, linguistic, and petty ideological feuds are a greater threat to the socioeconomic and cultural development of Brussels than en-during unemployment, the immigration issue, or petty criminality.

Nevertheless, there are clear indications of an emerging glocal elite. This is particularly evident in actions and strategies around urban spaces that have become examples of the impasse produced by "traditional" modes of governance. These are spaces characterized by a deep immobility and that need mediation and arbitrage. It is in these (politically) "vacant" spaces, with ambiguous, unclear, or absent power, that regulatory forces lose their grip. It is in such a stalemate situation, a liminal, interstitial, or in-between space, that we can find germs of the existence of a new and potentially promising glocal urban regime. These spaces generate urban "free" zones where the lo-cal and the global can meet, and collective or cooperative actions may ger-minate. This section describes three different examples and the dynamics of emerging glocal urban action they illustrate: (1) the debate around the inte-gration of the EU-facilities into the urban fabric, (2) the process of self-empowerment of the migrant community in Brussels, and (3) the rise of transgressive sociocultural practices.

The collective BruXXel.org[6] occupied the old Leopoldswijk railway sta-tion, now in the heart of Euro-land in front of the European Parliament, from October 13 to December 31, 2001. The timing of the action coincided with the Belgian presidency of the European Union. The place was strategically chosen because the nineteenth-century station symbolized the tension be-tween the "local" neighborhood and their uninvited guests, the Eurocrats. The building itself is perceived by employees of the European Parliament, as well as by the residents of the neighborhood, as a neutral zone, or buffer. The occupation of the railway station gave the campaigners the opportunity to create a free and autonomous zone as the protagonists actually silently welcomed the campaigners and their attempt to break the discommunication and the disjuncture between Eurocrats and residents. During those three months, the vacant railway station was transformed into a permanent meet-ing place. A busy program of debates on various themes concerning Brus-sels and the EU, music concerts, theater plays, food and drink successfully tempted a diverse audience to come to the location. Moreover, BruXXel.org used the media attention of the Summit of Laeken (European Union Summit) as a pivot to improve communication between the European institutions and the neighborhood groups.

In the same period, Brussels hosted, under the auspices of the prime minister, a high-level brainstorm session with a group of invited intellectuals.[7] The aim was to explore the needs and functions of a European capital and how Brussels could best express them (European Commission 2001). Belgian prime minister Guy Verhofstadt and the president of the European Commission, Romano Prodi, initiated the event. Although people living in Brussels were not invited to contribute to these brainstorm sessions, the group came up with some exploratory and innovative ideas. The group's report considered four initiatives to be of prime relevance (European Commission 2001): (1) to establish a Center for Advanced Studies, (2) to establish an institute for multilingualism, (3) to implement a transparent procedure for improving the architectural quality of European buildings and a better procedure to asses negative externalities, and (4) to adopt a partnership approach for specific issues of concern (e.g., schools, housing, transportation). These two "free" spaces, BruXXel.org and the brainstorming sessions, generated an extraordinary level of communication, exchange of ideas, and presentation of alternative views, something that is difficult, if not impossible, to achieve in the maze of traditional political power networks.

The presence of the transnational migrant community has resulted in the emergence of transnational networks and communities (in terms of trade, production, personal relations, exchanges, and the like) that are now deeply inserted into the economic fabric of Brussels but also remain absent from the institutional framework. Examples of multicultural practices are the shopping street, the Brabantstraat around the railway station Brussels North, and the emerging commercial district between the center of Brussels and the railway station Brussels South. These multicultural practices, which take shape in both "high" culture and popular "street" cultures (with boundaries that are rapidly blurring through a plethora of transgressive cultural practices), are internationalist and global in character. Furthermore, 36 percent of all retail entrepreneurs in Brussels are of foreign origin, yet they are absent from the current urban regime and institutional political framework.

Political blockage has resulted in an active struggle to seek new, alternative forms of political representation and to establish pressure groups among immigrants. The municipality of Brussels has pioneered, under pressure from such immigrant groups, the establishment of consultative committees such as the Commission Mixte de Consultation des Citoyens Bruxellois d'Origine Etrangère (Mixed Consultative Commission of Citizens of Brussels of Foreign Descent). Other autonomous initiatives jumped scales and found support in federal-level advocacy groups, often funded by the EU. Among these are the Centre pour Égalité des Chances et de la Lutte contre le Racisme (Center for Equal Opportunities and Opposition to Racism) and Le Mouvement contre le Racisme, l'Antisémitisme, et la Xénophobie (Movement against Racism, Anti-Semitism, and Xenophobia). All of these initiatives combine to support the struggle to obtain political voting rights for non-EU citizens in Belgium.

A third example of interstitial practices is the myriad of social artistic projects in the city that try to bolster multiscalar and heterogeneous partnerships in the city. A case in point is the project LimiteLimite, an initiative of City Mine(d) and Wijkpartenariaat.[8] The project LimiteLimite took place in the Brabantwijk[9] and lasted for two years, from initial conceptualization to final realization. The objective of the project was to ameliorate the image of the locality and to engender a new, inclusive, progressive urban regime. The idea was to construct a transparent tower 9m in height. The tower was artistically well defined and designed, geared to attract the interest of institutions that are not necessarily located in the neighborhood itself. At the same time, the project presented something tangible, whose progress the local residents could easily keep track of.

The location of the transparent tower was carefully chosen to obtain the optimal effect. It towers over a frictional zone. It is located in the middle of a deprived, popular neighborhood and in the proximity of the business district in the central northern part of Brussels. The project created a large partnership that went well beyond the neighborhood level. The core group consisted of RisoBrussel, an organization active in community work; City Mine(d); Rossaert and Gerben, who are architects; and APAJ-Classe Chantier, a polytechnical school. The neighborhood groups included the neighborhood committee Dupontstraat; three elementary schools; VIVA, a women's organization; Wijkpartenariaat, a community work association; and Sports Hall 58, a sport's association. They contributed by sensitizing the neighborhood and improving the conviviality between commuters, on the one hand, and students and the residents of the neighborhood on the other. The metropolitan actors were VLEKHO Business School; IRIS-Hogeschool, a school for higher education training social and cultural workers; St. Lucas, a school of architecture; JP Morgan Bank; Ondex; the Sociaal Impulsfonds (Social Investment Fund) of the Flemish Community; and the Koning Boudewijn Stichting (King Boudewijn Foundation). The project brought together unlikely partners from different geographical scales and from a heterogeneous social composition to engage collectively in the making of such a concrete, geographical project that transformed the "liminal," "interstitial," or "vacant" spaces referred to above.

Transgressive projects like LimiteLimite sensitize a wide network of local, metropolitan, and even international actors to support cosmopolitan initiatives in Brussels. It is precisely this creative fusion of differentiation, heterogeneity, and potential cosmopolitanism (which also characterized cultural life in turn-of-the-century Brussels) that can turn Brussels, at least potentially, into one of the exemplary sites for the enacting and celebration of a new, post-Fordist, and hybridized urbanism. It is those networks that are the potential harbingers of an inclusive culture of governance. Again, of course, this global-local cultural elite remains, at the moment, largely outside the traditional existing institutional networks of power.

CONCLUSION

The glocal city that Brussels already is remains embedded in a provincial and parochial institutional straightjacket. The economic and sociocultural future of Brussels is closely related to the integration of new glocal elites into existing networks of power. This leads to a very opaque, contested, and confusing maelstrom of power struggles and rapidly changing choreographies of power conflicts, alliances, and elite configurations. It is extremely difficult to disentangle the subtleties of power games and to identify key power brokers within this urban conundrum.

As the economy of Brussels has become more internationalized, a process supported by groups of international elites whose economic power expands in line with their growing presence, those same economic groups remain largely absent from the political arena. For example, foreign residents in Brussels still do not enjoy political citizenship rights. The construction sector, not surprisingly a major economic activity in the city, remains surprisingly local despite the opening up of the market (Timmerman 1992; Brukselbinnenstebuiten 1993; Papadopoulos 1996). The traditional local elite, composed of a dense network of politicians, financiers, and "merchants of concrete," attempts to weave the internationalization of Brussels into and through the traditionally existing power configurations. The alliance of money, politics, and concrete conclude lucrative deals in a highly exclusive and nontransparent manner. In addition, the political agenda for Brussels is still predominantly set and dominated by traditional elites. For example, the national bicultural "language question" dominates the political agenda, while the de facto, multicultural, hybridized reality of everyday life in Brussels remains neglected.

However, the power of the traditional elites is increasingly eroded, from both below and above. For example, international economic decision makers reinforce their grip on the city. This is particularly clear in the internationalization of the real estate market, which is now largely controlled and organized by international companies such as James Lang Wootton, Healey & Baker, and others. Another example, of course, is the continuing presence and involvement of international organizations and their physical expansion in the city. From below, locally marginalized, transnational communities (mainly Turks and North Africans) protest their exclusion in a variety of ways (such as regular rioting but also through the emergence of a new elite of immigrant community leaders and intellectuals) (Martiniello 1993).

In sum, there is a clear contradiction between the existing power configuration (white, Belgian, monocultural, male), which is increasingly at odds with the actual internationalization and multiculturalization of the social economy of the city. However, the new "glocal" economic elites often eschew coalition formation with local political or cultural actors and are often reluctant to engage strategically and cooperatively with local political or cultural elite networks. There is an urgent task ahead to forge new institutional and semi-institutional networks that are not only sensitive to the new hybridized identities of the key social and economic actors but that enable new alliances to form that connect local territorial interests with global ambitions.

NOTES

1. Many recent studies have identified Brussels as one of Europe's successful metropolitan areas. A report by Cheshire, Carbonaro, and Hay, for example, ranked Brussels fifth among 103 cities (Cheshire, Carbonaro, and Hay 1986; Cheshire 1990). Also, Taylor, in his ranking of fifty-five world cities, classified Brussels in the second group of "beta" world cities, together with San Francisco, Sydney, Toronto, Zurich, Madrid, Mexico City, Saõ Paulo, Moscow, and Seoul (Taylor 2000; See also Cattan 1994; Brunet 1989).

2. Other projects included the World Exhibition of 1958, "La Cité administrative" (1958–1984), the Berlaymont building (1967), the Tour du Midi (1967), and the World Trade Center/Manhattan project in Brussels North.

3. The actual share of the two language groups remains unclear. The "language" question was eliminated from the census in the 1960s. It was too controversial as a language count could be mobilized as a political "weapon," particularly by the French-speaking community. The elections provide an indication of the relative size of each language groups as voters choose between different linguistically divided lists. The election results indicate that the Flemish voters account for only 15 percent of the electorate (Favell and Martiniello 1999).

4. This decision was preceded by four different stages of state reform. The first stage of state reform (1970) formed the basis for the formation of the three regions, the Walloon (French speaking), the Brussels (bilingual), and the Flemish (Dutch speaking) regions. Nevertheless, the Brussels region was only formally established in 1989. The second stage (1980) created the three communities based on language (French, Flemish, and German). Also, the second stage created two community governments, one for the Flemish- and one for the French-speaking groups. The governments of these communities are responsible for cultural and personal affairs, whereas the regional governments are responsible, mainly, for economy and public works. The third stage (1988–1989) consisted of the formation of the Brussels Capital

Region. Finally, during the fourth stage (1992–1993), Belgium officially became a federal state.

5. Brussels hosts the following institutions of the European Union: the European Commission, the Council of Ministers, the European Parliament, the Economic and Social Committee, and the Committee of Regions.

6. The collective BruXXel.org is an initiative of a diverse group of citizens in Brussels concerned with the alleviation of the negative externalities of the expansion of the European Institutes on Brussels and, especially, on the European neighborhood.

7. The group included Michel Crozier, Umberto Eco, Bronislaw Geremek, Nicolas Hayek, Agnès Jaoui, Rem Koolhaas, Pasqual Maragall, Maryon McDonald, Gerard Mortier, Francois Schuiten, Geert Van Istendael, and Juan Ignacio Vidarte.

8. Other examples of such socially artistic initiatives are Cinema Nova, Zinnekes Parade, Brussel Behoort ons Toe/Bruxelles Nous Appartient, Ambassade Universalis, Brussels Gekleurd, and Festival Couleur Café.

9. The Brabantwijk is situated at the eastern side of the railway station Brussels North, close to the inner-center of Brussels. The main characteristics of the densely populated, blue-collar neighborhood are (1) an immigrant population, mostly of Turkish and Moroccan origin, accounting for 70 percent of the population of the neighborhood; (2) a population two-thirds of which is below thirty; (3) a high concentration of legally condoned prostitution and sex shops; (4) an average income that is 40 percent below the average regional income; (5) an unemployment rate of 25 percent, and (6) a lack of green, sport, and social facilities.

REFERENCES

Amin, A., Thrift, N., et al. 1994. *Globalization, Institutions, and Regional Development in Europe.* New York: Oxford University Press.

Aydalot, P. 1986. "Milieux innovateurs en Europe" [Innovative environments in Europe], *Groupement de Recherche sur les Milieux Innovateurs en Europe.* Paris: Sorbonne, Université de Paris I.

Bollens, S. A. 1999. *Urban Peace-Building in Divided Societies: Belfast and Johannesburg.* Boulder, CO.: Westview Press.

———. 2000. *On Narrow Ground: Urban Policy and Ethnic Conflict in Jerusalem and Belfast.* Albany: State University of New York Press.

BRES (Bruxelle Économique et Social). 1997. *Indicateurs Statistiques Bruxellois 1997.* Brussels: Iris.

Brukselbinnenstebuiten. 1993. *Een Trein van Troje. Verhalen over een Snelle Trein in een Slome Stad.* Brussels: Brukselbinnenstebuiten.

Brunet, R. 1989. *Les villes "Européennes": rapport pour la DATAR, délégation à l'aménagement du territoire et à l'action régionale.* Paris: La Documentation Française.

Castells, M. 1989a. *The Informational City: Information Technology, Economic Restructuring, and the Urban-Regional Process.* Oxford: Basil Blackwell.

———. 1989b. *The Informational Society.* Oxford: Blackwell.

———. 1994. "European cities, the informal society, and the global economy." *New Left Review* 204: 18–32.

Castells, M., and Hall, P. G. 1994. *Technopoles of the World: The Making of Twenty-first-Century Industrial Complexes*. London: Routledge.

Cattan, N. 1994. *Le système des villes Européennes*. Paris: Anthropos.

Cheshire, P. 1990. "Explaining the recent performance of the European community's major urban regions." *Urban Studies* 27, no. 3: 311–33.

Cheshire, P., Carbonaro, G., and Hay, D. 1986. "Problems of urban decline and growth in EEC countries: or measuring degrees of elephantness." *Urban Studies* 23, no. 2: 131–49.

Commissie, E. 1994. *Concurrentievermogen en Cohesie: Tendensen in de Regio's. Vijfde Periodiek Verslag over de Sociaal-economische Situatie en Ontwikkeling van de Regio's in de Gemeenschap*. Brussels: Europese Commissie.

Cooke, P., and Morgan, K. 1998. *The Associational Economy: Firms, Regions, and Innovation*. Oxford: Oxford University Press.

Cox, K., and Mair, A. 1989. "Urban growth machines and the politics of local economic development." *International Journal of Urban and Regional Research* 13: 137–46.

———. 1991. "From localised social structures to localities as agents." *Environment and Planning A* 23: 197–213.

De Beule, M. 1994. "Bruxelles, une ville industrielle méconnue." *Les cahiers de la fonderie* 1: 1–67.

De Keersmaecker, M.-L. 1998. "Staat van de Armoede in het Brussels Hoofdstedelijk Gewest. De Opbouw van Sociale Indicatoren" [State of the Poverty in the Brussels Capital Region. Constructing Social Indicators], in *20 Jaar OCMW. Naar een Actualisering van het Maatschappijproject* [20 Years OCMW. Toward an Actualization of the Societal Project], ed. J. Vranken, G. Vanhercke, and V. Menxel, 79–102. Leuven: Acco.

De Lannoy, W., Lammens, M. et al. 2000. *Brussel in de Jaren Negentig en na 2000: Een Demografische Doorlichting*. Brussels: Vrije Universiteit Brusse.

Demey, T. 1992. *De l'expo '58 au siege de la C. E. E.*, Volume 2 of *Bruxelles, chronique d'une capital en chantier*. Brussels: Paule Legrain/Edition CFC.

Elmhorn, C. 1998. "Brussels in the European economic space: the emergence of a world city?" *Bulletin de la société belge d'études geographiques* 1: 79–101.

———. 2001. *Brussels, a Reflexive World City*. Stockholm: Almqvist & Wiksell International.

European Commission. 2001. *Final Report: Brussels, Capital of Europe*. Brussels: European Commission.

Favell, A., and Martiniello, M. 1999. "Multi-national, multi-cultural and multi-leveled Brussels: national and ethnic politics in the 'capital of Europe.'" *Working Paper Series, Transnational Communities Programme* 4. Oxford: Economic and Social Research Council, at www.transcomm.ox.ac.uk/working%20papers/favell.pdf (accessed November 9, 2005).

Fitzmaurice, J. 1996. *The Politics of Belgium: A Unique Federalism*, Boulder, CO: Westview.

Harvey, D. 1973. *Social Justice and the City*. London: Edward Arnold.

———. 1995. "Globalization in question." *Rethinking MARXISM* 8, no. 4: 1–17.

———. 1996. *Justice, Nature and the Geography of Difference*, Cambridge, MA: Blackwell.

Hooghe, L. 1995. "Belgian federalism and the European community." In *The European Union and the Regions*, ed. J. B. Jones and M. Keating, 134–65. Oxford: Oxford University Press.

Hooghe, L., and Robert Schuman Centre. 1998. *Supranational Activists or Intergovernmental Agents? Explaining the Orientations of Senior Commission Officials towards European Integration*. San Domenico, Italy: European University Institute.

Iris Consulting. 1998. *De Sociaal-Economische Impact van de Europese en Internationale Instellingen in het Brussels Hoofdstedelijk Gewest. Verleden en Toekomst*. Brussels: KPMG.

Jessop, B. 1996. "A neo-Gramscian approach to the regulation of urban regimes: accumulation strategies, hegemonic projects, and governance." In *Reconstructing Urban Regime Theory: Regulating Urban Politics in a Global Economy*, ed. M. Lauria, 51–74. Thousand Oaks, CA: Sage.

Judge, D., Stoker, G., and Wolman, H. 1995. *Theories of Urban Politics* London: Sage Publications.

Lowndes, V., and Skelcher, C. 1998. "The dynamics of multi-organizational partnerships: an analysis of changing modes of governance." *Public Administration* 76, no. 2: 313–34.

MacLeod, G. 2000. "The learning region in an age of austerity: capitalizing on knowledge, entrepreneurialism, and reflexive capitalism." *Geoforum* 31, no. 2: 219–36.

Marks, G., Hooghe, L., et al. 1995. *European Integration and the State*. Florence: European University Institute.

Martiniello, M. 1993. "Ethnic leadership, ethnic communities' political powerlessness and the state in Belgium." *Ethnic and Racial Studies* 16, no. 2: 236–55.

Maskell, P., and Malmberg, A. 1995. "Localised learning and industrial competitiveness." *Regional Studies Association Conference on "Regional Futures,"* Gothenburg, Sweden.

Mens en Ruimte. 1994. *L'Impact socio-economique des institutions européennes et internationales à Bruxelles*. Brussels: Mens en Ruimte.

Papadopoulos, A. G. 1996. *Urban Regimes and Strategies: Building Europe's Central Executive District in Brussels*. Chicago: University of Chicago Press.

Sassen, S. 1988. *The Mobility of Labor and Capital: A Study in International Investment and Labor Flow*. Cambridge: Cambridge University Press.

———. 2002. *Global Networks, Linked Cities*. London: Routledge.

Scott, A. J. 1998. *Regions and the World Economy: The Coming Shape of Global Production, Competition, and Political Order*. Oxford: Oxford University Press.

Smith, N. 1996. *The New Urban Frontier: Gentrification and the Revanchist City*. London: Routledge.

Swyngedouw, E. 1996. "Producing futures: international finance as a geographical project." In *The Global Economy in Transition*, ed. P. W. Daniels and W. Lever, 135–63. Harlow, UK: Longman.

———. 1998. "Homing in and spacing out: re-configuring scale." In *Europa im Globalisierungsprozess von Wirtschaft und Gesellschaft*, ed. H. Gebhart, 81–100. Stuttgart: Franz Steiner Verlag.

———. 2000. "Territories of innovation: innovation as a collective process and the globalization of competition." *Technology Transfer and Industrial Change in Europe*, ed. H. Lawton Smith and E. Swyngedouw, 17–33. Basingstoke: Macmillan.

Taylor, P. 2000. "World cities and territorial states under condition of contemporary globalization." *The European Public Affairs Directory 1990*. Brussels: Landmarks.

Terhorst, P. J. F., and van de Ven, J. C. L. 1997. "Fragmented Brussels and consolidated Amsterdam, a comparative study of the spatial organization of property rights." *Netherlands Geographical Studies* 223.

Timmerman, G. 1991. *In Brussel Mag Alles. Geld, Macht en Beton*. Antwerp: EPO.

Vranken, J., Geldof, D., and Van Menxel, G. 1999. *Armoede en Sociale Uitsluiting: Jaarboek 1999*. Leuven: Acco.

Witte, E., and Velthoven, H. V. 1999. *Language and Politics: The Belgian Case Study in a Historical Perspective*. Brussels: VUB University Press.

Zukin, S. 1996. "Cultural strategies of economic development and the hegemony of vision." In *The Urbanization of Injustice*, ed. A. Merrifield and E. Swyngedouw, 223–43. London: Lawrence & Wishart.

9

The Processes Underlying Caracas as a Globalizing City

Miguel Lacabana and Cecilia Cariola

A new territorial pattern can be said to have emerged in the capitalist system beginning in the 1970s, one in which the cities have ceased to be the centers of expression of their respective national states' power in the world and turned into centers of the new global economy (Friedmann 1986). In spite of the growing geographic dispersal of economic activity, globalization tends to reinforce central control functions. The changes in the dominant forms of organization of cross-border flows and their key drivers; the processes of privatization, deregulation, and the opening of the national economies to foreign corporations; and national actors' growing participation in the global markets are the key components of the role played by cities as strategic territories in the new forms of economic organization of the global economy's strategic activities (Sassen 1999, 2002). Any territory's global articulation leads to the development of an urban node of provision of the advanced services that are essential to the new economy's control (Borja and Castells 1997).

It has likewise been proposed that the globalization process implies a reduction in state power and economic sovereignty. In fact, new forms of state regulation have emerged and contributed to an enhancement of global capital's competitiveness. Among these developments is the increased importance of certain territories, particularly the global cities and cities in the process of globalization. This reterritorialization of the state can be envisaged as a strategy pursued by national and local elites to favor their principal cities in the global urban hierarchy (Brenner 2003).

Attempts have been made to identify a causal relationship directly linking the globalization of cities to the impact of the new global economy. But though new processes are taking place, there is a simultaneous reinforcement of preexisting trends marked by the importance of endogenous factors and internal actors. Furthermore, the cities immersed in the globalization process continue to have basic features that reflect their identity (Marcuse and van Kempen 2000). The present-day urbanization processes are not entirely new, and today's metropolis can be viewed as a product of unequal development that has shaped and reshaped the city's spaces since the birth of urban industrial capitalism. However, new socioterritorial forms and combinations are being created, along with new identities; they do not entirely replace the previous ones, but they are significantly more complex than and different from them (Soja 2000; Marcuse and van Kempen 2000).

At least three major trends can be identified in the changes occurring in the cities caught up in the globalization process at the present time. The first trend has to do with extended metropolitanization, tied to the expansion of cities as a result of new post-Fordian modes of production and new global activities that require new "urban artifacts" to house them (de Mattos 2002). Urban megaprojects developed by national and transnational real estate capital spur the city's continued fragmentation. A second trend has to do with the changes in the urban economy and the resulting restructuring of the metropolitan labor markets, where highly skilled and high-paying jobs linked to the global economy coexist with informal and precarious occupations immersed in the economy of poverty. This trend has led observers to posit the presence of dual cities (Sassen 1999). The third tendency refers to the changes in the city's internal structure, induced by a growing residential segregation process that is reflected in an increasing sociospatial division of the city into segments that are more and more unequal. This trend goes beyond the erection of nonmaterial social barriers to embrace the raising of physical barriers in order to create a city of separate residential fragments. At the extremes we find, on the one hand, an isolation of the higher-income strata in closed enclaves, and on the other, an exclusion of the lower-income population expressed in a kind of apartheid (Marcuse and van Kempen 2000). Each of these changes is spurred by fear of the other, which acts as a basic factor in the structuring of the contemporary metropolis, closely linked to enclosure of communities and privatization of public spaces (Davis 1999).

The fractal city concept put forward by Soja (2000), which describes increasing social and spatial heterogeneity accompanied by an intensification of socioeconomic inequality, and the layered city concept offered by Marcuse and van Kempen (2000), according to which each layer houses different activities or spaces and reflects different ways of living depending on social status, describe a more complex and fragmented panorama than the one suggested by the dual city concept.

The perspective that focuses attention on the social and socioterritorial differentiation processes as effects of increasing exclusion and poverty in the city also calls that position into question (Cariola and Lacabana 2000, 2001).

The social transformations induced by the economic and political restructuring influence the way the metropolis is structured and experienced through the dynamic of socioterritorial segregation, which acquires a qualitatively different meaning associated with the juxtaposition of different ways of life, fostering a residential atomization and isolation and helping fragment the city into multiple unequal territories rather than into two mutually exclusive segments. This fragmentation is reinforced by each urban segment's functional specialization, depending on its greater or lesser articulation to the global network of economic relations and the unequal institutional segmentation provoked by the decentralization processes.

The "multiple cities" metaphor we adopt in our work gives expression to the urban changes associated with the globalization process and implies a critique of the dual cities concept. Its recognition of a greater complexity and fragmentation than envisioned by the traditional analysis of the dual city, on the basis of the labor market's behavior and its consequences in terms of social inequality, exclusion, and poverty, underlies our assertion that Caracas is subject not so much to a metropolitan dualization as to a heterogeneous and complex socioterritorial fragmentation, the latter being the defining feature of this city confronted by the challenge of turning itself into a global city. That is the most striking characteristic of the combined impact of globalization and internal factors, among which oil plays a key role, on the economic restructuring and opening processes that gave rise to significant changes in the urban structure, functional specialization, metropolitanization process, and new ways of living in the city.

These internal restructuring processes express themselves differently in a framework of sociopolitical transition characterized by institutional and policy changes that provoke intense conflict. Above and beyond the continuing territorial fragmentation, understood as a "hard" trend, the sociopolitical conflict gives rise to new forms of isolation or incorporation of urban space, which need to be analyzed in this context in order to visualize their reach and assess their ongoing trends.

Venezuela is immersed in a process of change that has engendered a massive sociopolitical conflict, which, in turn, affects Caracas's global position and role. As a result of these changes, new transformations emerge on top of the trends that had previously been influencing metropolitan society but, unlike those of the previous decade, are not favorable to the city's global integration. This chapter reflects the context of that sociopolitical conflict, which permeates the analysis since the changes now occurring do not allow for a clear visualization of future trends. The potential changes in the globalization of Caracas will be linked to scenarios of current government's permanence or disappearance, as well as to a new trend in the oil industry's activity and the global linkages in which Latin American integration plays a major role. Beyond the current uncertainty, the socioterritorial fragmentation of the metropolis appears as a permanent tendency, associated with the formation of Caracas as a global city.

From that starting point, we discuss the globalization of Caracas in a broad sense, embracing the economic, social, and political processes associated with the city's global integration and the behavior of the economic agents and social and institutional players that either support or oppose the ways in which that process plays itself out. In the first part of this chapter, we call attention to the key importance of oil in the globalization of Caracas. In the second and third parts, we analyze the trends prevailing in the 1990s regarding the labor market, social inequality, the city's socioterritorial fragmentation, and urban lifestyles, as well as some of the changes now taking place. The last part focuses on the role of Caracas in Venezuela's sociopolitical conflict, both as the territory in which that conflict plays out with maximum impact and as regards the scenarios for the city's globalization process in the framework of the changes now taking place in Venezuelan society.

OIL AND THE GLOBALIZING CITY

To speak of the processes underlying Caracas's emergence as a global city or of its integration into the hierarchy of global cities requires a focus on oil as the organizing principle of Venezuelan society, the force that determines both its internal and external linkages. Caracas is a small metropolis; although it has its place in the hierarchy of global cities, from the perspective of the global economy as an economy of flows, it stands outside the core. Its place in that hierarchy of global cities has been, is, and will continue to be closely linked to oil and to the fact that Caracas is the capital of a major oil-producing country, even though the nature of that linkage changes over time, and those changes have varying effects.

The rentier nature of the Venezuelan economy and its early integration into the international economy, especially as an oil supplier to the U.S. market, as well as the installation of the transnational oil and oil service companies' local headquarters in Caracas, were the key sources of the city's external linkage. Though this linkage was clearly subordinated to the circuits existing in the international economy, it changed, in part, following the oil industry's nationalization in 1976. But, although Venezuela took control of its principal economic activity, forms of subordination to the previous oil model (technology, management personnel, organizational culture, subcontractors, markets) remained.

These links to the U.S. economy were present not only in oil exports but also in the country's significant dependence on imports and in a culture linked to and penetrated by U.S. lifestyles. Miami became a key reference point; it was there that a sector of Venezuelan society favored by the distribution of oil income shopped, bought real estate, and experienced a milieu of well-being during the long period of exchange rate stability beginning in the 1960s and lasting until February 1983.[1] That is to say, the flow of goods, services, and people was very fluid, but the economy continued to be tied to the import substitution model, while, to a certain extent, global consumption took place outside the country's borders.

In spite of the high oil prices prevailing in the early 1970s, which created the oil boom and the "Great Venezuela" plan during the first administration of President Carlos Andrés Pérez, massive external public borrowing and the national economy's declining ability to absorb capital (the latter condition leading to a steady capital flight), plus the subsequent decline of oil prices, led to a foreign debt crisis that required the adoption of exchange controls and a devaluation of the bolivar in 1983.

As oil income lost its ability to finance internal accumulation, the exchange rate's stability was undermined, real salary levels declined, and the state lost economic and social legitimacy, the governing elites began to design a new plan for the country centered on the adoption of a neoliberal economic model. This plan, adopted in 1989, includes state reform and a program of adjustment and opening of the economy as a way of integrating Venezuela into the new global economy.[2]

The opening of the oil industry played an important role in that policy. In the framework of economic globalization, the proposal of the national elites was embraced by the "technocracy," which ran the state-owned oil company, Petróleos de Venezuela (PDVSA). A neoliberal economic position was increasingly adopted, with special stress on the state's inefficiency, and the oil company embarked on an internationalization policy beginning in 1983, followed by an opening to outside investment in 1992. The latter policy signified the return of the transnational oil companies, a progressive reprivatization of the national oil industry, and, in practice, a reduction of the state's power to control its own industry and a decline of fiscal revenue from oil exports (Mommer 2003). "As part of the general Opening of the Venezuelan economy to the outside world, PDVSA was tasked with the Oil Opening" (Mommer 2003, 6). "PDVSA began to play an important role in bringing the country into a global world where the territorial State is destined to disappear" (Mommer 2003, 7).

As a result of the oil opening, direct foreign investment in oil activity was essentially concentrated in production in different areas of the country's interior, while control over those geographically dispersed productive operations was located in Caracas. Local headquarters of the transnational oil companies and related firms were once again opened in Caracas,[3] where PDVSA's headquarters are also located. A similar trend occurred among transnational corporations active in other productive sectors (mining, industry, food processing) and with special force among those engaged in telecommunications, advanced services, and banking and finance. By the end of the 1990s, Caracas had acquired a clear specialization in the latter functions, expressed in a high concentration of nationwide employment exceeding the urban average (Barrios 1998). These functions expanded steadily to meet the needs of the productive activities stimulated by the opening. The concentration of workers with higher education in the metropolis, especially those employed in advanced services, finance, communications, mining, and oil, shows that Caracas also performs technical and control functions for important activities of material production, among which oil is the most outstanding (Barrios 1998). In a word, the development of advanced services, telecommunications, and finance, as well as the concentration of the control, direction, and management of productive activities, chiefly oil, characterize Caracas's economic leadership as a national center and its potential as a "globalizing city."

The impact of globalization and its correlates, the opening of the national economy and of the oil industry, reform of the state, deregulation, and privatization, stimulated major changes in the structure and function of Caracas at both the national and international levels, reflecting a process characterized by a new integration of Caracas into the global economy and the network of global cities. Acknowledging the city's status as the capital of an oil-producing country and the new functions it has been coming to perform, several works include Caracas in the hierarchy of global cities (Friedmann 1986; Beaverstock, Smith, and Taylor 1999; Taylor and Walker 2001), though its position in that hierarchy appears to have been declining in recent years (APEC 2002).

The city's globalization is not explained solely by the actions of transnational players; another major contribution is made by the practices conducive to global articulation undertaken by national economic agents and players. This process interacts with the economic changes induced by the opening and with other processes that had been occurring in the metropolis, reflecting the participation of different players who have been creating the territorial foundations for the new integration. Since the 1980s, alongside the progressive changes in the Venezuelan economy, Caracas has been undergoing a change in urban centrality fostered by national financial and real estate capital, which has resulted in the emergence of an area that has been turning into a global business district. Beginning in the 1990s, and in the framework of the decentralization of the state, Caracas has become institutionally fragmented by its division into five municipalities. One of them, Chacao, hosts the new business district, in line with this change of urban centrality, which is directly functional to the new forms of linkage to the global economy and the needs of national and international capital.

It is also important to stress at least two major initiatives to improve the city's competitiveness in the global context, undertaken by public and private institutions organized in the Venezuelan Council for Investment Promotion (CONAPRI), where a pioneering work titled "Venezuela: A Regional Strategic Center for the Americas" was written in 1997, and the Metropolitan Caracas Strategic Plan Foundation, which produced "A Proposal for the City: Metropolitan Caracas 2010" in 1998. Both institutions focus on enhancing the city's competitiveness with a view to turning Caracas into a regional metropolis for the Caribbean. CONAPRI made quite explicit the strategic role played by oil activity in the achievement of that position in the global hierarchy of cities (Chiappe 1998). However, neither of these initiatives had any significant impact since they were not taken up by the economic agents or the institutional players responsible for the city's governance.

Together with the practices driving the restructuring of the economy and the state and the new forms of linkage to the global economy, which can be summed up in the oil and global integration postulate, forms of resistance have also sprung up and have prevented the neoliberal economic model from becoming fully established. These forms of social and political resistance, ranging from popular protests like the "Caracazo" riots of February 1989 to the coup d'état attempts of 1992 and growing electoral abstention, ultimately became formalized in the political project now underway under President Chávez. That new political project calls for a change in the country's institutional structure and its global integration based on the oil and national development postulate. The changes are expressed in a new oil policy focused on strengthening the Organization of Petroleum Exporting Countries (OPEC) and keeping oil prices high by restricting production and in new hydrocarbon legislation that prescribes different forms of association with transnational oil capital. But these changes have not become dominant, and intense sociopolitical conflicts are now taking place that affect all spheres of Venezuelan society and make it impossible to predict the direction in which the globalization of Caracas will move in the future.

To sum up, a conjunction of internal and external factors has accelerated the global integration of Caracas and its incorporation into the hierarchy of global cities. Oil activity and the linkages it generates have given Caracas a place in the hierarchy of global cities, though not a position at the core of the global economy. Rather than the search for competitiveness under a strategy conceived for that purpose, this is a process driven by the pressure of the new forms of integration into the global economy and the impact of different kinds of transnational corporations' arrival, together with the proactive practices of national economic agents and other players. At the same time, there has not been a linear progression but a process full of contradiction, which has from the outset provoked social resistance to the neoliberal model and whose effects, as will be shown below, have produced changes in the urban economy, metropolitan society, labor market, and lifestyles of the inhabitants of Caracas, all of which are tending to make it an increasingly unequal and fragmented city in process of globalization.

RESTRUCTURING AND GLOBAL INTEGRATION PROCESSES: CAUGHT BETWEEN GLOBALIZED ACTIVITIES AND THE ECONOMY OF POVERTY[4]

Caracas strengthened its national and international control and management functions and modified its spatial structure to enable it to perform those functions as its incorporation into the hierarchical system of global cities replicated the dynamic associated with the new global economy and the quantitative and qualitative differences typical of a segregated and socially exclusive Latin American city.

The restructuring of the economy and the state, in the course of which internal institutional arrangements were adapted to the demands of the global economy, had a far-reaching impact on the metropolitan economy and gave rise to idiosyncratic changes in the city's labor market, which intensified still further in the opening years of the twenty-first century. The changes in question express themselves in the form of a growth of economic activities and employment tied to the new forms of global integration, together with the emergence of informal activities and employment associated with the economy of poverty. Key features of the new metropolitan economy include declining job stability in the economy's formal sector, a growing number of high-level jobs, increasing unemployment and work in the informal sector, a rise in service-sector employment and decline in manufacturing jobs, and growing inequality in the distribution of income among various labor-market sectors.

Employment in the formal sector of the metropolitan economy grew slowly in the 1990s and is thought to be on the decline under the current conditions of economic recession provoked by the country's political and economic crisis. Falling public-sector and industrial employment was offset until late in the 1980s by growth in commerce, services, telecommunications, banking and finance, and corporate services. Although the activities linked to the global economy generated few jobs, they were key to the expansion of specialized services for transnational corporations (advanced producer services) and high-income consumers (shopping centers, restaurants, recreation, cultural activities). The employment conditions prevailing in the formal sector have been extremely unequal in terms of quality and income, resulting in an intense labor and social vulnerability in sectors where jobs have become professionally, socially, and economically devalued and their holders' social status has deteriorated.

In general, this condition of labor vulnerability is closely linked to low incomes, though other variables, such as the absence of social security, also play important explanatory roles. In addition to this objective dimension, job instability and occupational vulnerability also have subjective dimensions. Low income, fear of unemployment, or descent in the hierarchy of job status generate insecurity and personal and family instability, due both to the loss of opportunities for personal and occupational self-realization and to the fear of social exclusion that accompanies departure from the labor market. These situations lead to an increasingly vulnerable identity among sectors of the population whose members had previously expected a stable path of upward mobility and social inclusion.

Parallel to the growth of economic activities related to the global economy, there has been an expansion of the economy of poverty, linked to increasing reliance on informal occupation characterized by low productivity and low incomes. This phenomenon gains in importance when associated with the growth of unemployment under present-day economic conditions. This sector has generated the largest number of jobs and has grown in construction, industrial, commercial, and service activities, reflecting individuals' pursuit of livelihood strategies and the informalization of companies. This trend has brought with it a decline in the number of stable jobs, a devaluation of work and workers, an undermining of the culture of work, and a loss of identity as a result of exclusion from the formal labor market.

Informality has not only grown but also become a way of life. It is not merely a short-term strategy to survive a temporary absence of employment in the formal sector; in a great many cases, it is a permanent activity that organizes poor households' livelihood strategies and its members' daily lives. This is a way of living characterized by family participation in many informal activities that are superimposed on the domestic spaces and normal activities, generating intrafamily conflicts for use of vital space, as well as use of the streets as an economic space. This provokes urban conflicts due to labor insecurity and the culture of "scrounging," as well as a fragmented social identity reflecting the absence of opportunities for upward mobility, a consciousness of belonging to the world of poverty, and a negative perception of the future (Cariola et al. 1992).

Falling incomes and rising inequality in the labor market have had a powerful impact on the positions people hold in the social structure, inducing greater heterogeneity and inequality. But inequality is not limited to income. The state's retreat from social policy widened the gap of poor households' unmet needs by the late 1990s (Cariola, Lacabana, and Velasco 1999). As a result of the increased volume of social investment and the inauguration of certain social-development programs by the new administration, there is now a modest improvement of educational and health care conditions for the lower-income population, but the overall trend has not been reversed.

Poverty continues to spread, and the number of poor households continues to increase.[5] There are more and more structurally poor households, and poverty is becoming more heterogeneous as a result of the impoverishment and downward mobility experienced by large numbers of formerly middle-class households. For these social sectors, emigration presents itself as an extreme strategy to be employed when there is no possibility of adaptation to the new conditions. But other processes are superimposed on this foundation of greater poverty. The modernization of opening the economy and integrating it into the global economy introduced new services and modernized old ones, thereby changing cultural and consumption patterns, demanding new skills, and generating high incomes in activities linked to the global economy. This speaks to the coexistence of simultaneous trends that expel, attract, and intermingle the economy of poverty and the global economy, the globally integrated social sectors, and those struggling to overcome their vulnerability and halt their downward mobility, as well as some of the excluded. In other words, differing forms of integration and exclusion, multiplicity and nonduality are the defining features of today's metropolitan society.

METROPOLITAN EXPANSION AND SOCIOTERRITORIAL FRAGMENTATION IN GLOBALIZING CARACAS: WAYS OF LIVING IN THE METROPOLIS[6]

The great economic and social transformations stemming from the globalization process are producing changes in the urban configuration and ways of living, inducing an expansion of our metropolitan areas toward their peripheries, reflecting the city-region complex model and involving a high degree of dynamism characterized by major socioterritorial inequality. They reflect great complexity, stemming both from the new functions and relations assumed by the metropolis and the social and cultural diversity represented by the social sectors integrated into the globalized system, which unequally share the city and its urban benefits with those subject to varying degrees of exclusion.

Caracas has overflowed its urban boundaries and expanded toward its periphery, while new dynamics and contents of urban segregation linked to the restructuring processes occurring in the framework of globalization are superimposed on the historical processes under which Caracas came into being in accordance with the oil rentier model, giving rise to increasing socioterritorial inequality and a growing metropolitan fragmentation.

In this respect, there is a functional specialization of each urban segment in terms of its greater or lesser articulation to the global network of economic relations (Ciccolella and Mignaqui 2000), as well as an institutional segmentation intensified by the administrative decentralization process.

Functional specialization is expressed in the emergence of differentiated financial and business districts within the city and the spread of large commercial and recreational installations linked to the expansion of import trade. A global business district has been created in the eastern part of Caracas in its richest municipality, serving as a symbol of modernity in urban government. It is complemented by hotels, cultural and recreational facilities, and shopping centers, which are added to the area's upper-income residential function. Chacao's multifunctionality has a clearly segregating effect, turning it into an enclave within the city (Mitchell 1998). It is a territorial unit directly linked to the global network of economic relations and socially specialized in upper-income sectors of the population. As such, it poses strong competition with the old business district located in the historic center of the city.

At the same time, other areas of the city serve as a refuge for marginalized sectors of the population, such as the street vendors, who reflect the growth of the informal subsistence economy and have taken over public spaces in the city's historic center. The spread of informality in the city has become more visible in recent years as unemployment has risen and the government has taken a permissive attitude toward it. The outcome of these trends is a proliferation of commercial activity on the streets, which only intensifies the city's polarization between areas integrated into the global economy and areas linked to the economy of poverty.

This functional specialization process is reinforced by the segmentation and differentiation among the local governments since the creation of new municipalities in response to metropolitan expansion and the emergence of local initiative as a result of the decentralization process have stimulated the fragmentation of the city's governments while calling attention to the socioeconomic inequality among the territories controlled by each (Negrón 1997; Mitchell 1998).

Parallel to these processes is an advancing socioresidential segregation related to the far-reaching transformation of Caracas society in the last decades. The restructuring of the economy and the state has provoked changes in the labor market and the social structure of the metropolis expressed in spreading poverty, social exclusion, and inequality. These transformations influence the way the city is structured and lived in by reinforcing the dynamic of segregation, which now acquires a qualitatively different form linked to the juxtaposition of different ways of living, conducive to atomization and retreat into the private sphere of life.

The current trends of socioterritorial segregation in Caracas imbue this process with a new meaning by associating it not only with the differential quality of urban space but also with the emergence and juxtaposition of ways of living that reflect the progressive differentiation of metropolitan society. The lifestyles proper to globalization, pursued by those who perform state-of-the-art activities and characterized by the incorporation of sophisticated consumption patterns, advanced knowledge, and modern communication technologies in daily life, intersect with those lifestyles emerging from the livelihood practices with which people react to exclusion and poverty, namely, those which take the form of economies of crime and transgression-oriented cultures and those developed by downwardly mobile, middle-income groups to cope with the consequences of their impoverishment. This is a juxtaposition of lifestyles whose greater or lesser articulation with each other reinforces the increasing urban fragmentation, incites conflict for the use of territory, and interferes with the inhabitants' identification with a city where the public space has yielded to the private and the values that used to orient citizen culture have weakened.

As occurs in other metropolises, fear of the other and fear of violence become decisive factors in the determination of ways of living and construction of the city (Davis 1999). In Caracas, they are keys to an explanation of the dynamics of socioterritorial segregation and the ways of life associated with it. Violence is perceived as a problem of key importance by the inhabitants of Caracas, reflecting the capital's objective position as the country's most unsafe city, and it is the principal argument for enclosing residential neighborhoods and privatizing public spaces. In subjective terms, fear of the other conditions the times and forms of use of residential streets and neighborhoods, and it contributes to the organization of day-to-day life in the different parts of the city.

Housing, as an orienting value and a goal to be pursued, is a part of families' household projects in every stratum, and achieving it is a goal that absorbs all the vital energies among the most excluded and vulnerable groups. It is in this process of building and sharing a residential space that important relations of sociability are strengthened and a fundamental aspect of the different social sectors' identities takes shape. In this respect, the residential strategies pursued by the different groups help define the different ways of living in the metropolis. They reflect sociocultural practices that imply particular forms of production of residential space as a result of the formulation of the livelihood strategies with which the most excluded cope with poverty, "globalized" reproduction strategies on the part of those who are included, or a combination of both among those who inhabit other vulnerable sectors of the population.

INCLUDED SECTORS, HIGH INCOME AND UPWARDLY MOBILE MIDDLE INCOME: INTEGRATION INTO GLOBALIZATION AND MODERNITY WITH TERRITORIAL SELF-ISOLATION

The upper-income groups tend to segregate themselves by privatizing the production and use of their residential urban space and maintaining a socioterritorial homogeneity that reinforces their social identity.

The search for security is the chief motivation for this urban tendency, in combination with socioterritorial exclusivity and the conservation of a high quality of life. The outcome is the organization of enclosed and exclusive urban ghettos, equipped with private security systems and electronic access-control devices, with high-quality infrastructure and advanced technology and with internal open spaces, all of which reproduce the standards prevailing in the developed countries. These are luxury condominiums, which play host to ways of living typical of the dominant groups in globalized society. The development of communications allows these groups to stay in direct contact with the globalized world, including the other sociourban sectors of the city that are part of that world, while maintaining distance and isolating themselves from the rest of metropolitan life. These housing developments are not integrated into the city; they are globalized segments of it whose advantages are enjoyed and where daily life goes on in globalized fashion.

IMPOVERISHED AND VULNERABLE MIDDLE SECTORS: CAUGHT BETWEEN INCORPORATION INTO GLOBALIZATION, OR MODERNITY, AND SURVIVAL

For the heterogeneous set of impoverished middle-status groups, deteriorating living conditions give rise to ways of living subject to a variety of dilemmas: survival versus incorporation into the globalized world and modernity, territorial isolation and integration into the city, privatization of urban residential space and deterioration due to the difficulty of maintaining it, and both the strengthening and vulnerability of social identity associated with the different residential spaces.

Lifestyles are oriented by values regarding the importance of housing as a contribution to security and the family as the core of social solidarity, citizen culture, and neighborliness. The latter factors strengthen community integration and identity when they are shared by different segments of inhabitants, but they can give rise to socioterritorial conflicts in case of socially heterogeneous communities.

Note that in the framework of the current political conflict, the middle sectors give priority to strategies and ways of living that tend toward greater territorial isolation. This trend reflects their need to assert their social identity, which is threatened by impoverishment, and an intensification of their fears, especially fear of the other. In this case, the other is represented by the lower-status groups who are stigmatized as violent and from which they must defend themselves through a clear territorial separation.

POOR, LOWER-STATUS SECTORS: CAUGHT BETWEEN SURVIVAL AND STIGMATIZATION

In the context of the labor market's restructuring and the state's social retreat during the 1990s, the poor sectors of the population have resorted to adaptive strategies focused on the private sphere of the home more than on collective action at the community level. Clearly, their short-term orientation has led to the abandonment of long-term expectations. However, these trends appear to be changing at present in the context of a government that champions these sectors and has generated new expectations for inclusion through greater participation and initiative by the lower-status groups. The progressive implementation of a popular participation project appears to provide the necessary framework for new collective experiences arising from the need to respond to the contingency of political conflict or to the government's own initiatives, as well as to articulate old, collective experiences oriented toward coping with impoverishment, whose dispersion and continuity in time prevented their consolidation.

An expression of the prevailing short-term orientation is the type of residential strategy pursued by these groups to solve their housing problems or to earn an alternative income in the form of rent. Its most widespread form since the 1960s has been the self-building of substandard housing units on illegally occupied land, creating the *barrios*, or slum neighborhoods.

For the lower-status groups, profound impoverishment has intensified preexisting segregation as a qualitatively different phenomenon associated with the population's concentration in a state of extreme poverty, the serious deterioration of living conditions, and lifestyle changes in their habitats where the radicalization of violence influences their patterns of social integration into the city. These are ways of living that tend toward territorial self-enclosure within the barrio, the devaluation of lower-class habitats, and a weakened sense of belonging to a community, hence, a reduced positive construction of identity.

Strong links exist between urban segregation, access to social rights, and preservation of individual rights; living in a barrio poses a barrier to gaining access to basic rights that is increasingly difficult to overcome. Livelihood strategies in the barrios have enabled their residents to achieve a citizenship status denied them by the city: there they obtain housing, largely generate their own employment, and have access to the most heavily devalued educational facilities. The result of living in poverty and exclusion in the Caracas barrios is the creation of a sociourban apartheid in which the inhabitants' identity is also constructed on the foundation of a hostility toward other sectors of the city's population that stigmatize the barrios as hotbeds of crime and violence, an image that legitimates any level of repression against these communities.

The ways of living developed by the different metropolitan social sectors clearly help accentuate the segregation trend and have a common thread: all of them tend to reinforce behaviors that, taking different paths and having different meanings, lead to ever-increasing socioterritorial exclusion.

In contrast to concepts that posit a dual city, divided into two mutually exclusive socioterritorial segments as a consequence of globalization and social polarization, the condition of Caracas strengthens the view of a sometimes conflict-ridden coexistence of multiple cities within the metropolitan territory. The heterogeneous socioresidential differentiation produced by old and new segregation processes, which is reflected in the creation of exclusive ghettos for the upper-income groups, middle-income residential areas suffering from deterioration or displaced to the city's periphery, and true social apartheid for the lower-income groups, is further reinforced by a territorial differentiation proper to the economic transformations in production and consumption, expressed in the emergence of financial and business districts and large shopping centers, while important inner-city areas become the economic space for an informal economy of bare subsistence. Moreover, the prevailing model of city government, characterized by the absence of a comprehensive vision and by a multiplicity of isolated institutional initiatives, only strengthens the city's fragmentation and territorial inequality. The feature that defines this city caught up in the globalization process is not a duality of socioterritorial structuring but a complex and heterogeneous fragmentation of its territory.

HAS THE GLOBALIZATION PROCESS OF CARACAS GONE INTO REVERSE? THE GLOBALIZING CITY TRAPPED IN THE SOCIOPOLITICAL CONFLICT

The new processes and practices, both global and local, that are driving the globalization of Caracas superpose themselves on others already under way, giving rise to the city's territorial fragmentation. This trend becomes especially prominent during periods of sociopolitical conflict, even though the urban structural processes continue operating. Hence, both the changes in the urban structure and the city's globalization trend are tied to the evolution and potential resolution of that conflict.

The situation at the present time is one of conflicts of high and low intensity in all spheres of society, generated by the emergence of new leadership groups and the changes pursued by President Chávez, which are institutionalized in the constitution of 1999. The country's sociopolitical conflict intensified in 2002 with the coup d'état, the lockout, and the oil strike. In 2003, the conflict has played out mainly in the political and institutional sphere. Caracas was, and continues to be, the territory in which the political conflict is most intense, reflecting a polarization of metropolitan society.

The sociopolitical conflict has a macroterritorial expression directly related to the particularities of Caracas. It is the capital, the seat of the national government and of multiple national and subnational jurisdictions, and it is a primate city in the sense of being the place where the dominant elites (political, economic, cultural, religious, etc.) come together (Myers and Dietz

2002). In addition, the highest-income members of society tend to concentrate in Caracas, which is the geographic core of the sociopolitical conflict mounted by the opposition to the current government. The opposition leadership in Caracas can be associated with that concentration of elites and upper-income sectors, as could be observed in the lockout and shutdown of oil activity.

The microterritorial expression of this conflict reflects the socioterritorial and institutional fragmentation of the metropolis, where each social pole of the conflict is associated with a fragment of the city. The opposition has its greatest center of strength in Caracas, concentrated in the middle- and upper-income sectors of the population and in the municipalities that are emblematic of modernity and integration into the global economy. It is in these microterritories in the east of Caracas that the opposition groups come together and concentrate, and it is here that they plan and launch their mass mobilizations in opposition to the government. The marches from east to west in Caracas are emblematic of the collective image of a "rich east" and a "poor west." At the other pole of the conflict are the lower-status urban groups that hope the political inclusion in which they now participate will turn into an economic and social inclusion as well. Their identification with the Chávez political project, which reflects their distrust of the traditional political parties, the catastrophic effects of the economic policies pursued in the last two decades, and the certainty that they will have no opportunities in the future, mobilizes them in defense of the government from their segregated microterritories, especially in the west of Caracas. The downwardly mobile middle sectors, or the new poor, having a diffuse territoriality, join one or the other pole in the conflict according to their greater or lesser social identification and the continuation or dissipation of their expectations of reversing the socioeconomic decline to which they have been subjected in the last two decades (Lacabana and Cariola 2002).

As a result of the sociopolitical conflict, the features that define the city's socioterritorial fragmentation have become even more complex. On the one hand, we observe the emergence of lower-income groups through a sociopolitical inclusion process that partially overcomes residential apartheid, even though socioeconomic exclusion mechanisms continue to operate. On the other, there is a retreat of the middle- and upper-income groups, who strive to fortify their residential ghettos. While the boundaries of the lower-income urban fragments are becoming more permeable, the other groups tend to isolate themselves even further within their residential spaces through individual and collective self-defense practices. The ecology of fear (Davis 1999) is an urban reality. Fear of the other continues to intensify among the middle- and upper-income sectors of the population, driven by the emergence of the popular sectors and the possibility of a social model break. The poor are increasingly stigmatized and feared because they are associated with the government's political project; the upshot is a classist fear in response to the prospects for greater social equality and a more equitable distribution of wealth that is perceived as implying a loss of privileges rather than the construction of a full and egalitarian citizenship. In spite of the popular sectors' emergence and newfound political participation, fear acts as a determining factor in their social action as well: they fear that the current political model might be overturned, that the new mechanisms for sociopolitical inclusion and responsiveness to their demands might be lost, and that their expectations of improving their socioeconomic condition and becoming fully empowered citizens might be frustrated.

This simultaneous opening and closing of the urban boundaries has many forms of expression:

- Advances by the lower-income population in the use of the city's public spaces, while the middle- and upper-income residents concentrate in the new private spaces for collective use tied to global consumption patterns.
- New identities in which the lower-income population's cultural patterns are given a positive valuation, with public expressions that range from defense of the new constitution as a tool for change to music as a medium for transmitting the new conditions. The middle- and upper-income groups perceive those expressions as symptoms of social disintegration and accentuate a cultural pattern tied to globalization.
- The sociopolitical conflict's visibility itself, taking the form of political rallies in the streets of Caracas in which both sides measure and compare their strengths.

Broadening the meaning of the concept proposed by Soja (2000), we can state that what is now occurring is a socioterritorial implosion and explosion referring to a little-studied characteristic of the metropolis: the territorial expression of sociopolitical conflict, which, in turn, introduces particularities into the globalization process experienced by Caracas.

The lockout and oil strike, used as weapons to resolve the sociopolitical conflict in the opposition's favor, have had a powerful impact on the urban economy. The preexisting recession has deepened; the number of firms going out of business has increased; and unemployment and the informal sector have grown. A great expansion of the economy of poverty, taking the form of street vending, has taken place in the city's public spaces; this trend only calls more attention to the differences between the globally integrated and nonintegrated segments of the city. However, it is important to note that the integrated segment has also been, and will continue to be, adversely affected by the recession, business failures, and falling consumption since the crisis and the restructuring of the oil industry launched by the government will have an impact on the high-level consumer-service sector and that of advanced services to companies. In fact, some of those companies had already been shutting down even before the current administration came to power as a result of the recession. The paradoxical aspect of this process is that in the midst of the most serious economic and political crisis in many years, the government continues to award concessions to joint ventures involving transnational oil companies. This may lead to a partial reversal of the urban economy's deterioration and, especially, to the integration of its core into the global economy.

Once again, oil appears to be the organizing element and the decisive influence on the future of Venezuelan society, and oil is at the core of the current sociopolitical conflict. The collapse of the oil strike and the government's new strategy to revive oil production without dependence on the old top management and many related companies, as well as its strategy of internalizing oil (as opposed to the industry's internationalization and opening), also imply changes at the national and global levels. The effects of all this on Caracas as a city in the process of globalization are not yet clear. Will there be a retreat or new forms of global integration? That is a question that is still up in the air.

The two scenarios we envisage regarding the direction of the globalization of Caracas may reflect either an intensification of the current strategy of change or a return to neoliberal economic premises.

In the first such scenario, the restructuring of oil activity and the development of internal productive chain effects may reduce the industry's stimulative effect on the metropolitan economy. That reduction will be partly offset by new foreign investment and the need for centers for the control of productive activities. But there will also be a change in the direction of opening that will favor Latin American integration, which may give rise to new forms of relations and leadership for Caracas in the Andean and Caribbean spheres. Furthermore, the place Caracas holds in the global hierarchy of cities may change if it is conceived solely in terms of the presence of advanced service companies and the view of the global economy as an economy of flows, though the new integration could give Caracas a higher rank for its economic and political influence over the change processes that are expected to sweep Latin America.

PDVSA's actions to internalize the oil industry, ranging from supporting the social economy through the creation of cooperatives to stimulating an urban focus of productivity and innovation, are oriented by this same perspective of a new global competitiveness for Caracas. Moreover, though the city's socioterritorial fragmentation will continue, the lower-income groups' increasing social organization and participation based on the new local institutional structure could partially reverse the inequalities and lead to more local investment to improve those groups' quality of life. In turn, the lifestyles of the middle- and upper-income groups will continue to be associated with territorial self-enclosure and practices of resistance, which will continue fluctuating between political opposition and the extreme option of emigration.

In the second scenario, the government's fall would pave the way for a return to, and a reinforcement of, neoliberal economic policy, marked by greater opening of the economy and the oil industry and, possibly, a privatization of PDVSA and other state-owned energy companies. Under those circumstances, the trends of the previous decade in the globalization of Caracas (weakened since the current government's coming to power) will be reinforced, and the tendency toward greater urban inequality will deepen. The process of territorial self-enclosure by the middle- and upper-income groups will not be reversed; a similar trend will intensify among the lower-income groups prevented from advancing in the processes of construction of citizenship that are visualized in the previous scenario. The strengthening of the global business district as an emblematic center of the process will be accompanied by a reorganization of the city designed to regulate the use of public space to the detriment of the lower-income groups that rely on street vending to survive. In this scenario, Caracas will again come to hold a position in the global hierarchy of cities, as measured by the presence of advanced service companies, since the opening and privatizations will replicate, with even greater intensity, the process under way over the past decade, which set in motion the trends examined above.

This review of scenarios in the context of the country's sociopolitical conflict and its effects on Caracas confirms the importance of the oil dynamic's influence on potential changes in the city's globalization process and the persistence of socioterritorial fragmentation. As well, the city's future is linked to the sociopolitical conflict's outcome since that will determine the choice among different models of national development.

Returning to the initial question, does the fact that Caracas is caught up in a sociopolitical conflict that confronts two different development models imply a reversal of its globalization? The answer must be grounded in the acknowledgment of a more complex situation. In both cases, the process will continue advancing, but it could move in different directions. Rather than a reversal of the city's globalization process due to the loss of activities integrated into the global economy, the new model carries with it an alternative way to participate in that economy, which, in addition to giving attention to economic activities, also proposes a form of sociometropolitan development centered on social cohesion and justice, in which the improvement of living conditions for the bulk of the population is a goal in and of itself, not just a factor in the city's competitiveness.

NOTES

1. In the collective imagination of potential and real migrants, Miami now represents both an escape from Venezuela's economic crisis and the possibility of getting a job and participating in a global lifestyle.

2. The policies adopted in 1989 and thereafter clearly reflected the so-called Consensus of Washington, which called for a minimization of the state, privatization of state-owned enterprises and public institutions, elimination of subsidies, and balancing of the budget. Emphasis shifted from improving living conditions to structural adjustment, in connection with which the key objective was economic efficiency (Stewart 1998).

3. Shell, British Petroleum, and Amoco opened headquarters offices, but HP, Placer Dome (gold mining), and Bellsouth (telecommunications) did so as well.

4. The following analysis reflects the results of the "Labor Transformations and Social Restructuring in Caracas Metropolitan Area" study (CENDES-CDCH), which continued until the late 1990s (Cariola and Lacabana 2002, 2001, 2000).

5. This growth of poverty, under way since the late 1980s, was contained, to a certain extent, in the early years of the current decade as a result of a short-term improvement in salaries' purchasing power. But the current political and economic crisis augurs for a new intensification of impoverishment.

6. Cariola and Lacabana 2002, 2001, 2000.

REFERENCES

Asociación Plan Estratégico de Caracas (APEC). 2002. Visión 2010. *Boletín Electrónico* no. 24, año 4, marzo–julio.

Barrios, S. 1998. "Caracas metropolitana: actividades y ocupaciones básicas." In *Fundación plan estratégico Caracas metropolitana* (FPECM). Caracas Metropolitana: Temas Prioritarios para el Futuro de la Ciudad, edición FPECM, Caracas.

Beaverstock, J., Smith, R. G., and Taylor, P. J. 1999. "A roster of world cities." GaWC Research Bulletin 5. University of Loughborough, Department of Geography, at www.lboro.ac.uk/departments/gy/research/gawc/rb/rb5.html.

Borja, J., and Castells, M. 1997. *Local y global: la gestión de las ciudades en la era de la información*. Madrid: Taurus.

Brenner, N. 2003. "La formación de la ciudad global y el re-escalamiento del espacio del estado en la Europa occidental post-Fordista." *Revista EURE* 29: 86.

Cariola, C., and Lacabana, M. 2000. "Transformaciones en el trabajo, diferenciación social y fragmentación de la metrópoli: el área metropolitana de Caracas." *Revista Cuadernos del CENDES* 43, Caracas.

———. 2001. "La metrópoli fragmentada. Caracas entre la pobreza y la globalización." *Revista EURE* 27: 80.

———. 2002. "Pobreza, nueva pobreza y exclusión social. La heterogeneidad social en la Caracas metropolitana." Informe final de Investigación, El Centro de Estudios del Desarrollo (CENDES), Universidad Central de Venezuela, Caracas.

Cariola, C., Lacabana, M., and Velasco. F. J. 1999. "Impacto socio-ambiental del ajuste estructural. Mercado de trabajo, pobreza y medio ambiente urbano." Temas para la discusión 5, El Centro de Estudios del Desarrollo (CENDES), Universidad Central de Venezuela, Caracas.

Cariola, C. (coord.), Bethencourt, L., Darwich, G., Fernández, B., Gutiérrez, A. T., and Lacabana, M. 1992. *Sobrevivir en la pobreza. El fin de la ilusión.* Caracas: Editorial Nueva Sociedad.

Castells, M. 2000. *La era de la información. Economía, sociedad y cultura.* Vol. 1. Madrid: La Sociedad Red. Alianza Editorial.

Chiappe, D. 1998. "La estrategia gigante." *Venezuela Now.* Caracas: CONAPRI.

Ciccolella, P., and Mignaqui, I. 2000. "Economía global y reestructuración metropolitana: Buenos Aires ¿ciudad global o ciudad dual del siglo XXI?" *Revista cuadernos del CENDES* 43, Caracas.

CONAPRI (Venezuelan Council for Investment Promotion). 1997. *Venezuela.* Caracas: Centro Estratégico Regional para las Américas.

Davis, M. 1999. *Ecology of Fear: Los Angeles and the Imagination of Disaster.* New York: Vintage.

de Mattos, C. 2002. "Transformación de las ciudades Latinoamericanas. ¿Impactos de la globalización?" *Revista EURE* 28: 85.

Friedmann, J. 1986. "The world city hypothesis." *Development and Change* 17, no. 1: 69–84.

Fundación Plan Estratégico Caracas Metropolitana. 1998. "Una propuesta para la ciudad." Caracas: FPECM.

Lacabana, M., and Cariola, C. 2002. "Desigualdad socioeconómica y polarización política en Caracas. Algunos elementos para entender la territorialidad del conflicto sociopolítico en Venezuela." Ponencia presentada al I Congreso Latinoamericano de Ciencia Política. Salamanca.

Marcuse, P., and van Kempen, R. 2000. *Globalizing Cities. A New Spatial Order?* Oxford: Blackwell.

Mitchell, J. 1998. "Political decentralization: a new tool for the segregation of urban space? The case of Chacao in Caracas, Venezuela." Chicago: Ponencia al Encuentro de LASA.

Myers, D, J., and Dietz H. A., eds. 2002. *Capital City Politics in Latin America: Democratization and Empowerment.* London: Lynne Rienner Publishers.

Mommer, B. 2003. "Petróleo subversivo," August 1, 2003, at www.soberania.org/Articulos/articulo_007.htm (accessed November 10, 2005).

Negrón, M. 1997. "La planificación urbana local y el contexto metropolitano." *Urbana* 19, FAU-UCV, Caracas.

Sassen, S. 1999. *La ciudad global: Nueva York, Londres, Tokyo.* Buenos Aires: Eudeba.

———. 2002. *Global Networks, Linked Cities.* London: Routledge.

Soja, E. 2000. *Postmetropolis: Critical Studies of Cities and Regions.* Oxford: Blackwell.

Stewart, F. 1998. "La insuficiencia crónica del ajuste." In *Todos entran. Propuesta para sociedades incluyentes,* ed. E. Bustelo and A. Minujin, 25–65. UNICEF. Colección Cuadernos de Debate. Santillana. Buenos Aires: UNICEF.

Taylor, P., and Walker, D. R. F. 2001. "World cities: a first multivariate analysis of their service complexes." *Urban Studies* 38, no. 1: 23–47.

10

Reconsidering the Social Structuration of Globalization

M. Mark Amen, Kevin Archer, and M. Martin Bosman

The preceding chapters have, in their varying ways, served to provide a deeper empirical understanding of cities not often treated in the global cities literature. As discussed in the introductory chapter, the significance of such work is that it brings to greater light how all cities are affected in some way by globalizing forces. One of our goals as editors has been to provide the greatest latitude to our authors to determine for themselves what to focus their research sights on for each city. To this end, we did not provide very tight parameters for their individual investigations. Analysis guided by social structuration theory requires consideration of both market-based structural exigencies and the human agency that contributes to and resists such exigencies. To our minds, therefore, this requirement is best accomplished via a deeper understanding of the varying degrees of power agents have to make decisions that effect happenings in reality, both more globally and more locally in scope.

Each of the preceding empirical chapters provides a window through which unique constellations of such power relations come into view as the very basis for urban differentiation in a globalizing world. It is clear that each city treated in this volume encounters global flows and networks in varying ways and with varying intensity. Each city also reflects a unique constellation of global and local flows and networks of differential economic, political, and cultural power. They each thereby require a close empirical analysis to determine the precise contours of powerful globalizing agents and agency emerging within them.

Understood in this way, our theoretical approach to globalizing cities in the introductory chapter is very close to that of those who consider cities to be the result of the "glocalization" of global-local flows, as briefly discussed in chapters 8 and 9 (see also Brenner 1999). However, this rather inelegant term connotes to us a rather static conception of what is really an ever-changing constellation of differential power relations within not just economic, but also political and cultural, global-local flows and networks. Indeed, Salmon and Swyngedouw and Moyersoen begin, in their respective chapters, to broaden this conception in this very way in their empirical investigations of political relations in Sydney and Brussels. The changing constellation of differential power relations is confirmed in all the case studies, reinforcing our belief that the power relations of globalization within cities can be mapped from many different empirical directions.

In this concluding chapter, we offer some observations specifically grounded in our understanding of the empirical evidence provided for all eight cities. For example, it appears that powerful globalizing agency is penetrating and preempting local agency, rendering all of our case cities potential global wannabes. This is apparently based on the overwhelming dominance of neoliberal discourse and practice. The privileged position the neoliberal project now holds has, in effect, tended to depoliticize the urban development process, both in practice and in the scholarly reflection thereof. Based on these observations, it is necessary, we believe, to reassess our initial endorsement of social structuration as the way to merge the market- and agency-driven approaches we still believe characterize the global cities literature.

FIVE OBSERVATIONS ABOUT OUR CASE CITIES

On the basis of the specific empirical work in the preceding chapters, it is possible to gain further theoretical insights into relations of power that cut across all of these globalizing cities. Our reading of the specific cases leads us to first observe that while powerful global economic agencies have emerged in each of these cities, the response of local agency to these flows of power is remarkably mixed. In some cities, such as Tampa Bay, Frankfurt, and Johannesburg, local political and business leaders appear to be somewhat disconnected from these powerful global agents. Leaders in Tampa, for instance, are far more concerned about parochial issues than they are about how globalization has emerged as a force with which to contend. Within the political sector, mayors and county commissioners are so preoccupied with long-standing local debates (e.g., downtown development versus support for neighborhoods) that one gets the impression that the world has passed them by. Even new initiatives within the business community, such as those proposed by the Tampa Bay Partnership and by the I-4 Corridor initiative, are cast within traditional marketing approaches or concerns about how to attract the high-technology sector, the so-called sunrise sector, to move to the corridor. Something similar also appears to be occurring in Johannesburg, where leaders are busy creating different blueprints for how the city can regain its prior world city status. These leaders are living in the past as they attempt to recoup a lost, rather than create a new, status in the world. Frankfurt's fate is, apparently, not all that different. Its future is being determined by global networks of flows among advanced producer services firms and the financial sector businesses that need their services. As these global agencies are negotiating outcomes that impact Frankfurt, that city's local leaders are apparently standing on the sidelines awaiting the results.

In other cities, local agency has been overridden or mediated by national government policy. In some instances, government has accommodated global power flows in hopes of bringing benefits to the country, even if such benefits come at the expense of the city. For the last thirty years, for example, the Philippine state has supported a policy of exporting contract labor to establish a niche in the global market. Local agents appear to have very little control over the socioeconomic consequences of this policy for Manila. And in Thailand, the national government's efforts to attract short-term capital investments have devastated the built environment of Bangkok while local agents have been largely incapable of altering the situation. Even in richer Australia and Belgium, national policies of accommodation have had important consequences for Sydney and Brussels. These two nation-states have pursued the presumed benefits that come to countries when they increase the presence of global financiers, international realtors, expanded stock market activity, or European Union representatives in their cities. Local agents in Brussels and Sydney, who have been largely excluded from these negotiations, are now left to deal with the results of these national policies. The local response has been mixed. Leaders are divided, and citizens who are not part of the formal negotiation process are now mobilizing local resistance. Only in Venezuela, it appears, has the national government consciously attempted to resist powerful transnational agents. In chapter 9, Lacabana and Cariola explicitly identify those responsible for denationalizing the oil industry at the end of the 1980s to further hegemonic neoliberal privatization schemes. But, paradoxically perhaps, the Chávez government's reversal of oil privatization has brought about, for different reasons, intensified socioeconomic polarization in Caracas akin to that now also emerging in Sydney and Brussels.

On the basis of our case studies, then, we cannot yet conclude that local agency in these cities is making much of a difference to the global "position" each city appears to be assuming. These cases do not establish that local agents have uniformly acknowledged the emerging presence of global agents in their communities well. Nor, then, do the cases demonstrate that people in these cities have mounted a concerted effort to resist or propose alternatives to the emerging global role of their cities. Of course, local decision makers—economic, political, and cultural—continue to make decisions in the daily courses of their lives. Yet, only some are doing so increasingly with a view to the wider, global implications of such for each of the cities investigated. Even in relatively rich cities, like Frankfurt, Sydney, Brussels, and Tampa, global economic forces are not considered with the same degree of urgency as something to contend with in the continuing development, or competitiveness, of each. In poorer cities, like Johannesburg, Manila, Bangkok, and Caracas, of course, such powerful global forces loom even larger on the horizon of local decision makers, in both corporate and quasi-public (IMF, World Bank) institutional forms. Their impact is such that there is even reason to ask how much difference local agents could make, even if they tried.

Second, and in the most general terms, it seems clear from these empirical investigations that this urban reality of powerful globalizing economic agents has indeed created its own hierarchy of command-and-control centers wherein the position of any city is never secure and all urban areas become global city wannabes. In fact, we would argue that this increasingly common view both in the scholarly literature and in policy circles has considerably strengthened the power wielded by global neoliberal economic agents—so much so that even cities like New York, London, Paris, and Tokyo cannot presume that their established position as global cities is guaranteed to last. More precisely, there does not seem to be any viable counterhegemonic discourse emerging from our cases concerning the need to be integrated into the global market to remain competitive in the ongoing quest for urban development. In all the case studies of this book, save perhaps for those on Caracas and Brussels, a wider picture emerges of mostly national and sometimes local agents' mostly accommodating, if not actually promoting, decisions made by more powerful global economic agents concerning their respective cities. Perhaps the Manila case study offers the clearest example of government efforts to integrate the Philippines into the global economy by espousing that globalization is a natural, inevitable force over which even government itself has no control. This point is made, however, with equal force in the case study of Frankfurt where, apparently, the very status of the city is determined almost exclusively by the locational decisions made by advanced producer services firms and the businesses that need their services. Certainly, Caracas's potential global city status is largely driven by the atypical organization, through OPEC, of oil as a critical resource in the global production process.

This, we feel, is one way in which an uncritical, market-driven, global cities approach actually reinforces a sense of urgency for cities around the world. Looking closely at the case studies more concerned with political agency, like those of Sydney, Brussels, Johannesburg, Bangkok, and Tampa, merely confirms this assertion as most local decision makers in these cities never appear to question the need for deregulation, privatization, or structural adjustment in the continuous quest for city competitiveness. In this respect, powerful, global, neoliberal, economic agents are increasingly successful at creating real change in cities around the world, as well as in creating and maintaining an enabling discursive space among global and local economic and, as chapter 5 on Manila indicates, political agents.

A third observation based on our empirical cases is that perception of the increasing ability of powerful global economic agents to invest and disinvest even productive capital rapidly across the planet has tended simultaneously to depoliticize traditional political agents while also creating urban liminal spaces wherein polarization has led to resistance. On the first point, the case studies of Manila, Frankfurt, Tampa, Bangkok, and Johannesburg provide evidence that, to the extent national (and occasionally local) elites are playing a role in response to the emerging presence of global agents, that role is mostly one of accommodation. In service to the interests of these agents, they have adopted a managerial approach, that is to say, the business of negotiating deals and providing incentives and support. This approach is devoid of politics, which requires making choices among competing societal interests and different societal priorities concerning the satisfaction of diverse values like wealth, health, enlightenment, and justice (Lasswell and Kaplan 1950).

Concerning the urban polarization that is occurring, the impact of the global economy on Brussels, Caracas, and Sydney has sharpened basic conflicts between the old and the new and between the haves and the have-nots. One outcome of increased economic competitiveness and rising sociospatial inequalities is, for elites in these three cities, the construction of their own spatial and socioeconomic realms within or adjacent to the city's limits. The attempt, for instance, by traditional political elites to redraw city limits so that Sydney could advance its global city status was met with resistance from residents and city council members in Leichardt and South Sydney. Their contesting of the proposal to change the boundaries brought out cultural and political differences and economic inequalities among residents within the region. Such polarization is far more pronounced in Caracas; Lacabana and Cariola provide a detailed description of an emerging fractal city wherein the rich have isolated themselves in their own exclusive, urban, economic environment that, in many respects, is far more linked and networked to the global than to the local economy. The rich quarters of Caracas (and also of Brussels and Johannesburg) are increasingly decoupled both spatially and socially from the rest of their respective societies and economies and more tightly linked to the commanding heights of global economic and political elites. The middle class and the poor in Caracas have been increasingly marginalized, spatially, socially, economically, and culturally. In a similar vein, the glocal elites of Brussels have moved to suburban Brussels, leaving in their wake a melange of indigenous and immigrant communities that are showing new signs of resistance in three interspatial initiatives to improve the built environment and to empower immigrant communities politically. A similar kind of polarization is occurring in Johannesburg, although forms of resistance tied to this polarization are not identified as clearly in the case study presented.

The "depolitization" trend we observe among local and global elites in the empirical evidence presented here can be rendered even more profound, even quite critical of our very project. Our fourth observation, which may well be the foundation for those preceding it, is that the seemingly overwhelming dominant power, both practical and discursive, of global economic actors is actually reinforced by the very way in which we theoretically frame our approach to empirical study, including our own attempt to consider the "structuration" of globalization as outlined in the introductory chapter. What is striking about the empirical evidence reported in the preceding chapters is that both the authors and those public and private agents they discuss appear to work within a framework of discourse and action that, at least implicitly if not fully explicitly, leaves largely unquestioned the inevitability of global "winners" and "losers" among all global city wannabes. The key to being a "winning" city is actually to be more fully or better integrated into global economic flows and networks. What is left unquestioned, save partly in the case studies of Sydney, Caracas, and Brussels, is whether integration of this sort, even on the best possible terms, is actually a good thing socioeconomically for cities. It appears, after studying the cases, that we remain largely blinded by our own conceptual global cities framework, which makes it that much more difficult to propose, let alone actually, empirically, to discover, alternatives to market- and agency-driven global cities approaches, both of which are premised on the inevitable presence of a global economy. That is, we all have more or less caught what Beck calls, in a different context, the "thought-virus of globalism," the symptoms of which include a relative blind eye to alternative forms of city development in an era of intensifying global relations (2000, 122).

It is no wonder then, as described in the various case studies, that most policymakers, both global and local, hardly question the need to adapt policy to best fit the exigencies of the global market and global economic agents. If even most scholars cannot conceive of alternatives in this post–cold war era, it is hardly surprising that most policymakers emphasize the inevitability of having to adapt to global pressures in order to "succeed" economically in the new world, neoliberal, economic order. In this context, Hugo Chávez's attempt to resist such forces in Venezuela, described in the case study of Caracas, is merely an exception that proves the rule and, indeed, is more destined than not actually to conform to such an order (or die trying) as his apparently like-minded colleague Luis Inacio ("Lula") da Silva seems to be doing in neighboring Brazil. Again, the lack of a more powerful, counterhegemonic discourse and, then, practice concerning the globalization of cities has led to much scholarship that has only reinforced the depolitization of the policy process in the face of apparently overpowering global forces. From this perspective, it is only natural that some cities will "win" and some will "lose" in the race to global city status based on their ability, or not, to adapt themselves to what Ryner calls the global "disciplinary neoliberalism" of such hegemonic discursive and practical forces (2002, 121).

It is not just that policymakers are now all trained with the same neoclassical, liberal, economics textbooks, although this is surely a major part of the problem, if one that is, as yet, too little researched (although, see Nelson 2001 and Coats 1997 for a start). There is certainly a globally hegemonic, neoliberal, epistemic community and not just in the economics profession itself (McCloskey 1996). The neoliberal dogma concerning the alleged benefits resulting from privatization, openness, free markets, and overall structural adjustment is, in this manner, openly purveyed as if it were a nonideological objective take on reality, not open to debate or discussion, particularly not in political terms. This is most manifest in recent treatises on globalization like those by Bhagwati (2004) and Legrain (2004), who maintain the now well-worn, but still pervasive, idea that neoliberal economics is a form of applied science, above and beyond political debate. Indeed, Bhagwati (2005) suggests that free trade can also meet social objectives (e.g., reduced child labor and gender inequalities) and that public policy needs only to use moral suasion to determine the pace at which such objectives are reached.

We believe that this problem of a lack of alternative visions is even more insidious than this, pervading even the global cities literature, including this very volume. The very conception of the necessity to "integrate" better with global forces in order to "attain" a more global status is a heavy, if not explicitly stated, presence in all of the preceding chapters, including our own introduction. The notion that all cities are globalizing suggests a certain inevitability of a certain specifiable process that some cities will facilitate better than others. Using our own chapter on Tampa as an example, the worry there is that Tampa's economic and political elite cannot get their act together to provide a more conducive image for the generation or attraction of global economic agents or activities. Similarly, the worry about Brussels seems to be that the parochial local elite have not integrated with the glocal elite in a way conducive to the rise of Brussels as a global city player. This seemingly inevitable competition for global status can even be seen in the narratives on Bangkok, where better things might have been done with the bonanza of finances in the 1990s, and Johannesburg, where local crime, lingering ethnic rivalry, and unskilled labor impede the city's progress up the global hierarchy. Finally, from the opposite angle, the message from Caracas appears to be that, to resist the inevitable, national policymakers actually have to delink from global forces altogether, surely a quixotic quest at best.

This is in no way a criticism of our authors' empirical work, as this latter has been quite edifying, as already discussed, particularly in its discussion of cities not often treated in the literature. Rather, the suggestion is that the very conceptions of "global cities," "comparative city status," "global nodes and networks," and even our own "agency and structure," then, "structuration" are potentially reifying enclosures that discursively construct a world where unilinear inevitability and lack of alternatives more or less follow, both in how we understand and act in the world. The point is that it is not just the same neoliberal economics texts that are being read across the globe. It is also potentially more critical global cities texts that replicate an overly deterministic worldview on the basis of which both global and local agents act.

A somewhat similar argument along these lines has been made by Hirst and Thompson (1999) and Rosenburg (2000) in their criticism of the growing literature on globalization. Unlike these authors, however, we believe that there really is something qualitatively new about global relations today, and not only economically, that is manifested most in cities. That is, globalization is not just a new, obfuscating conceptualization of a state or process that is actually quite old. Rather, it signifies real economic, political, and cultural processes that are now both more rapidly expanding all over the globe and intensifying in their impact, as manifested, at least in part, by the very empirical evidence presented in the preceding chapters of this book. To make sense of these new processes necessitates, to our mind, the attempts to theorize their causes and characteristics that Rosenburg (2000), for his part, criticizes as inadequate. Put differently and making use of this latter author's own terms, globalization theory is necessary and not necessarily prone to folly, even though some attempts at it may turn out to be.

Using our own attempt at such theory included in the introductory chapter, we believe now, based squarely on the empirical work of our invited authors, that a fifth observation can be made: it appears that even the looser conception of the structuration of human activity lends itself to a certain inevitability and lack of alternative options for human agents. And, yet, we still do not think that what we called in the introduction the "agency-driven" conception of transnational or hybrid or cosmopolitan urbanism is a successful alternative theoretical conception either. Again, the examples of such transnationalism that, say, Smith (2001) or Flusty (2004) provide are not convincing in this respect as they tend to lose sight of the more powerful forces, both global and local, that make it necessary for some human actors to act in certain ways in certain places, not entirely of their own choosing.

REDIRECTING OUR UNDERSTANDING OF GLOBAL CITIES

Not surprisingly, based on the preceding observations, we think more embedded, empirical studies of actual cities are needed to help construct a more sophisticated theoretical framework from which to make sense of the actual processes behind, and the resulting impact of, globalization. This is certainly not, however, a turn to some form of empiricism on our part. The key is to consider each city as a very complex field of interacting human actors with varying amounts of more global or local economic, political, and cultural power to shape their own and their city's destiny. Already talk of "actors" as opposed to "agents," it seems to us, suggests a necessarily close empirical examination of real people, outside of theoretically reified structural contexts. Within this interaction, decisions are made, or not, to render the city more or less integrated with growing global relations, and the results of these decisions are manifested in both the built and social environments of the city. But the emphasis in analysis has to remain focused on the contingencies of such decisions. That is, both the extent and results of globalization in this respect are always a result of negotiation, however unequal, among people with varying kinds and degrees of power, and the actual results of such negotiation can never be entirely foreseen, even by the actors themselves; nor are they necessarily long enduring. Put differently, this negotiation is an ongoing give and take, not one that ends, once and for all, even in cities in the least democratic of countries.

Less abstractly, we would like to spend more time in the cities our authors have reported on in order to determine more precisely who, in fact, made certain decisions that impacted the various cities as they did. Was there any discussion of possible alternatives, not just among disaffected, usually less powerful, groups, but even among more powerful economic, political, and cultural decision makers? What were these alternatives, if any? Why, eventually, was the day carried by some decision makers as opposed to others, and what are those who did not carry the day doing about it now? Specifically, how have various kinds of people in Frankfurt taken to the decision, apparently made elsewhere, that it would be better for Frankfurt to become a big control center for European financial flows—if still secondary to London— than, say, a more locally embedded cultural center or something else? Have any of these groups proposed alternative visions for Frankfurt's future in a globalizing world? If so, what are they, and why did they not carry the day? Or who, in fact, decided that Johannesburg would be better off not seeking global city status in the way that it has not? Who determined that, in the process, the city would develop socially and spatially in a Los Angeles sort of way, and were or are there no dissenting voices?

This line of questioning, it seems to us, opens up the very real possibility of constructing an alternative conceptualization of globalization and cities that is run through with contingencies and possible avenues for alternative theories and practices. All cities are affected by globalizing forces, but precisely how they are affected is neither inevitable nor knowable a priori. Instead, the extent to which all cities are affected by globalization is the result of a particular constellation of contingent decisions that are made by differentially powerful human actors, both global and local. If, for example, the locally embedded Brussels elite were actually to be better integrated with the glocal Euro-elite, might this mean that the built and social environment of the city would undergo a Los Angelization process described so well in the cases of Johannesburg and Bangkok? In this case, achieving higher global city status as a result of a growing hegemony of more glocal decision makers may not be such a good thing for the Brussels community. Maybe, in other words, the more parochial local elite, by its very parochialism, has opened up the very possibility for other, more locally embedded human actors to explore alternative city-development possibilities, as Swyngedouw and Moyersoen seem to suggest. But who, in fact, are these actors, what are they saying and doing, was there debate among their ranks and between such groups, and how did their message(s) affect, or not, the actions of the more powerful glocal and local economic, political, and cultural elite?

Again, answers to such questions simply demand more careful, theoretically informed empirical work on individual cities. The key, as noted, is to determine what Massey (1993) calls the veritable "geometry of power" that is forever constituting and reconstituting itself in cities by what we have called the negotiation among glocal and local economic, political, and cultural actors in terms of what kind of city each city is to be. From this perspective, a much fuller empirical picture of each individual city must be painted than is possible in the short space of one chapter. What we have been able to make of our cities based on the cases provided by our authors is, then, merely a first cut at how each is globalizing. Other empirical studies of, say, Frankfurt (e.g., Friedmann and Lehrer 1997), Bangkok (e.g., Webster 2004), Johannesburg (e.g., Crankshaw and Parnell 2004), or Brussels (De Corte and Goyens 2004) necessarily widen our empirical view, thereby allowing for an ever-clearer understanding of the evolving glocal-local geometries of power in each city. The point is that this type of theoretically informed, empirical investigation necessarily does not assume that globalization is an inexorable extra-actor force from outside pressuring city actors to either conform (that is, achieve "success") or resist (that is, suffer "failure"). Nor does it assume that actors act independently of extra-actor, even discursive, pressures and biases to act in certain ways. As Bhaskar puts it so eloquently in more macroterms, such an approach assumes, rather, that

> people do not create society. For it always preexists them and is a necessary condition for their activity. Rather society must be regarded as an ensemble of structures, practices and conventions which individuals reproduce or transform, but which would not exist unless they did so. Society does not exist independently of human activity (the error of reification). But it is not the product of it (the error of voluntarism). (1998, 216)

Again, we believe, such talk of "people," "practices," "conventions," "activities" and "societies," as well as "structures," renders it that much more difficult to lose sight of the very contingencies of social structuration, which are both global and local, however this process may be biased in certain directions by varying preexisting geometries of power, both practical and discursive.

This focus on contingency is absolutely crucial. Local geometries of power relations differ in different places at different times, and their precise constitution is forever in flux, due to ongoing negotiations among human actors with varying degrees of power. That this is so makes in-depth study of cities all the more imperative. But even more significantly, that this is so also renders it that much easier to conceive of, and set into practice, possible alternative, non-, or even anti-neo-liberal globalizations of cities in today's world. What needs to be determined in each city is how some coalition(s) of human actors are able to forge a hegemonic project (or not, as in the case of Tampa) with regard to its development and how this hegemony is maintained or, indeed, may be under threat by the ideas and actions of other coalition(s) of human actors, both global and local. Such an investigation immediately underscores the negotiated nature of city development, as well as the contingency of outcomes even in a rapidly globalizing world. But, more importantly, such an investigation also immediately opens up a space for more critical discursive and practical work toward alternatives, perhaps even some sort of more "distributive," as opposed to neoliberal, "growth coalition," as suggested by Hirst and Thompson (1999).

Less abstractly and considering again our own work on Tampa, it would appear that, unlike, say, Bangkok, Manila, Johannesburg, or even Frankfurt and Sydney, it is a rather good thing that the Tampa business and political elites cannot get their act together well enough to integrate better into the global economy of neoliberal discipline. While it may be that there is a hegemonic neoliberal stance in these elite communities—although, based on the case studies in this book, even this is unclear—there appears to be much in dispute as to how best to act on this basis, for the alleged good of Tampa as a whole. Not only that, there does not seem to be any explicit hegemonic coalition developing even among the glocal and local economic and political elite, to say nothing about the cultural elite. If this is the case, although more empirical work is necessary to fully determine this, then it opens up the possibility to shape Tampa's future development in a wholly different direction from what seems destined by attempting to attain global city status, as described in the dominant scholarly and policy literature. Put differently, the very fact that Tampa's business and political elite cannot get its act together means that a discursive and practical space is opened up for an alternative development play to be written and performed.

This certainly suggests that, in the case of Tampa, what Swyngedouw and Moyersoen call a possible "liminal space" for alternative globalism is writ quite large. While the Brussels elite may be "reluctant" globalizers, the Tampa elite appear all the more embedded in their local context as more or less "ignorant" globalizers in the most literal sense of this term. As the Tampa

political elite continue to bicker over jurisdiction, legitimacy, and development vision at the most local levels, the business elite is quite riven with
competing ideas about the best possible avenues for the future development
of Tampa. And both elites—surely, in many cases, the same individuals—for
the most part seem blissfully unaware of, or unconcerned with, globalizing
forces so on the minds of elites in the other cities treated in this volume.
Surely, this is a greater parochialism than even that of the local Brussels elite.
But just as surely, such a parochialism offers the wholly unintended consequence that Tampa eventually may, through ongoing debate and negotiation, develop policies to mitigate the discipline of global neoliberalism,
thereby perhaps losing the battle for global city status but winning the battle
for a more thoughtful, equitable, and just city development.

This analysis may be unduly idealistic, particularly with regard to Tampa
in the contemporary American political context, but it certainly underscores
the very contingency of city development in the age of globalization. Maybe
it really is better for cities *not* to integrate more fully into the neoliberal discipline of globalization in order to rise in stature in the global cities hierarchy so touted even in the seemingly more reflective scholarly literature. Yet,
what we really need to determine more fully is whether or not this alleged
liminal space for an alternative globalization of cities is, indeed, a real possibility (Magnusson 1996). To this end, we need to determine in much more
depth just what, for example, are the specific conflicts between city and
county political officials in Tampa and between more glocal and more locally embedded economic elites in the chamber of commerce, the Tampa
Bay Partnership, and the I-4 Corridor initiative. And what about the cultural
elite? We have noted that some in Tampa have become quite taken with
Florida's conception of the importance of generating or attracting the so-
called creative classes as a key to city development. But who, exactly, has
taken the initiative to form "Creative Tampa Bay," and is there any dissention
within the group or between the group and more traditional political and
economic elites? And, finally, what about citizens' groups from the varying
neighborhoods and social contingents of Tampa? What are they saying about
what Tampa means to them and how to attain the goal of a more inclusive,
equitable, and just city-development process?

In the end, we are suggesting that a much thicker empirical description of
the coalescence of competing citizen's interests and organizations, both elite
and nonelite, is necessary to actually get at the ongoing negotiation within
localized geometries of economic, political, and cultural power in order to
determine the precise trajectory of globalization in any given city. Globalization, in this respect, is not something caught from outside or generated
fully from inside on the basis of the actions of localized individuals. Nor, indeed, is globalization an inexorably homogenizing process, as suggested by
neoliberals and many global cities scholars alike. Rather, globalization is a

profoundly contingent, because fully contested, process, the result of ongoing social conflict and negotiation. To really know how all cities of the world are globalizing, or, more precisely, the differing manners in which they are globalizing, necessitates a fuller empirical description of this ongoing social conflict and negotiation in specific cities at specific temporal conjunctures all over the world. Our belief is that, by doing this kind of thick empirical work on individual cities, the liminal spaces for alternative city development in this age of intensifying globalization will, in fact, be rendered more explicit and, thereby, discursively and practically recognizable and attainable on the part of both scholars and policymakers alike.

REFERENCES

Beck, U. 2000. *What Is Globalization?* trans. Patrick Camiller. Cambridge, MA: Polity.

Bhagwati, J. 2004. *In Defense of Globalization.* New York: Oxford University Press.

———. 2005. "Trade in the world of globalization." In *Florida's Global Frontiers: Impacts of Trade Liberalization*, ed. M. M. Amen. Tampa: University of South Florida Globalization Research Center.

Bhaskar, R. 1998. "Societies." In *Critical Realism: Essential Readings*, ed. M. Archer, R. Bhaskar, A. Collier, T. Lawson, and A. Norrie, 206–57. New York: Routledge.

Brenner, N. 1999. "Globalization as reterritorialization: the re-scaling of urban governance in the European Union." *Urban Studies* 36, no. 3: 431–51.

Coats, A. W., ed. 1997. *The Post-1945 Internationalization of Economics.* Durham, NC: Duke University Press.

Crankshaw, O., and Parnell, S. 2004. "Johannesburg: race, inequality, and urbanization." In *World Cities beyond the West: Globalization, Development, and Inequality*, ed. J. Gugler, 348–70. New York: Cambridge University Press.

De Corte, S., and Goyens, C. 2004. "Neighborhood contracts: towards participatory planning?" In *The Contested Metropolis*, ed. INURA, 88–95. Basel, Switzerland: Birkhauser.

Florida, R. 2002. *The Rise of the Creative Class and How It's Transforming Work, Leisure, Community and Everyday Life.* New York: Basic Books.

Flusty, S. 2004. *De-Coca-colonization: Making the Globe from the Inside Out.* New York: Routledge.

Friedmann, J., and Lehrer, U. 1997. "Urban policy responses to foreign in-migration: the case of Frankfurt-am-Main, Germany." *Journal of the American Planning Association* 63: 61–78.

Hirst, P., and Thompson, G. 1999. *Globalization in Question.* Cambridge, UK: Polity Press.

Lasswell, H., and Kaplan A. 1950. *Power and Society: A Framework for Political Inquiry.* New Haven, CT: Yale University Press.

Legrain, P. 2004. *Open World: The Truth about Globalization.* Chicago: Ivan R. Dee.

Magnusson, W. 1996. *The Search for Political Space: Globalization, Social Movements, and the Urban Political Experience.* Toronto: University of Toronto Press.

Massey, D. 1993. "Power-geometry and a progressive sense of place." In *Mapping the Futures: Local Cultures, Global Change*, ed. J. Bird, B. Curtis, T. Putnam, et al., 59–69. London: Routledge.

McCloskey, D. 1996. "Missing ethics in economics." In *The Value of Culture: On the Relationship between Economics and Art*, ed. A. Klamer, 187–201. Amsterdam: Amsterdam University Press.

Nelson, R. H. 2001. *Economics as Religion: From Samuelson to Chicago and Beyond.* University Park: Pennsylvania University Press.

Rosenburg, J. 2000. *The Follies of Globalisation Theory.* New York: Verso.

Ryner, J. M. 2002. *Capitalist Restructuring, Globalisation and the Third Way.* London: Routledge.

Smith, M. P. 2001. *Transnational Urbanism: Locating Globalization.* Oxford: Blackwell.

Webster, D. 2004. "Bangkok: evolution and adaptation under stress." In *World Cities beyond the West: Globalization, Development and Inequality*, ed. J. Gugler, 82–118. New York: Cambridge University Press.

Index

About the Authors

M. Mark Amen is academic director for the Dr. Kiran C. Patel Center for Global Solutions at the University of South Florida and has been a member of the faculty in the Department of Government and International Affairs since 1982. He received his doctorate in political science from the Graduate Institute of International Studies (Geneva, Switzerland) in 1978, and his research interests are in global political economy, theories of the state, and globalizing cities.

Kevin Archer is former chair of the Department of Geography at the University of South Florida. He received his Ph.D. from Johns Hopkins University. His research interests include globalizing cities and sociospatial polarization, as well as the production of postindustrial nature.

Jonathan V. Beaverstock is professor of economic geography at Loughborough University, UK. His research focuses on the strategic organizational management of professional and financial services in contemporary globalization and the spatialization of knowledge networks in international financial centers, particularly the city of London, Singapore's "Golden Shoe," and Manhattan, New York City. In his current work, he is investigating financial clustering in London and transnational labor mobility in professional service firms.

Keith S. O. Beavon is professor of geography and head of the Department of Geography, Geoinformatics, and Meteorology at the University of Pretoria, South Africa. He has previously held teaching positions at Rhodes University and the University of Cape Town in South Africa, University College of Swansea in Britain, and the University of the Witwatersrand in Johannesburg. He obtained an MSc from the University of Cape Town and his Ph.D. from the University of the Witwatersrand.

Pornpan Boonchuen is lecturer at the School of Architecture, King Mongkut's Institute of Technology Ladkrabang, Bangkok, Thailand. She teaches architectural design, site planning, and introduction to urban planning for undergraduate students. She earned an M.A. in architecture from Texas A&M University and an M.A. in urban and regional planning from the University of Hawaii at Manoa. Her research interests include urban form and the use of civic space in Bangkok.

M. Martin Bosman is assistant professor of geography at the University of South Florida in Tampa, Florida. He received his M.A. in geography from the University of Natal in the Republic of South Africa and his Ph.D. in geography from the University of Kentucky in 1999. He has published widely on the geography of the digital divide, and his current research is on globalization and newly emerging city-regions.

Cecilia Cariola is an architect with an MSc in urban planning. She is a professor in MSc and Ph.D. programs in development planning and a researcher on regional urban affairs at the Centre for Development Studies (CENDES) at the Central University of Venezuela. She has over twenty years of research experience in regional and urban planning, urban labor markets, and poverty, and her research has appeared in various journals, magazines, and books.

Mike Douglass is director of the Globalization Research Center and professor and former chair of urban and regional planning at the University of Hawaii. He received his Ph.D. in urban planning from the University of California, Los Angeles (UCLA), and has been a visiting scholar and professor at Stanford University, UCLA, the National University of Singapore, and Thammasat University. His books include *Japan and Global Migration: Foreign Workers and the Advent of a Multicultural Society; Cities for Citizens: Planning and the Rise of Civil Society in a Global Age;* and *Culture and the City in East Asia.*

Michael Hoyler is lecturer in human geography at Loughborough University, UK. His current research focuses on the impact of contemporary processes of globalization on the restructuring of European metropolitan regions. He also has research interests in the historical geography of Europe, especially the role of knowledge and education in the social and economic development of European cities and regions.

Miguel Lacabana is an economist with a doctorate in social sciences, and he also has completed postdoctoral training at the Development Planning Unit, University College of London. He is a professor in MSc and Ph.D. programs in development planning and a researcher of regional urban affairs at CENDES, at the Central University of Venezuela. He is currently editor of *CENDES Magazine* and has over twenty years of research experience in regional and urban planning, urban labor markets, and poverty. His research has appeared in various journals, magazines, and books.

Johan Moyersoen is a Ph.D. student in the School of Geography and the Environment at the University of Oxford. He holds degrees in political science (University of Ghent, Belgium), social and cultural anthropology (Catholic University, Leuven, Belgium), and regional science (Cornell University, Ithaca, New York). His current research is on urban political economy and peace science. He is assistant editor of the *Journal of Peace Science, Peace Economics and Public Policy.*

Kathryn Pain is a research fellow at the Institute of Community Studies, London. She has a diploma in town planning and a Ph.D. from the University of Reading and is a corporate member of the Royal Town Planning Institute. She has been a senior researcher and lecturer in geography at Loughborough University and an academic at the Open University and the Centre for Urban and Regional Studies, University of Birmingham.

Scott Salmon is on the faculty at the Eugene Lange College and Milano Graduate School at the New School for Social Research in New York City.

Saskia Sassen is the Ralph Lewis Professor of Sociology at the University of Chicago and Centennial Visiting Professor at the London School of Economics. Her new book is *Territory, Authority and Rights: From Medieval to Global Assemblages* (2006). She has just completed for UNESCO a five-year project on sustainable human settlement for which she set up a network of researchers and activists in over thirty countries.

Erik Swyngedouw is university reader in economic geography at Oxford University and a fellow of St. Peter's College. He has written extensively on urban and regional political economy, globalization, political ecology, and the politics of water. His most recent books include *The Globalized City* (coedited with F. Moulaert and A. Rodriguez, 2003) and *Social Power and the Urbanization of Water* (2004).

Peter J. Taylor is professor of geography at Loughborough University, UK, and visiting professor at the Metropolitan Institute at Virginia Polytechnic

Institute. Founder of the Globalization and World Cities (GaWC) Study Group and Network, his current research focuses on cities as networks and how to measure them. His latest book is *World City Network: A Global Urban Analysis* (2004).

James A. Tyner received his Ph.D. from the Department of Geography at the University of Southern California. He is associate professor of geography at Kent State University. His research and teaching interests include population and urban and political geography. He recently published *Made in the Philippines: Gendered Discourses and the Making of Migrants* (2004).